T0329746

Boom and Bust in Puerto Rico

BOOM

and

BUST

in

PUERTO RICO

How Politics Destroyed an Economic Miracle

A. W. MALDONADO

University of Notre Dame Press *Notre Dame, Indiana*

Library of Congress Control Number: 2021941548

ISBN: 978-0-268-20097-8 (Hardback)
ISBN: 978-0-268-20096-1 (WebPDF)
ISBN: 978-0-268-20099-2 (Epub)

CONTENTS

Prologue   viii

Introduction   1

PART I. THE RISE AND FALL

ONE. Operation Bootstrap   15

TWO. Operation Bootstrap and the Statehood Surge   30

THREE. The Demise of Section 936   52

FOUR. The Turning Point   73

FIVE. The Breakdown of the Public Corporations   83

SIX. The Demise of the Government Development Bank   97

SEVEN. "That Is Nuts": Puerto Rico's Labor Policy   118

EIGHT. Will Puerto Rico Become a State?   131

NINE. The Future of Puerto Rico   158

PART II. THE HISTORICAL CONTEXT

TEN. A "Troubled" Relationship   177

ELEVEN. A Century of Miscommunication
and Misunderstanding   190

EPILOGUE. The Pandemic, the "Curse," the "Fix"   207

Notes   217

Index   233

PROLOGUE

On March 16, 2020, three days after President Donald J. Trump declared a national emergency to confront the growing coronavirus pandemic, Avik Roy, *Forbes* policy editor, published an article titled, "Puerto Rico Can Help the U.S. End Its Dependence on Chinese Pharmaceutical Ingredients." The virus crisis, Roy pointed out, dramatizes the fact that the "U.S. is too dependent on China for critical active pharmaceutical ingredients." A U.S. Department of Commerce study "found that 97 percent of the antibiotics used in the U.S. now come from China[, and] 40 percent of over-the-counter and generic prescription drugs used in the U.S. now come from India."[1]

A major reason for this dependence was a 1996 act of Congress. On August 20, 1996, at a ceremony on the South Lawn of the White House, President Bill Clinton signed the Small Business Job Protection Act that eliminated Section 936, the tax incentive that Puerto Rico used to attract industry and that converted the island into one of the world's largest manufacturers of pharmaceuticals and medical devices. Critics of the tax break, Roy pointed out, "hailed" the repeal as "ending corporate welfare as we know it," producing a windfall of new tax revenue for the U.S. Treasury.[2]

But that was not the result. Instead, "the end of Section 936 dispersed the global pharmaceutical industry (from Puerto Rico) to other parts of the globe,"[3] to Ireland but primarily to China and India. The Puerto Rican economy was devastated: "Not coincidentally [it] marked the beginning of a deep recession which has lasted until today. . . . [T]he loss of pharmaceutical industry jobs helped crash the Puerto Rican economy, turning economic growth from positive to negative."[4] As the island lost jobs, the Puerto Rican government lost tax revenue and became increasingly dependent on borrowing. In 2014, the government of Puerto Rico lost its credit. A year later, Governor Alejandro García Padilla declared that its monstrous $73 billion debt was not payable.

On the morning of September 20, 2017, Hurricane Maria struck Puerto Rico, causing massive destruction. The U.S. media reported not only on the humanitarian crisis but also on the effect on the island's pharmaceutical and medical device industry, its importance to the United States, and the consequences of having eliminated Section 936.

U.S. Food and Drug Administration commissioner, Scott Gottlieb, expressed his concern on October 20, 2017, that the damage, especially to the electric power infrastructure, would create "shortages of critical medical products" in the United States. "There are currently more than 50 medical device manufacturing plants in Puerto Rico," he said, "employing about 18,000 people. Collectively they manufacture more than 1,000 different kinds of medical devices. These include simple but essential products like surgical instruments and dental products as well as highly complex devices such as cardiac pacemakers and insulin pumps." These devices, he went on, "are critically important to patient care, because they may be life-sustaining or life-improving."[5] Further, particular styles of the devices were manufactured by a single company.

Soon after, on October 28, 2017, *Forbes* published an article making the same point. The "lesson . . . of Hurricane Maria," according to the article, "is not [just] about the suffering of the Puerto Rican people, an astonishing three in four of whom remain without power more than one month after Maria clobbered the island. This is about whether Puerto Rico's powerful pharmaceutical industry, which is responsible for about 25% of all U.S. pharma exports, is really going to weather the storm." The article referred to the repeal of Section 936 in 1996: "More than a decade after the favorable tax treatment that enticed the industry to the island has expired, how long will the owners of the roughly 50 drug manufacturing plants wait for a fully functioning electrical grid. . . . So here's the lesson that we might learn from Hurricane Maria: Drug companies can pick up and leave."[6]

A September 26, 2017, CNBC report emphasized the effect of the repeal of Section 936 on Puerto Rico. The island, it stated, has been devastated not only by the ferocious hurricane but also by President Clinton signing the law in 1996 "that would phase out Section 936 over 10 years. Plant closures and job losses followed. Ten years later[,] . . . left with a dwindling tax base, the Puerto Rican government borrowed heavily to replace the lost revenue. . . . [T]oday the U.S. territory has over $70 billion in debt, and an unemployment rate 2.5 times the U.S. average, a 45 percent poverty rate." "Between 1980 and 2007," the report continued, "Puerto Rico's economy added jobs at roughly the same pace as the rest of the U.S. But its economy began to shrink shortly after the repeal of Section 936. . . . [D]uring the decade . . . Puerto Rico lost 40 percent of the manufacturing job base."[7]

This book on the rise and fall of the Puerto Rican economy is the story of bad politics and economic decisions in Washington and in Puerto Rico. In Puerto Rico, the government mismanaged the economy, sinking it into unpayable debt. It is the story of the 120-year troubled relationship between Puerto Rico and the United States and where it is likely headed in the future. As the movement to make Puerto Rico a state grew, it had a profound effect on the island's economic policies and decisions. As Puerto Rico and the United States seek to lift the island out of the economic and fiscal crisis, the question remains, will Puerto Rico become a state?

This book is also the story of Section 936. The question posed by the March 16, 2020, *Forbes* article was, in view of the critical importance of the pharmaceutical and medical device industry not only to Puerto Rico but also to the United States and now dramatically evident in the coronavirus pandemic, why did the government of Puerto Rico petition Congress to eliminate it, and why did Congress and the president agree? The demise of Operation Bootstrap shows how politics destroyed an economic miracle.

Introduction

Tears came to his eyes. Visiting the John F. Kennedy Library and Museum in Boston, the Puerto Rican attorney José Alfredo Hernández Mayoral saw a photograph that covered most of the entire wall at the far end of a long room. He recognized it, as he had seen it many times in several books on President Kennedy. In the photograph, the short, portly figure of the famed cellist Pablo Casals bends forward toward Kennedy; Luis Muñoz Marín, governor of Puerto Rico, is next to Kennedy and to his right is Muñoz's wife, Inés Mendoza; to his left, a smiling, radiant Jacqueline leans forward toward Casals; next to her, the young, beautiful Marta Casals, the Puerto Rican cellist student whom Casals had married four years earlier.

There was reason for a Puerto Rican to feel deep emotion before this familiar photograph. The November 13, 1961, Casals concert became, after Kennedy's death, the White House event that heralded the Kennedy years as a lost Camelot. The eighty-four-year-old Catalan cellist was the international symbol of resistance to the Franco dictatorship in Spain. He refused to perform in the United States or any country that had

1

recognized the regime. Now Casals, returning to the White House after performing before President Theodore Roosevelt fifty-four years earlier, had agreed to do so in part to express his admiration for the young president but mostly his admiration for the governor of Puerto Rico.

In 1948, Muñoz became the island's first elected governor. A former independence supporter, he came to believe that neither independence nor statehood was viable for Puerto Rico and led the effort to achieve autonomous commonwealth status in 1950–52. Maximizing the island's federal tax exemption and unique position under the U.S. flag, he carried out a massive industrialization program that transformed Puerto Rico from the "poorhouse of the Caribbean" to a "showcase of democracy,"[1] inspiring the admiration of President Kennedy and others, including Casals.

Back in 1956, Muñoz and Teodoro Moscoso, head of Operation Bootstrap, the economic development program that modernized Puerto Rico, convinced Casals to live in Puerto Rico, his mother's birthplace. Accepting Muñoz's argument that hosting a music festival in Puerto Rico would not violate his anti-Franco crusade because Puerto Rico, while part of the United States, had a distinct juridical and cultural identity as a commonwealth, Casals went on to organize the Casals Festival, which became a renowned classical music world event.

Now, at the White House, among the 153 guests was the seventy-seven-year-old Alice Roosevelt Longworth, the famous "Princess Alice" who had heard Casals perform before her father, Theodore, half a century earlier. There were many American and foreign composers and conductors in attendance: Aaron Copeland, Leonard Bernstein, Leopold Stokowski, Eugene Ormandy. There were labor and business leaders, David Dubinsky, Henry Ford, and Paul Mellon, as well as the nation's top journalists, Walter Lippmann, Edward R. Morrow, and Randolph Hearst. One of the composers, Gian Carlo Menotti, commented to the media, "In no place in Europe can an event like this be seen."[2]

In 1963, two years later, President Kennedy revived the awarding of the Medal of Freedom, the nation's highest civilian honor, naming Muñoz as one of the recipients.

Just as the photograph and the idea of Camelot provoked in many Americans a feeling of loss, it did also in Hernández Mayoral. This was more than a historic Casals concert; this was also a state dinner in honor of Muñoz. All those luminaries, the elite of the United States, were there to honor a Puerto Rican. And as a Puerto Rican, the emotion he felt was so sharp because the photograph recalled that Puerto Rico had also had its Camelot—and that it too was lost.

Hernández Mayoral knew well what Puerto Rico had lost. His father, Rafael Hernández Colón, three times governor of Puerto Rico, had dedicated his long political career to extending and saving the Muñoz legacy, repeatedly fighting the battle to save Operation Bootstrap. He expanded Bootstrap by obtaining Section 936 from Congress in 1976. Nine years later, returning to power after losing the 1976 and 1980 elections, he succeeded against efforts to repeal the incentive. But under a new administration and new economic policies in the 1990s, the island's government asked Congress to repeal Section 936, effectively ending Operation Bootstrap and triggering an economic decline that engulfed the island around the time the lawyer stood before the moving memory of Camelot.

The Endless Nightmare

What had once been a beautiful dream had turned into a seemingly endless nightmare. The Puerto Rico that took off under Operation Bootstrap—which inspired Kennedy's Alliance for Progress, celebrated as the free, economically prosperous alternative to the Cuban Revolution—was now suffering what seemed a bottomless economic decline. It was burdened with a larger debt per capita than any U.S. state, a decade-old recession, and little hope. In June 2015, Governor Alejandro García Padilla declared that the government was unable to pay its $70 billion debt plus unfunded pension liabilities, totaling $120 billion, "the biggest government financial collapse in United States history."[3]

Meanwhile, Puerto Rico's unique political and economic relationship to the United States, its commonwealth status, which Muñoz and his followers believed had finally resolved the half-century-old political status issue in 1952, extolled by American constitutionalists and jurists as "the most notable of American governmental experiments in our lifetimes,"[4] was now degraded in Washington and under relentless attack in Puerto Rico. In 2015, the United States shifted views on the commonwealth, arguing before the Supreme Court that the island was subject to congressional power under the territorial clause.[5] The following year, on June 30, 2016, President Barack Obama signed the Puerto Rican Oversight, Management and Economic Stability Act (PROMESA). The act created a seven-member fiscal board appointed by the president and Congress with two mandates: first, restructure the island's gigantic debt, overseeing negotiations with creditors; and second, oversee and approve the government budget process to ensure that the giant annual deficits would be eliminated by 2022. To ensure that the island government would approve and function under balanced budgets, the Fiscal Board was granted authority to override Puerto Rico's elected officials in all spending matters.

Congress and the president were reacting to the island government's desperate SOS. Puerto Rico had reached a dead end. On the one hand, it could not declare bankruptcy under Chapter 9, a federal bankruptcy relief available only to municipalities. On the other hand, its constitution mandates the government pay its debt *before* any other expenditure. The island government asked the U.S. government to intervene to prevent creditors from effectively shutting it down. For once it seemed that Puerto Rican partisan politics were suspended. Governor García Padilla, of the pro-commonwealth Popular Democratic Party (PDP), joined Puerto Rico's nonvoting member of Congress, Resident Commissioner Pedro Pierluisi, of the pro-statehood New Progressive Party (NPP), in sending the SOS.

But political status politics is unavoidable in Puerto Rico. Congress creating the PROMESA Fiscal Board was not seen as another case of a government going bankrupt and seeking federal rescue, as had occurred in American cities like New York and Detroit or in the District of Columbia, the U.S. capital. The ultimate power of the Fiscal Board over the island government was seen as an attack on Puerto Rico's status and constitutional order, as the annulment of the island's constitution, as Puerto Rico returning to the pre-commonwealth, shameful status of a U.S. colony.

Days before Congress acted, former governor Hernández Colón, the pro-commonwealth elder statesman, sent an unusually harsh, uncharacteristically emotional letter to the House leadership. "This bill deprives the people of Puerto Rico of their right of self-determination and thereby tramples on their right to vote," he argued. Listing the Fiscal Board's powers, which include the authority to unilaterally override the governor's and legislature's fiscal policy, he continued, "The above are flagrant examples of a long list of appropriations by the Board under H.R. 5278 of the powers of the government belonging to the people of Puerto Rico under our Constitution. Such an encroachment of our governmental powers renders null and void our right to vote. Democracy and the consent of the governed ceases to exist the very moment the right to vote is denied. No circumstances warrant such action. Fiscal crisis like wars do not upend core democratic principles."

Hernández closed by attacking what to him and other pro-commonwealth supporters was most demeaning. The law declares that Congress is acting on the basis that Puerto Rico is still a U.S. territory subject to the plenary powers of Congress under the U.S. Constitution. In island status politics, Congress, for the first time in sixty-four years of commonwealth status, was declaring that Puerto Rico remained a "colony." He wrote, "I oppose this bill because of its shameless invocation of the territorial power to impose these encroachments." These powers "hark back to the discredited racist premises" of the Insular Cases, which established the unfettered power over Congress over Puerto Rico in the early 1900s, and "are no longer acceptable," he argued. "Unrepentant colonialism is not the way to help the people of Puerto Rico and we will oppose this affront to their dignity every step of the way."[6]

Hernández Colón had followed Muñoz's insistence that Puerto Rico had ceased being a U.S. colony when it became a commonwealth in 1952. Now, accusing Congress of "unrepentent colonialism," the island's political status conflict once again erupted. The pro-statehood movement saw PROMESA as confirmation that in fact the island had always been a "colony," that Congress had never relinquished its sovereignty but had merely authorized the island to enact its own constitution. As the NPP leader Jenniffer González Colón, then candidate for resident commissioner, put it, "[PROMESA] represents the best sample of the plenary powers that Congress has over Puerto Rico, and evidences that our colonial status ties up Puerto Rico's economic development model."[7] For the NPP leadership, the root cause of the economic and fiscal crisis "is our colonial status."

Rubén Berríos, leader of the small but influential Independence Party, agreed. He wrote that while it is right to feel indignation and protest the "abusive and humiliating" PROMESA board, no one should fool themselves: "The colony is the cause: the Board is the consequence."[8]

In 2017, with the pro-statehood NPP back in power, Governor Ricardo Rosselló and Resident Commissioner Jenniffer González Colón launched in Congress the biggest drive for statehood in island history. On January 4, González Colón filed a bill in the House aimed at admitting Puerto Rico as the fifty-first state by 2025.[9] A month later, the governor signed a law to host a nonbinding plebiscite between statehood, independence, and free association, excluding commonwealth status.[10] The plebiscite was boycotted by the pro-commonwealth and pro-independence parties. Statehood leaders trumpeted a victory of 97 percent, but voter turnout was only 23 percent, by far the lowest for any plebiscite in history.[11]

Undeterred, in July, the governor appointed a team of former governors, public figures, and the famous baseball player Ivan Rodriguez to serve as shadow members of Congress and lobby for statehood in Washington.[12] As the economy continued to decline, the recession entering its eleventh year, Puerto Rico found itself in a battle over political status that had not been seen since the 1930s.

The Hurricanes

In early September 2017, Puerto Rico was lucky for once. Hurricane Irma, with category 5 winds of up to 185 miles per hour, the most powerful Atlantic hurricane in recorded history, seemed to be on the way to a direct hit on the island. On September 7 it just missed the island, however, passing north; it caused power outages but not much more damage.

But Puerto Rico's luck was short-lived. Two weeks later, on September 20, category 4 Maria, the third costliest hurricane in history, hit Puerto Rico directly, crossing the length of the island and leaving $92 billion in destruction and 3,059 dead. It took eleven months to restore power to the entire island. As the weeks went by, Puerto Rico received hundreds of millions of dollars in U.S. emergency relief funds, millions of dollars from numerous civic and philanthropic organizations and from Puerto Rico's many entertainment and sports celebrities, and thousands of workers to slowly restore power and water. Scores of political leaders came: President Trump in a short visit, New York's governor Andrew Cuomo repeatedly, other governors, members of Congress, and an emissary of the pope. In the opposite direction, thousands of Puerto Ricans migrated to Florida and other states, many with their homes destroyed, without jobs, leaving behind unpaid mortgages and car loans. For the first time in centuries, Puerto Rico's most fundamental problem was not overpopulation but depopulation.

As the island fell into the recession in 2006, the exit increased from 15,288 in 2011 to 69,343 in 2017. Then, after the hurricane, it soared. Federal and island demographers project the island's population, 3.2 million in 2018, to drop to 2.7 million by 2022. The loss of a great part of Puerto Rico's productive population is still another grave economic problem.

The Political Crisis

In July 2019, the nightmare continued. Near midnight on July 24, in a recorded message, Governor Rosselló resigned. He had resisted ten days of nonstop protests, including by far the biggest in island history, as hundreds of thousands cried out, "Ricky resign!" And the legislative leadership of his party had had enough and gave him an ultimatum: resign or be impeached.

The crisis erupted on June 24 when Rosselló fired Treasury Secretary Raul Maldonado, who also held the two other highest offices in government finance: head of the Management and Budget Office and chief financial officer. Maldonado had long been considered the governor's right-hand man, also having served as his chief of staff. A day earlier Maldonado had rocked public opinion when he declared that there was an "institutional mafia" in the Treasury Department. Rosselló responded by implying that Maldonado himself was being investigated for corruption.

Two weeks later, the media began to receive transcripts of chat messages between the governor and his closest aides and advisers in which he insulted other political and governmental leaders, gays, and many others, at times using obscene language. This was followed by the U.S. Attorney's Office in San Juan indicting the former secretary of education, the former head of the Health Insurance Administration, and four others for "conspiracy, wire fraud, theft of government funds, and money laundering."[13]

The protests began, and the NPP called for Rosselló's resignation. On July 22, the island's leading newspaper, which had supported him, demanded his resignation on its front page. Rosselló had resisted the escalating pressure, but he could resist no more.

On July 30, Rosselló announced that he was naming Pedro Pierluisi, an attorney, to fill the vacant post of secretary of state, who according to the constitution would replace him. The announcement was met with a collective sigh of relief. Pierluisi had served as resident commissioner and president of the NPP. The private sector was especially pleased, confident he would focus on the economic and fiscal crisis.

But from the beginning, it was evident that the crisis was not over. The legislature first had to confirm Pierluisi as secretary of state. The House did, but the Senate did not. Citing legal arguments, Pierluisi decided that he could still swear in as governor, and he did. Five days later, on July 8, Puerto Rico's supreme court ruled otherwise. Secretary of Justice Wanda Vasquez, a career public official next in line in succession, took the oath of office. Puerto Pico had its third governor in a week.

Then came the earthquakes. As Puerto Rico celebrated the Christmas season, on December 28, 2019, the island began to shake, with eleven of the earthquakes magnitude 5 or greater. On January 7, a magnitude 6.4 earthquake permanently damaged and shut down the principal power plant that supplies over one quarter of the island's energy. The island lost power for a week. Governor Vázquez declared a national emergency, and the following day President Donald J. Trump followed suit. Eight thousand people lost their homes, refugee centers were established in fourteen municipalities, forty thousand people camped outside the hard-hit city of Ponce, and the economic damage was estimated at $3.1 billion. Two months later, on March 13, Vázquez again declared a national emergency, and two days later she placed Puerto Rico on lockdown to prepare the island for the coronavirus pandemic—another devastating blow to a Puerto Rican economy relentlessly battered by economic and fiscal crisis, hurricanes and earthquakes, and political crisis.

Is Puerto Rico "Cursed"?

How can we explain such a remarkable run of misfortune? Was Puerto Rico "cursed"? In 1899, a prominent Catholic prelate believed it was. Hurricanes were then seen as acts of God and were named after saints. After the devastation of San Ciriaco on August 7, 1899, which killed 3,369 Puerto Ricans, the prelate explained in a long letter why God had "punished" Puerto Rico. Like most Catholic priests on the island, the native Spaniard was hurt and offended that the Puerto Ricans had welcomed the Americans with open arms, turning their backs on Mother Spain. San Ciriaco, the prelate wrote, was "God's punishment."[14]

The threat of hurricanes every year between June and November, resulting from the many storms and hurricanes that form off the African coast and cross the Atlantic toward the Caribbean, has always been part of the island's reality. Every year there are official storm and hurricane alerts and warnings and the frantic rush to prepare for the worst. The hurricanes are terrifying, of course, causing deaths mostly by drowning in the floods and mudslides and wiping out the island's rural agricultural economy. Although the danger is real, most hurricanes miss the island; there is a direct hit on average every seven and half years.

In 2018, there was no evident explanation for Puerto Rico's extraordinary bad luck. Not one but two hurricanes struck one after the other after twelve years of economic recession. They occurred after Puerto Rico suffered the humiliation of being told that it no longer could borrow money, of admitting that it could no longer pay its debt because it was bankrupt, and of having imposed on it a fiscal board capable of overriding its government.

It was not bad luck. And though they inflicted tremendous damage, neither the hurricanes nor the earthquakes were the causes of the economic crisis. So who is to blame? The response of most of the political leadership in all the parties, especially after the creation of the PROMESA Fiscal Board, is the island's political status. It is "colonialism." As Governor Rosselló invariably pointed out, if Puerto Rico were not a "colony," if Puerto Ricans had the political power of citizens living on the mainland, voting representation in Congress, and the presidential vote, none of this would have happened.

On May 9, 2019, the pro-statehood senate president, Tomás Rivera Shatz, wrote, "The colonial crime against Puerto Rico has been provoked principally by the U.S. Congress. . . . [The United States] has always discriminated economically as it has politically, because we are a colony. . . . [T]hat is why the problem of Puerto Rico is colonialism and those that promote it."[15] Puerto Rican political leaders supporting statehood or independence are of one voice: the Americans are to blame.

Puerto Ricans are Latin Americans. The Venezuelan intellectual and journalist Carlos Rangel, in his influential and controversial 1977 book, *The Latin Americans: Their Love-Hate Relationship with the United States*, asks what has been a terrible question for Latin Americans: how can we explain the economic and political success of North America and the relative political and economic failure of Latin America? Rangel is far from being an apologist for the United States, recognizing "Washington's misuse of power, its clumsiness and exactions." But he calls on Latin Americans to stop "blaming American imperialism" for Latin American failure.[16] Stop wallowing in self-pity, in resentment and humiliation, Rangel pleads, and face the reality that Latin Americans themselves are to blame, that Latin America's failure is due to defects in its culture and politics.

Rangel dedicated less than two pages to "the case of Puerto Rico." Like most Latin American intellectuals, he is confused by Puerto Ricans. He writes, "It is in Puerto Rico that we find the most extreme form of the bitterness and resentment that Latin Americans in general feel towards their northern neighbors."[17] Yet Puerto Rico has benefited from the United States as no other Latin American country has: "Its economic development has been quite extraordinary."[18] At the time, Puerto Rico's per capita income of $2,000 was five times that of Central American countries.

But in fact the theme of Rangel's book — the love-hate relationship with the United States — is precisely the foundation of Puerto Rico's status politics. When he writes that Puerto Rico "suffers from an acute case of the Latin American complex," he is effectively describing Puerto Rico's obsession with the political status issue. This is the key to answering the question of how the Puerto Rico of the Camelot event, of Operation Bootstrap, of the economic miracle that turned the poorhouse of the Caribbean into the showcase of democracy, descended into a seemingly endless nightmare.

What Caused the "Death Spiral"?

In 2016, Governor Alejandro García Padilla described what he called Puerto Rico's "death spiral."[19] Part I of this book ends with a summary of six factors that account for this. Part II gives the historical context.

On July 25, 2019, a *Wall Street Journal* editorial expressed no doubt that corruption, bad policies, and resistance to the efforts of the PROMESA Fiscal Board to impose fiscal responsibility had brought about the collapse of Puerto Rico's economy.[20] It is evident that in the political crisis, Puerto Rico *is* responsible. In the economic and fiscal crisis, it was the U.S. government that eliminated Section 936, without an alternative, ruining Puerto Rico's economic development, killing Bootstrap. But it was the government of Puerto Rico that asked Congress to eliminate Section 936. In the end, the economic, fiscal, and political crises are the result of the breakdown of Puerto Rican self-government.

Of course, Puerto Rico has been "unlucky" in that it has been hurt repeatedly by acts of nature, hurricanes, earthquakes, and the pandemic. But the economic and fiscal crisis, the "fall" of Puerto Rico, is not the result of "God's punishment." There is no "curse." Like Rangel's Latin America, Puerto Rico has no one to blame but itself.

PART I

The Rise and Fall

CHAPTER ONE

Operation Bootstrap

In 1953, Rexford Tugwell, Puerto Rico's last American governor, wrote, "It is not too much to say that a transformation is in progress [in Puerto Rico] which for a long time will be one of the wonders of human history."[1] In 1954, Chester Bowles, anticipating Puerto Rico's role as the "showcase of democracy" after the 1959 Cuban Revolution, wrote, "At a time when we Americans urgently need to burn deeply into our private conscience and public policies a sympathetic grasp of the hopes and striving of the underdeveloped world, it is both fortunate and arresting that Puerto Rico can teach us so much. . . . [T]he United States should take special pride in its own recent and enlightened co-operation with Puerto Rico's 'Operation Bootstrap.' That is why this test case in American attitudes towards the generic problems of underdeveloped areas could be so pertinent elsewhere, if we wanted it to be. Let us make full use of the opportunities given us by this instant of special success."[2]

In 1961, the economist Kenneth E. Boulding wrote, "There is a type of revolution which does not fit into any type . . . of category and which may be the most fundamental in the long run. I call it the 'Fomentarian

15

Revolution' in honor of a remarkable institution in Puerto Rico which embodies it known as Fomento."[3] In 1965, the Harvard constitutionalist Carl J. Friedrich wrote, "Rare are the instances in which the transition to self-government of a former colonial territory has been achieved with comparable success."[4] And in 1987, Eric Hobsbawm wrote that Puerto Rico had experienced "the biggest and most intense, fastest and universal transformation in the history of humanity."[5]

On August 24, 1977, the *Wall Street Journal* associate editor and sup-ply-side economist, Jude Wanniski, wrote a column, "A Conversation with Muñoz Marín," that sought to explain Puerto Rico's remarkable economic growth. Muñoz, once an ardent critic of U.S. "colonialism" and passionate advocate of independence, described his transformation: "At the time I had held the classical theory of empire — that empires are good for the empires but not for the colonies. But here I saw Roosevelt, the head of the American empire, willing to back us in our fight against the capitalists in Puerto Rico. It showed me that I had to revise my theory of empire."[6]

Convinced that the United States was not the enemy but would now support his ambitious social and economic reforms, Muñoz campaigned in 1940, not on independence, but exclusively on his social justice agenda. Against all odds, he was elected president of the insular senate in 1940, becoming the island's top political leader.

But power brought about another change in Muñoz. As he told Wanniski, "When you are the party in opposition, you can afford to be the party that demands redistribution of wealth. But as we became the party of government we had to give more room to the idea of growth, so there would be more to distribute."[7]

This was the turning point in the island's history. Muñoz prioritized economic growth, upending the island's political culture by putting aside the political status issue. And he focused his government on the creation of wealth, the industrialization program called Operation Bootstrap.

That the United States would support Puerto Rico was manifest when President Franklin D. Roosevelt appointed Rexford Tugwell, famous as a member of Roosevelt's original New Deal "brain trust," the last of the American governors and by far the most successful. His personal relationship with Roosevelt was crucial, especially in the height of the war when the island, totally dependent on marine transportation, was effectively isolated by Nazi submarines seeking to impede the sea lanes and the flow of petroleum to the United States and Europe.

Tugwell, appointed governor in 1941, known for his academic career as an economist and an early admirer of the Soviet Union, would collaborate with Muñoz's left-wing agenda. Known by his critics as "Red Rex" because of his socialist tendencies, he was determined to introduce powerful economic planning into Puerto Rico's governance. He had served in the Roosevelt administration Department of Agriculture and was an expert in land reform, which made him an ideal ally for Muñoz. Forced by conservative Republicans in Congress to leave Washington because of what they considered his socialist ideas, he now believed and resented that Roosevelt's early New Deal was being overtaken by what he perceived as the return of conservative capitalists to power in Washington, in part as the result of World War II. Now he was delighted to have another opportunity, with Muñoz running the island government, to finally bring the New Deal spirit and programs to Puerto Rico.

Working in tandem, they created the first modern, efficient, honest government bureaucracy in Latin America and, according to some historians, among the best in the world.[8] They established numerous new government agencies and public corporations, including the Department of Transportation, the Budget Office, and Fomento, an agency in charge of attracting U.S. industry to the island. Among his initiatives, Tugwell was particularly proud of the powerful Planning Board—convinced that economic planning was indispensable to good government—and the Water Resources Authority. After a long legal battle with the private, Canadian-owned power company in San Juan, he had achieved his goal of a government monopoly on electric power.

Tugwell left the island in 1946, after five years as governor. World War II had ended, and he was convinced, as he wrote in his memoirs, *The Stricken Land*, that his usefulness to Puerto Rico and to Roosevelt had also ended. He was aware that he and Muñoz had accomplished a change comparable to the early New Deal on the mainland, but he left feeling skeptical about Teodoro Moscoso's new agency, Fomento, doubting that Puerto Rico could replace agriculture with industrialization. He was also skeptical about Puerto Rico's future under Muñoz's leadership. He admired Muñoz the man but distrusted Muñoz the politician, just as he distrusted most politicians in Puerto Rico and Washington. In his memoirs, he wondered if all that he and Muñoz had accomplished would survive what he saw as the viciousness of Puerto Rican politics.[9]

Tugwell's skepticism in 1946 was rooted in what had been the island reality. He well understood the power and destructiveness of island politics. He had been a witness to the attempt to extend the New Deal to Puerto Rico in the 1930s and its breakdown due to ferocious island political conflicts. Now he wondered, would Puerto Rico revert to the sense of hopelessness?

Hopelessness

"As for Puerto Rico," President Roosevelt lamented to Ernest Gruening in 1934, "the place is hopeless, *hopeless*," throwing his hands up for emphasis and in frustration.[10] Gruening was director of the Division of Territories and Island Possessions of the Interior Department and led the effort to extend the New Deal to Puerto Rico. Roosevelt and his administration, under the enormous weight of lifting the nation from the Great Depression, dedicated extraordinary time and effort to the small island territory in the Caribbean. This was partly because Eleanor Roosevelt had visited the island with Tugwell in 1934 and had taken a personal interest in Puerto Rico after witnessing the deplorable condition of these U.S. citizens—worse than anything she had seen on the mainland.

But the massive effort of millions in federal spending floundered. Pro-independence violence during the decade and the ambiguous reaction of local politicians triggered resentment in Gruening and others. Convinced that Puerto Rican politicians were not only ungrateful, but favored anti-American sentiment, Washington's enthusiasm for extending the New Deal to Puerto Rico waned. The sense of hopelessness reached all the way to the First Lady. "Increasingly frustrated," wrote Ruby Black in her biography of Eleanor Roosevelt, "her ambitious plans snarled by petty politics in Puerto Rico, incompetent administrators and congressional opposition, the First Lady began to withdraw."[11] Muñoz, politically damaged by the effort's failure, pronounced, "And so ends the most glorious, the most fair-minded, the most generous, and the most dastardly four years of the American regime in Puerto Rico."[12]

The fundamental cause for the sense of hopelessness was the perception that Puerto Rico represented an American failure. In their visit, Eleanor Roosevelt and her team could not believe that after nearly four decades of American rule, they were witnessing men, women, children—U.S. citizens since 1917—living in putrid slums, sleeping in shacks propped up over running sewage. "The misery of the people," Tugwell wrote, "was very nearly as deep as that of any people in the world." Speaking for the president who had ordered U.S. troops to take Puerto Rico, General Nelson Miles had issued a solemn proclamation in 1898: America had come to bestow "the advantages and blessings of enlightened civilization." More than an American failure, it was seen as a shameful "broken American pledge."[13]

It was not that the Americans did not try. In the early 1900s, there was an extensive effort to build infrastructure, roads, schools, and hospitals. Diseases that decimated the islanders were nearly wiped out, including bilharzia, caused by parasitic flatworms found in contaminated bodies of water that sapped the energy from its victims, leaving Puerto Ricans weak, passive, and indifferent. Then, in the 1920s, pro-business presidents promoted private spending, all in agriculture—sugar harvesting and refining, tobacco, and rum—but failed to lift the island out of poverty. Now liberal New Deal spending, despite its successes in surmounting the Great Depression on the mainland, had also failed.

The inevitable conclusion was that nothing worked. But why? Was it, after all, a problem with Puerto Rican culture? Efforts to "Americanize" Puerto Ricans—by conducting public instruction in English, for example—had failed. Was Puerto Rico, regardless of its political relationship to "enlightened civilization," destined by its Spanish heritage to follow the failure of Latin America?

Was it the nature of Puerto Rican politics? Except for outbreaks of nationalist violence that lacked popular support, Puerto Rican politics was pacific, unlike that of many of its Latin American neighbors. But it was also abstract, idealistic, personalistic, sterile, and at times destructive.

Or was it simply the fundamental economic reality of size and population? Puerto Rico, a small island, one hundred miles long by thirty-five miles wide, was already overpopulated in 1898, with nearly one million inhabitants. As Tugwell found during his 1934 trip, American success in wiping out disease had triggered a population explosion, now approaching two million. Although there had been significant improvements under the Americans, Puerto Rico was losing the race against population growth, and living conditions kept worsening. As an overpopulated island where 80 percent of the land was not suitable for large-scale agriculture, lacking sufficient valuable natural resources, a thousand miles from the U.S. mainland, what chance did Puerto Rico have to lift its exploding population from misery?

For many in Puerto Rico, and increasingly in Washington, the answer was none. But seven years after leaving Puerto Rico, Tugwell changed his mind. By 1953, he knew that his administrative revolution had not only survived, but thrived beyond his dreams. He wrote that now he saw the economic, political, and social changes that he and Muñoz had carried out had led to a "transformation . . . which for a long time [would] be one of the wonders of human history."[14] He no longer had doubts about Muñoz as a political leader: he wrote a book in 1958 on the art of politics, comparing Muñoz to Roosevelt and New York mayor Fiorello La Guardia.

For Tugwell, it was not hyperbole. His five years in Puerto Rico had left him with the pessimism that Puerto Rico was a "stricken land" where nothing, even his own best efforts, would last. Now he believed that he was witnessing a true economic miracle.

The Sleepless Night

Muñoz and Tugwell's sweeping reforms and creation of an efficient and honest government administration had made possible the remarkable economic takeoff. And it began on an early morning in 1947. It was still dark outside, and Teodoro Moscoso, head of Fomento, had not closed his eyes. Hours earlier, something terrible had happened to him and, he was convinced, to Puerto Rico.

A year before, he had convinced senate leader Muñoz to approve legislation to offer tax exemption for American job-creating investment on the island. Since the island's status gave it exemption from federal income tax laws, this would give the investments total tax exemption. But the 1946 law, Moscoso believed, was seriously defective and needed to be amended. The Moscoso proposal, however, reignited what had always been strong opposition within the Popular Party leadership and within the administration. After what seemed an endless meeting with his entire economic team and other political leaders, Muñoz yielded to the cacophony of opposition and finally decided to reject Moscoso's plea.

Muñoz's rejection should not have surprised the thirty-six-year-old Moscoso. He had always known that the very idea of offering full tax exemption provoked in Muñoz strong and conflicting emotion. He was, after all, an anti-capitalist, a Marxist in his youth, and until recently a radical proponent of Puerto Rican independence. His program of deep social and economic reforms, including land redistribution, was aimed at breaking up the stranglehold of absentee corporations on the island economy and politics. And, most important, as governor, Tugwell, who had recruited most of the administrators and economists, some of them with Ivy League degrees and who saw him as their mentor, had been firmly opposed to tax exemption.

Tugwell's Opposition

It was Tugwell who had plucked a restless and unhappy Moscoso from a family pharmacy in Ponce and made him his principal Puerto Rican aide, impressed by his talent for getting things done. Moscoso, however, became a nuisance at La Fortaleza, badgering the governor about the need to create an agency dedicated to promoting the island's industrialization. But like almost all island economists, Tugwell believed that Puerto Rico's economic future depended on agriculture. Although people had talked about industrialization since the early 1900s, it was always in the context of agriculture-dependent industries such as sugar mills and rum distilleries. Nonagricultural industrialization, as Moscoso envisioned it, had never materialized, and Tugwell was convinced it never could.

But somehow Moscoso got Muñoz and the Popular Democratic Party–controlled legislature to create a small agency, the Puerto Rico Development Company, which would become known as Fomento, with a budget of $500,000, and the Government Development Bank. On May 11, 1942, Tugwell signed the law creating the agency. A few months later, he got around to naming Moscoso to head it, saying, "This is your idea so you might as well run it." As he admitted in his memoirs, he didn't think much about it then.[15]

World War II gave Moscoso an opportunity to advance his industrialization goal. Since the early 1900s, Puerto Rico had benefited from a federal excise tax rebate; every dollar paid in rum excise taxes on the mainland was deposited into Puerto Rico's Treasury. When the United States limited liquor production during the war, rum consumption on the mainland skyrocketed, giving Puerto Rico a revenue windfall. Using this revenue, Moscoso set out to build government-owned and government-operated factories, mostly related to the booming rum industry. It soon became evident that this was not enough. Believing that Muñoz was more ideologically flexible than Tugwell, Moscoso persuaded him in 1944 to approve a tax exemption bill to try to bring investment to the island. Tugwell promptly vetoed it.

For Moscoso, it was still a victory. He believed that he had finally convinced the anticapitalist Muñoz to at least try tax exemption. Muñoz was changing. He and his party were overwhelmingly reelected in 1944. After the Philippines obtained its independence with economic conditions that he believed would have been terrible for Puerto Rico, mostly losing free access to the U.S. market, Muñoz revealed to his party leadership and the people that he was giving up his support for independence.

As always, his program of economic justice had priority, and by now he was convinced that the wide economic and social reforms that were visibly and dramatically lifting the people from centuries of extreme poverty were not enough. There was land and wealth distribution, electric power, water and sewerage extended to thousands of families, but Muñoz realized that real social and economic justice was possible only by creating new wealth. This created a conflict for him: would he stay true to his lifelong socialist convictions or accept the reality that to create wealth meant industustrialization—and this meant capitalism.

Moscoso saw the opportunity he needed. After Tugwell left in 1946, Moscoso tried again and this time succeeded in persuading Muñoz and his party to approve a new tax exemption bill. With World War II over, the rum tax windfall had ended. The early government industrial plants, while for Moscoso and Fomento of important learning value, were evidently not going to make a dent in the increasing numbers of unemployed. Moscoso informed Muñoz that Fomento would need a $300 million government investment, which was obviously unrealistic. The 1946 law had not worked; Fomento had established fewer than ten small private industries. Moscoso decided to return to Muñoz to try to convince him that Fomento needed a much more robust tax exemption law.

But that early morning in 1947, sleepless, Moscoso concluded that his battle was finally over. He had faced persistent opposition since the beginning of Fomento: he was accused of wanting to bring back the absentee corporations that had exploited Puerto Rico for decades and that effectively, through vote buying, had controlled island politics.

Muñoz was already fighting a difficult ideological battle within his party. He had to overcome an internal party rebellion when he decided to give up independence and seek a new form of autonomy. The harshest opposition now came from the new Puerto Rico Independence Party. Attacked for betraying the island by supporting Moscoso and Fomento, Muñoz was denounced for also betraying his reformist, social justice ideals.

But the worst opposition was not political or ideological but came from a close friend of Moscoso, another of the professionals recruited by Tugwell, generally regarded the island's best economist. Muñoz's secretary of the treasury, Sol Luis Descartes, adamantly argued that Moscoso was dead wrong, that tax exemption was the wrong economic development strategy. To the meeting at Muñoz's home, he brought along an American tax expert who had written extensively on how high-taxed economies produced high economic growth and low-taxed economies, low growth. In the end, they argued, tax exemption was simply immoral. How could one justify taxing a hardworking Puerto Rican entrepreneur but not the wealthy American owner of a brassiere factory?

That night, Descartes and the tax expert prevailed. Muñoz was convinced. Exhausted by the long hours of heated arguments, he finally cut it short. He had decided. They would not amend the tax bill; they would repeal it.

Moscoso knew that this decision ended his industrialization dream. With great effort a small number of small factories would continue to trickle in, but that was not the Fomento Puerto Rico desperately needed. If there was one thing he and his Fomento team had learned, it was that Puerto Rico needed a tax incentive big enough to overcome the great disadvantages of Puerto Rico as an industrial site. He had argued emotionally that night that tax exemption was not a gift, a favor for the rich, but the essential *equalizer* that made Puerto Rico competitive with the mainland.

Of course, he would have to leave. What would he do? He was a trained pharmacist working in the family business when six years earlier he got the call from Tugwell. His father had hoped that he would run the big family pharmacy business. But this was out of the question.

Then he got an idea. It was still dark outside, but he got dressed and drove to Muñoz's home.

"Don Luis," he told a stunned Muñoz, still in his pajamas, "I have a question."

After a long pause: "What do we have to lose?"

Another pause: "If they are right, and it won't work, we'll be where we are now. But if it works, . . . what do we lose by trying?"[16]

Muñoz reversed himself. And this was the beginning.

The Rise: The "Economic Miracle"

That early morning conversation in 1947 triggered what became known as Operation Bootstrap, the beginning of what became the "economic miracle." The Industrial Incentives Act, approved on May 12, 1947, exempted private companies from income and property taxes, among others, for a ten-year period that would later be extended through amendments to the act. This local exemption, alongside the federal income tax exemption applicable in Puerto Rico, meant that American companies that resettled in the island would pay no income tax. Adding to the equation was the fact that Puerto Rico was not subject to federal minimum wage increases and had free trade with the United States.[17]

Operation Bootstrap began to take off. Whereas Fomento attracted only 13 manufacturing plants between 1943 and 1948, in 1948 alone it attracted 24. In 1949, the number doubled, to 50, and the next year it increased to 80. By 1955, there were 300 factories. A little over a decade after his conversation with Muñoz, in 1959, there were 530 factories operating and 91 more on the way.[18]

Many of these plants were labor-intensive garment factories and paid better than the island's agrarian industries. These factories not only benefited those who worked for them but also had an indirect impact on industries necessary to sustain them, like water, electricity, housing, roads, health, and education.[19]

The island's per capita income grew by nearly 400 percent from 1950 to 1973, becoming the highest in Latin America. The island's gross national product grew from 1950 to 1977 by 300 percent.

The political effect was inevitable. In 1948, Congress approved the first gubernatorial elections. Muñoz and the Popular Democratic Party won in a landslide, with 61.2 percent of the vote, 32.5 percent more than the nearest rival. With the economy for the first time in history experiencing sustained economic growth and with Muñoz having achieved political hegemony, he decided the time had arrived to tackle the political status issue. He proposed the adoption of commonwealth status, a novel arrangement whereby Puerto Rico would consent, for the first time, to a relationship with the United States and adopt its own constitution. In 1952, Muñoz was reelected overwhelmingly with 64.9 percent of the vote, more than three times the runner-up, the Puerto Rico Independence Party.

Still, Moscoso's battle to defend Bootstrap continued. In the 1920s, Muñoz and others had bitterly criticized what they called the "era of flattering statistics"—ridiculing the official reports of American governors describing the "progress" taking place on the island.[20] These statistics, he said, hid the reality that the vast majority of Puerto Ricans were not only still struggling to survive in abysmal conditions, but were now victims of American laissez-faire capitalist exploitation. Bootstrap's "flattering statistics," the critics pointed out, while undeniably lifting many from poverty, hid the reality that it was failing to resolve the island's most fundamental problem: massive chronic unemployment. The growth in manufacturing jobs could not compensate for the rapid fall of agricultural employment in rural areas, which triggered migration to urban areas.[21] Unemployment hovered between 11 and 16 percent during the 1950s and 1960s.[22]

But Bootstrap, always unavoidably entangled in the island's political status conflict, now became the center of the new Puerto Rico Independence

Party's challenge to Muñoz. The leading opposition party in 1948–52, it strongly attacked Bootstrap as a new form of American capitalist exploitation: the flood of American capital was exploiting the island, paying no taxes on big profits while paying workers starvation wages.

For the *independentistas*, Bootstrap was a conspiracy devised and implemented by Muñoz—the man who had betrayed the independence movement that he had led for many years—to favor this new form of "Yanqui imperialism." Bootstrap was nothing but a Machiavellian Muñoz plot to make Puerto Rico totally dependent on the Americans—on American factories and welfare payments—in order to finally crush independence sentiment on the island. At the same time, the independence advocates argued, Muñoz and Moscoso were seeking to reduce the island's abysmal, persistent unemployment by effectively pushing hundreds of thousands of poor Puerto Ricans to migrate to New York City slums. Muñoz responded that while there was no policy to promote the massive migration that took place in the 1950s—470,000 in that decade alone—the government did indeed open government offices in New York and elsewhere to assist the migrants.

The assault from what in island politics is considered the Left—the independence movement—did not surprise Muñoz and Moscoso. The fact was that the success of Fomento was making closer and stronger not only the economic but also the political and cultural links of Puerto Rico to the United States. But what seemed to make no sense was the attack from the right—the conservative, pro-American sector—led mostly by the island's Republican pro-statehood party. At the beginning, in the 1940s, the attack was that Fomento was really a Muñoz socialist plot to take over the private economy. As industrialization took off, the argument was that Muñoz was now guilty of the "flattering statistics" that he had denounced in the past, that the Fomento economic growth was really due to three factors: the great postwar industrial expansion in the United States, American Cold War policies to ensure stability in the Caribbean, and the mass migration of Puerto Ricans to the United States.

But there was a vital change in the anti-Bootstrap campaign from the conservative sector. By the 1970s, with the pro-statehood New Progressive Party in power, the attack on Bootstrap became essentially identical to that of the Independence Party two decades earlier: Bootstrap was in fact a Muñoz "conspiracy"—this time not to crush independence but statehood. The essential anti-Bootstrap argument was the same as that Moscoso had confronted from the beginning of Fomento in 1942 and that had never really abated. Bootstrap was based on a bad, wrong, and in the end destructive economic policy: tax exemption.

The Fall: The Anti-Bootstrap Crusade

In 1965, Carlos Romero Barceló, a thirty-two-year-old San Juan attorney, testified before the U.S.–Puerto Rico Commission on the Status of Puerto Rico, launching a frontal attack on the Bootstrap program. "The problem that we have in Puerto Rico," he said, "is that there are too many industries which are being artificially maintained by the government for political purposes, which solve a short-run problem but create greater and more serious long-run problems."[23]

"One of the most widely used arguments against statehood," he continued, "is the fact that our economy is now becoming increasingly dependent upon tax-exempt industry and that when we become a State we would not be able to offer tax exemption, and, therefore, industry would disappear." The other, "more valid argument used to attack statehood," he said, "is that Puerto Rico cannot pay the minimum wages that can be paid by all other States of the Union."[24]

In the following half century, Romero Barceló went on to become one of Puerto Rico's prominent pro-statehood leaders. He was elected mayor of San Juan twice and governor of Puerto Rico twice; he served in the insular senate and was elected twice as resident commissioner, Puerto Rico's representative in Congress. He was also the leading opponent of tax exemption.

Romero Barceló argued, as economists did from the beginning, that tax exemption was simply bad economic policy. But he went much further. He confronted the unavoidable reality that the federal tax exemption that Congress had granted Puerto Rico in the first Organic Act in 1900 was incompatible with statehood. Article 1, section 8, of the U.S. Constitution states that "all Duties, Imposts and Excises shall be uniform throughout the United States."

When Romero Barceló testified in 1965 that tax-exempt industries are "artificially maintained by the government for political purposes," that the real purpose of Bootstrap was not economic but "political," this became the core of his lifelong crusade against the Bootstrap program. The real purpose, as he would spell out in a 1973 pamphlet, *Statehood Is for the Poor*, was to crush the statehood movement.[25]

Romero Barceló's crusade culminated on the afternoon of August 20, 1996, on the South Lawn of the White House when President Bill Clinton signed the Small Business Job Protection Act, among other things, raising the federal minimum wage from $4.25 to $5.15 in two years. The increase had wide bipartisan support in Congress; its approval was not in doubt. It was a joyful ceremony: the president surrounded by smiling lawmakers from both parties; the lawn filled with happy children. Among those who were most jubilant was Romero Barceló, Puerto Rico's resident commissioner in Congress. He had long supported extending the federal minimum wage to Puerto Rico, but there was a much bigger motive for his celebration. He had carried out in Congress, with the support of the island's pro-statehood government, an intense campaign to eliminate Section 936, which had extended the island's federal tax exemption incentive, allowing companies to repatriate their island profits to the mainland tax-free. It had aroused great controversy on the island, but he succeeded in attaching a clause to the minimum wage bill that decreed a ten-year phase-out of the exemption.

It was evident that it would have a big economic impact. The president and several members of Congress, in fact, had opposed its elimination without replacing it with an alternative. President Clinton knew it would hurt the island's economy. The White House press release acknowledged, "This legislation ignores the needs of our citizens in Puerto Rico, ending the incentive for new investments now and phasing out the incentives for existing investments."[26] He called on Congress to provide the island with new tools for economic investment. It didn't.

But for Romero Barceló and the statehood movement, this was a vital step forward in the century-old march to statehood. The government agency Fomento still existed. Puerto Rico remained a commonwealth. But for them, the elimination of Section 936 removed a giant "obstacle to statehood."

The defense and survival of Bootstrap had always been an uphill battle for Moscoso and for Puerto Rico, from Tugwell's veto of the first tax exemption law in 1944 to Muñoz's wavering in 1947, the early morning meeting with Muñoz, and the battle against Descartes and the other opponents to tax exemption. It survived the devastating Yom Kippur oil crisis of 1973 that temporarily brought economic growth to a screeching halt. Bootstrap had always survived. But it and the Puerto Rican economy would not survive the killing of Section 936.

CHAPTER TWO

Operation Bootstrap and the Statehood Surge

Although not quite as dramatic as October 18, 1898, when the Spanish flag was lowered at La Fortaleza and the American flag was raised, the election in 1968 of Luis A. Ferré as the first pro-statehood governor of Puerto Rico marked a historic moment in Puerto Rican history. It ended the twenty-eight-year hegemony of Muñoz and the Popular Democratic Party. Puerto Rico again had a two-party system, which many in Puerto Rico, including PDP followers, celebrated as a big advancement for Puerto Rican democracy.

But there was an important question. Would there be continuity in Puerto Rico's economic development programs? Given the incompatibility of statehood and the tax exemption incentive and the outspoken opposition of Romero Barceló, elected mayor of San Juan, and other party leaders, there were concerns about what Ferré's attitude would be toward Operation Bootstrap.

Bootstrap advocates and the island's private sector had reason to feel confident. The sixty-four-year-old Ferré was Puerto Rico's leading industrialist and humanist. He had graduated from MIT with a degree in engineering, and later served on its board of governors. An accomplished pianist, he was the island's leading patron of the arts. In 1959, he founded the Ponce Museum of Art, with a collection of nineteenth-century European and Puerto Rican paintings housed in a building designed by Edward Durell Stone, an architectural landmark in the southern city of Ponce.

People respected him as a politician. He served as the local Republican Party's national committeeman and was active in GOP politics, and although he was considered a conservative, he was admired on the island for adopting liberal labor policies in his many industries and businesses. Many Puerto Ricans also admired his dogged opposition to Muñoz and the PDP during the decades in which they won elections overwhelmingly, capturing almost total control of the legislature and municipal governments.

So dominant were Muñoz and his party that he was often accused in Washington, as in much of Latin America, of being if not a dictator, then another Latin American strongman. In the United States, it was hard to understand what was effectively a one-party system. Many in the Latin American Left—never understanding why this "Latin American nation" did not demand its independence, particularly after the Cuban Revolution—denigrated Muñoz as an American puppet who had crushed the independence movement. Although Ferré himself often accused Muñoz of being a dictator, his perennial opposition candidacy election after election, along with the success of his business empire, strengthened Muñoz's argument that democratic political competition on the island indeed existed. Ferré had been running for elective office since Muñoz's and the PDP's first elections in 1940. Now, in 1968, he had launched his fourth attempt at the governorship.

Why, people often asked, did this wealthy, cultured man run for governor when he had no opportunity of winning? Because opposing the all-powerful Muñoz was vital to Puerto Rican democracy, he answered. But he had a deeper motivation. He did not run to win and administer the island. As he often explained, he had a mission: to keep the statehood ideal alive. And it was precisely Ferré, when the statehood flame was dangerously flickering in the 1950s and on the verge of dying, who reignited it.

The Statehood Movement

The statehood movement was born thirty-three days after American troops landed on Puerto Rico's southern coast. On August 27, 1898, José Celso Barbosa, a black physician educated at the University of Michigan, founded the local Republican Party, declaring, "We aspire to become another state within the Union."[1]

In the 1930s the conservative Republican Party, representing the business elite, mostly in the sugar industries, formed a coalition with its ideological opposite, the pro-labor Socialist Party, getting control of the legislature in 1932 and 1936. The odd coupling of a capitalist party with a labor-socialist party, in fact, revealed the nature of island politics. At the beginning, the Socialist Party downplayed the political status issue. But its leadership, which had strong links to the U.S. labor movement, came out for statehood, allowing it to form the "coalition" with the pro-statehood Republican Party.

Island politics was not driven by economic theory or policies. The rhetoric was about the much-professed political status "ideals," but there was a more mundane motivation: to gain control of the legislature in order to control the island's budget and thus the government jobs that sustained its political machines.

By midcentury, overwhelmed by the Muñoz–Popular Democratic Party hegemony, the coalition had broken. The Socialist Party disappeared, and it seemed that the Republican Party was destined to follow. In the 1952 elections, the Republican Party received only 85,591 votes, compared to the PDP's 431,409 votes. It even lagged behind the new Independence Party's 126,228 votes.

On July 25, 1952, the island became a U.S. commonwealth under its own constitution, its proponents proclaiming that the island was no longer a colony. Not only was Muñoz's political power at its height, but the island economy had begun to take off under Operation Bootstrap. Was there a place in island politics for a statehood party? The highly emotional opposition to the PDP came from the pro-independence sector, along with sporadic acts of violence on the island and the mainland. But no one expected it to become dominant, as in fact it did not: it declined in the coming decades to a small fraction of the electorate. Ferré, with his brother-in-law, Miguel Ángel García Mendez, a wealthy sugar mill and real estate owner, took over the Republican Party in 1952. Ferré ran for the legislature that year and began running for governor in 1956. The Republican Party became the Statehood Republican Party. He proved to be an effective politician, transforming the image of Republicans as stodgy reactionaries. He was charismatic, lacking the hard edges of many island politicians, and projected himself as "pro-American" without being anti–Puerto Rican. He reversed the statehood movement's decline, and the party began to climb dramatically. It doubled its share of votes from 12.9 percent in 1952 to 25.1 percent in 1956 and then to 32.1 percent in 1960.

Ferré and García Méndez understood that status politics was the only way to oppose the Muñoz-PDP juggernaut. The Operation Bootstrap "economic miracle" was a palpable reality. They insisted that the new commonwealth was at best a temporary arrangement that gave no guarantee against independence and that Muñoz had never stopped being a radical *independentista* but was using commonwealth status as a smokescreen. Their campaign slogan was that one day Puerto Ricans would wake up to find that the PDP had "brought independence through the kitchen."

Ferré argued that in spite of Puerto Rico's obvious economic improvement, once it became a state it would benefit greatly from much more in federal funds and not have to depend on "gimmicks" such as tax exemption. He appealed to what seemed to be common sense: if all the states are rich, it makes sense that statehood will make Puerto Rico rich. Muñoz and statehood opponents denounced this as demagoguery and unrealistic.

But for Ferré the basic reality was that since almost all Puerto Ricans opposed independence, they were "pro-American." The tight grip of the PDP on the vast number of Puerto Ricans dependent on the island government, fearful of losing public housing and all the other welfare benefits, was not permanent. Without Muñoz, commonwealth status, a Muñoz "myth," and the PDP itself, would inevitably wither and die. Muñoz was not immortal. It was a matter of time.

The End of the Muñoz Era

In 1964, it seemed as if the time had arrived. Muñoz decided to retire. Wanting to dramatize the transition to a new generation of PDP leaders, he proclaimed the end of the Muñoz era.[2] Overcoming deep resistance to his retirement, he convinced the PDP to nominate Roberto Sánchez Vilella, who had been his closest aide since 1940 and was then serving as secretary of state and was admired as a good administrator.

But the 1964 election was a disappointment for Ferré and the statehood movement. Muñoz and the PDP campaigned hard for Sánchez Vilella, and he won overwhelmingly. This was Ferré's third consecutive defeat as gubernatorial candidate, this time to a lackluster opponent. He announced that this was his last election.

Muñoz was delighted that the big victory now seemed to disprove that that the PDP could not win without him. But Ferré's party had again increased the pro-statehood vote from 32.1 to 34.7 percent. What was it that seemed to be driving the statehood movement relentlessly forward? Ferré's charisma and political talents obviously were a big part of the answer. But was there a deeper explanation? Was it because of the economic changes taking place as the island modernized and industrialized? Was the deeper cause Operation Bootstrap?

On the surface, it did not seem to make sense. Logically, Puerto Rico's extraordinary economic growth vindicated its commonwealth status. It worked. As more and more Puerto Ricans got good jobs and climbed out of poverty, it would seem to undercut the old argument that only statehood meant prosperity. But the growing urban middle class created by industrialization was proving to be precisely the breeding ground for statehood sentiment. In San Juan, the PDP underperformed, barely surpassing 50 percent of the vote in 1956, 1960, and 1964.

And there was an even deeper factor, the cultural transformation. From the beginning, PDP intellectuals and ideologues had warned that Moscoso's industrialization would result in what U.S. colonial policies in the 1920s and 1930s had failed to achieve: the "Americanization" of Puerto Rico. The PDP that Muñoz had created considered itself the "*jíbaro* party" — the party of rural workers — and its electoral strength emerged from the rural areas.

Operation Bootstrap was not only radically changing the economy, but it was radically undermining its traditional, jíbaro values, creating what Muñoz decried as an excessively consumerist society. In the 1950s he had begun talking about Operation Serenity — as he put it, the need to make

Bootstrap's progress the servant, not the master, of good Puerto Rican cultural values, of a "good civilization." Muñoz lamented that he had not done enough for Operation Serenity. He gave Moscoso the command to grow the economy. Moscoso had done just that, and now Muñoz was worrying about the cultural effects. Was Ferré right, after all? Was Moscoso's industrialization, the "Americanization" of Puerto Rico, leading irrevocably to eventual statehood?

The Juridical Defect

But there was another factor. Among Puerto Rico's political class, including the PDP and most of its professional and academic elite, it was evident that commonwealth status had a serious juridical defect. It left U.S. citizens living in Puerto Rico without the right to vote for president, only one resident commissioner with restricted right to vote in the House, and no representation in the Senate. Doubts about the juridical legitimacy of the commonwealth and repeated efforts by Muñoz and subsequent PDP leadership to resolve the juridical defect gave the statehood movement a critical boost.

Leading up to the creation of the commonwealth in 1952, particularly as the proposal made its way through Congress, Muñoz had a difficult time with his own legal and juridical advisers. For him, resolving the status issue was straightforward enough. As independence and statehood were not possible, Puerto Rico had to be accorded some form of autonomy within the American constitutional system. Legally, Puerto Rico was still a U.S. territory. But Muñoz, who had eschewed his father's attempt to get him to study law, selling his law texts for much-needed money for liquor and cigarettes, now insisted that while the juridical issues were important, what guided him was the reality.

And the "reality" was that since electing its own governor in 1948 and its own legislature, Puerto Rico was effectively exercising self-government. It also had an autonomous status, if not de jure, certainly de facto. The goal now was to get Congress to approve a constitutional process whereby, governed under its own constitution, Puerto Rico would no longer be a "juridical colony."

What had always interested Muñoz was his program of economic and social justice, so the goal was to create a commonwealth that allowed the island to continue its economic growth. In his thinking, Puerto Rico had more real power with fiscal autonomy than as a state with voting representation in Congress. It seemed to him common sense. Puerto Ricans paid all their taxes to the island Treasury controlled by a legislature elected entirely by the Puerto Rican voters. As a state, Puerto Ricans would pay most of their taxes to the federal Treasury controlled by a Congress where Puerto Ricans would elect a fraction, 6 representatives, 2 senators, of the 535 members.

Muñoz used this argument often in defense of Puerto Rico's commonwealth status, especially in the 1967 status plebiscite. But it satisfied no one, beginning with many in his own party.

In 1959, Muñoz, however, decided to return to Congress to make improvements in Puerto Rico's commonwealth status, including correcting the "juridical defect." The Fernos-Murray bill failed, in large part because of its complexity, which confused members of Congress. Since its creation in 1952, the commonwealth had generated considerable positive media attention due to the wide perception of Operation Bootstrap's success. Why change something that seemed to be working so well?

There was still another factor. Muñoz and the PDP expected that their initiative to "perfect" the commonwealth would arrest the growth of the statehood movement. But it had the opposite effect: seeking greater autonomy was decried by statehood leaders as a move toward independence.

A new pro-statehood, nonpartisan militant group was organized to combat the Fernos-Murray bill, Ciudadanos Pro Estado 51 (Citizens for State 51), among them young professionals, many of them federal employees on the island fearing that the changes Muñoz was seeking could cost them their jobs. The new group was led by the young lawyer Carlos Romero Barceló and marked his entry into island politics. He would become a pivotal leader in the statehood movement.

The 1967 Plebiscite and the Birth of the New Progressive Party

In 1961, Muñoz made a decision that set off a chain of events culminating in the November 1968 election of Ferré and his pro-statehood New

Progressive Party (NPP). After the glittering White House banquet in his honor, still smarting from the defeat of the 1959 Fernos-Murray bill, Muñoz decided to try again to get Congress to "perfect" the common-wealth, this time with President Kennedy's enthusiastic support. The plan was to first get Congress to approve the changes and then hold a three-sta-tus plebiscite, the first in island history.

This was a big change in Muñoz's thinking. Statehood leaders had been demanding a plebiscite, believing that given the opportunity to vote for statehood in a nonpartisan plebiscite, statehood would win. Muñoz had resisted insisting that Puerto Ricans had already expressed themselves in the 1951 status referendum. Statehood leaders countered that it was limited to a yes or no vote on commonwealth status. A three-status plebi-scite, Muñoz had argued, would be a waste of time. What was the point of asking Puerto Ricans if they supported statehood when it was in fact not possible economically and when everyone knew that Puerto Ricans overwhelmingly rejected independence. By 1960, the pro-independence vote had dropped to less than 3 percent, where it would remain.

But there was another element in Muñoz's thinking: his decision to retire in 1964. Secretary of State Roberto Sánchez Vilella's resounding victory in 1964 had proven that the PDP remained a powerhouse with-out him. A resounding commonwealth victory in the plebiscite, crushing the statehood movement, would prove that the commonwealth would also survive without him.

But nothing went as planned. First, the Muñoz initiative in Congress to perfect the commonwealth again floundered. As much as the Kennedy administration wanted to help, as had happened with the Fernos-Murray bill, again there was confusion over what exactly Puerto Rico wanted, whether the grand design of virtual total autonomy was feasible under the U.S. Constitution.

Ferré, the island's Republican Party chairman, mobilized GOP members in the House hearings to submit Muñoz to harsh questioning. Finally, Con-gress decided to defer action on the status issue, instead creating the United States–Puerto Rico Commission on the Status of Puerto Rico, a study com-mission that would inform the electorate on the economic, political, and cultural consequences of changing to statehood or independence.

This was not what Muñoz and the PDP wanted, but there was a silver lining. They hoped that if the Commission's technical, professional, and political studies were done right, the perennial status conflict would be changed from the world of fantasy, wishful thinking, and partisan demagoguery to the cold economic and political realities of Puerto Rico and the United States. In the end, Muñoz was confident, this would achieve his goal of securing commonwealth status. In this also, Muñoz and commonwealth supporters were disappointed.

Meanwhile, as the monolithic, invincible Popular Democratic Party began to mobilize for the 1967 plebiscite battle, there was an unexpected crisis. Governor Sánchez Vilella divorced his wife to marry a young assistant and announced that he would not seek reelection. This caused a media frenzy. He refrained from participating in the plebiscite campaign to avoid becoming a distraction. Cracks began to appear in the PDP between the old and the new political leadership and then between Muñoz and Sánchez Vilella. In what for commonwealth advocates was to be the decisive battle, the PDP was clearly weakened.

A similar conflict arose in the Statehood Republican Party (SRP) that seemed to likewise divide and weaken the statehood movement. Ferré and his brother-in-law, García Méndez, who throughout their careers had complemented each other politically, fought and split. Ferré, as he had in the past, endorsed the plebiscite. García Méndez, convinced that the Muñoz-PDP behemoth would crush the statehood vote, was just as strongly opposed. Controlling the Statehood Republican Party machinery, the party decided to boycott the plebiscite. Since the Independence Party had already decided to boycott, García Méndez believed this would delegitimize the Muñoz plebiscite.

Their partnership had succeeded in lifting the statehood movement in the 1950s, and it seemed that they needed each other. Ferré was the charismatic vote getter who would return to his businesses after each election; García Méndez, who had been Speaker of the House in the 1930s and was now one of the island's wealthiest businessmen, ran the party machine from his Senate seat. Ferré argued that he could simply not abandon his lifelong ideal; García Méndez argued that if the SRP participated, it would have to abide by the results — effectively killing the statehood "ideal." Ferré took a huge gamble that he, the perpetually optimistic idealist, was right, and his brother-in-law, the hardcore realist, was wrong. Ferré organized his own group, Estadistas Unidos (United Statehooders), with a new generation of statehood militants that had carried out the effective Citizens for State 51 campaign in 1959.

Commonwealth won the July 23, 1967, plebiscite with 60 percent of the vote. But this was far from the decisive defeat of statehood that Muñoz and the PDP wanted. The results dramatized what had been evident: the PDP was seriously divided and weakened. Accustomed to at most losing one or two of the small, rural towns, now it lost in the biggest cities, San Juan and Ponce, and three other municipalities.

Ferré and his followers celebrated what they considered remarkable statehood strength. It had overcome the SRP boycott with 39 percent of the vote. Unlike what occurred in the PDP, the split in the SRP *strengthened* the statehood movement. For the new statehood leaders, the plebiscite revealed that what had been holding it back was precisely the Republican label — identified in the past with the sugar corporations and now with the reactionary business oligarchy. Many of them identified themselves as Democrats. Casting off the now-empty shell of the SRP, the statehood ideal was liberated to represent Puerto Rico's rapidly growing middle class.

Ferré had pledged to his brother-in-law that he would not convert Estadistas Unidos into a rival political party. But faced with the reality that more than 96 percent of the SRP electorate had followed him, Ferré quickly converted Estadistas Unidos into the New Progressive Party. The SRP, the oldest party, founded in 1899, received only 4,057 votes in 1968 and disappeared.

In the PDP, the division degenerated into its worst crisis. In March 1968, Sánchez Vilella reversed his decision to retire and announced that he was running for reelection. The generational war broke out, the new generation supporting him and the old rallying behind and nominating the veteran Senate leader Luis Negrón López, a shy rural lawyer who had always worked behind the scenes as the Senate majority leader and who had never aspired to the governorship. Puerto Rico's political world was upended. Governor Sánchez Villela organized his own party and launched an emotional campaign not only against the PDP and Negrón López but also against Muñoz.

After three decades of political continuity, stability, and predictability, the 1968 elections seemed bizarre: Sánchez Villela was running by attacking his mentor and party; Ferré was running against his old party and against his brother-in-law and closest colleague. There was a reversal in the perception of the political parties. The PDP had always been seen as the progressive, forward-looking, and, by some, even radical and dangerous party. Now led by Negrón López, who prided himself on being an authentic Puerto Rican jíbaro, never natural or relaxed and sometimes awkward in his campaign, was seen as appealing to a country that no longer existed. Puerto Rico was no longer jíbaro country. And there was the Muñoz protégé himself, Sánchez Villela, and the new generation of PDP leaders saying exactly the same thing: the PDP had become the party of the past.

Ferré and his new party were seen as the party of the future. Using modern television and advertising techniques, Ferré ran a sophisticated campaign. He projected himself not as the typical Puerto Rican politician but as a no-nonsense doer: his most effective TV ad showed him banging his fist on a table and saying, "This has to change!"

In addition, Ferré introduced a new element into the statehood campaign. Statehood leaders made it clear that being pro-American did not mean being pro-Americanization. The statehood ideal had to be liberated from the accusation that it was anti–Puerto Rican. He came up with the concept of *estadidad jíbara*, or native statehood, insisting that Puerto Rico would not lose its distinct Hispanic identity under statehood.

Taking advantage of the PDP division, Ferré went after the disaffected PDP voters, organizing groups of "statehood populares." The strategy worked. The PDP vote fell to 40.7 percent, the Sánchez Villela insurgent party got 11.7 percent of the vote, and Ferré won with 43.6 percent.

After the initial shock of seeing the Popular Democratic Party lose for the first time, and it became evident that this was more than a change in party, Puerto Ricans began to ask themselves: what exactly will change?

When the New Progressive Party was organized weeks after the status plebiscite, it left no doubt that it had a mission. Many of the young leaders had always expressed doubts about whether the Statehood Republican "old guard," the mixture of professional politicians who lived off their legislative salaries and reactionary businesspeople, were really committed to statehood. Some had even doubted Ferré himself. Why would a wealthy Puerto Rican want to change to a status where he would have to pay full federal taxes? Now there was no doubt: the new party they created had one and only one purpose: statehood.

For many others, leaders and members of the Popular Democratic Party, it was not clear what would change. Ferré, after all, attempted to appeal to the disaffected PDP, pro-commonwealth voters with his pledge that a vote for him was not a vote for statehood. But this pledge was also quickly forgotten. In the wild celebration on the night of the election victory, the cry of the party leaders — including Ferré — was that statehood won. In his swearing-in ceremony, he vowed eventual statehood. Could anyone realistically expect Ferré and his party not to drive toward statehood? And if they did, what would happen to the Fomento program, and what would happen to Operation Bootstrap?

Ferré, Moscoso, and Operation Bootstrap

Moscoso always considered Ferré a good friend and admired him as an industrialist and patron of island culture, but as head of Fomento he was exasperated, at times angry with him precisely because of the ambiguity in his attitude toward Fomento.

Ferré had benefited greatly from Fomento. In the early 1950s, in one of Moscoso's most controversial and contested proposals, he urged Muñoz to have Fomento sell a profitable cement plant, originally built by the federal government, to the Ferré family. This not only made the Ferré family the island's largest industrialists, and perhaps the wealthiest, but gave it a monopoly on cement production since the Ferré family already owned the only other cement plant.

For Moscoso, the sale was critical to the Bootstrap program. He convinced the Ferré family to take over four other Fomento plants, all of which were suffering losses and two of which had serious labor problems. The sale would permit a fundamental change in the Fomento program. No longer would it depend on government-owned operations and cooperatives, as conceived by Tugwell, Muñoz, and the PDP in 1942. It would privatize the Fomento program. Now Moscoso could focus on the promotion of private capital, using the new tax exemption law to carry out aggressive campaigns in the United States. Muñoz reluctantly agreed. Ferré was already his principal adversary, and throughout the years, Muñoz would allude to the sale of these plants to counter the accusation that he was a dictator.

Now, after the 1968 election, the question was, what would the new governor's attitude toward Fomento be? As a statehood leader, there had been no ambiguity as to Ferré's attitude toward Fomento. His official biographer, Guillermo Baralt, points out that he had been one of Fomento's fiercest critics.[3] In his first campaign for governor in 1956, he severely criticized Fomento for benefiting foreign industrialists at the expense of Puerto Rican entrepreneurs.[4] In the 1967 plebiscite campaign, when the president of a petrochemical plant in Puerto Rico stated that the company would not have settled in Puerto Rico but for the tax exemption, Ferré countered that he preferred that the poor benefit from the economic benefits of statehood over the company's $20 million earnings. Then, campaigning for governor in 1968, he promised to reduce the tax exemption from 100 percent to 80 percent.[5]

For Moscoso, this was Ferré the politico; Ferré the industrialist knew better. In fact, if anyone in Puerto Rico knew the vital benefits of tax exemption, Moscoso often ranted, it was Ferré. He was deeply involved in the Fomento program, sitting on the board of Fomento-promoted industries, such as Textron, the big American needle company. He knew firsthand that the island's economic development depended on Fomento, which was now operating at top speed. By 1968, it had promoted 2,385 factories and created 83,824 jobs.[6]

But the political reality was that Ferré had swept into power riding the enthusiasm and expectation of a new generation of leaders that meant it when they cried, "Statehood *now!*" They demanded and expected concrete steps toward statehood.

So now, as governor of Puerto Rico, would Ferré be the industrialist Fomento ally or the anti-Fomento politician? How would the new governor reconcile his statehood promise with the inescapable reality that it was incompatible with tax exemption and the Fomento program?

A Different Battle for Fomento

While it was not clear what the Ferré–statehood party election meant to Bootstrap, it was evident to Moscoso, who throughout his career had had to explain, defend, and at times fight for the program, that Bootstrap was now in a different fight. And he knew that he and Fomento would have to engage in a new kind of psychological warfare.

Ferré's idealistic optimism that somehow statehood would work out economically obviously had worked to lift the statehood movement. And that optimism was fed by the sense that Puerto Rico's economic growth was secure. Even the early skeptic of Fomento, Rexford Tugwell, predicted in 1953 that "before long, Puerto Rico may well be more prosperous than many regions of the Union." This rapid economic growth, he wrote, would make it "likely" that it would become a state.[7]

Muñoz himself, as strongly as he opposed statehood, predicted that in time Puerto Rico would reach the same per capita income as that of the United States. Although he would still oppose statehood, he said then, Puerto Rico would be free to choose it without suffering economically.

Fomento was now promoting multimillion-dollar industries, like petrochemicals, that, unlike the early garment factories, which could easily pack up and leave, seemed secure, even permanent. Many felt that the island's phenomenal economic growth was effectively on autopilot.

Moscoso knew that this was a big mistake: there was nothing preordained, much less automatic about the success of Operation Bootstrap. On the contrary: it was vulnerable; Bootstrap, in fact, was essentially insecure because it was *unnatural* to Puerto Rico. Puerto Rico's *natural* state for centuries had been economic stagnation, poverty, and gross economic injustice. There was a reason that for so long the mind-set in Puerto Rico was hopelessness.

Bootstrap was called a "miracle" precisely because it defied Puerto Rico's long history: it was not supposed to happen. The economic liftoff, like the takeoff of a giant aircraft, defied gravity. Everything has to work perfectly. This, Moscoso believed, was the vital lesson: Puerto Rico's economic growth depended on extraordinary hard work, talent, and creativity in Fomento. Of course, it also depended on conditions in the United States and the world beyond Puerto Rico's control. But in the end it depended on good government, on good economic policy. Ironically, the danger now, as Moscoso saw it, was that Puerto Rico would go to the other extreme, from hopelessness to unrealistic optimism: the danger that political leaders did not understand that mistakes and bad decisions and tampering with the delicate engines of economic growth could prove fatal.

The threat to Fomento now, for the first time, was political status ideology. In the past, Moscoso and the Fomento proponents battled over tax policy and economy theory: Did tax exemption actually work, would it produce sustained growth, and was it, in the end, "morally" defensible? It had been in large part a family battle within the Popular Democratic Party leadership and a conflict within Muñoz himself. Now the battleground had crossed the profound gulf that historically divided the Puerto Rican political leadership. Tax exemption, the Fomento program itself, would now be at the core of the political status war.

In the euphoria of a new era in Puerto Rico as Ferré and his new party took power, there was reason to wonder whether, in their deep, sincere passion for statehood, they would make policy and economic mistakes that would prove catastrophic. In the final analysis, it was Puerto Ricans who had made the "economic miracle," and it was Puerto Ricans who could kill it.

An Ideological Tightrope

Ferré walked a political and ideological tightrope during his governorship. His attitude was that although Operation Bootstrap and statehood were incompatible, he acknowledged that statehood needed a period of continued Bootstrap economic growth. The political battle cry was, "Statehood now!," but the reality, he sometimes admitted, was that it would take years to achieve that goal.

Walking the tightrope required continuing to criticize tax exemption. He disparaged it as a "gimmick," a temporary necessary evil. Bootstrap supporters were pleased when a week after the election he backtracked on his campaign promise to reduce the tax exemption rate. But they were unhappy when Ferré named a soft-spoken, amiable corporate lawyer to head Fomento, not another hard-driving promoter in the Moscoso mold. Months later, the new head was out. Fomento began to deteriorate.

Other factors converged to affect the Fomento program. A fifty-seven-day labor strike on the island, a recession affecting the mainland, and a new agreement reducing U.S. tariffs on imported textiles, in addition to the questions raised by Ferré's persistent pro-statehood campaign, triggered the first decline in manufacturing in nineteen years.[8]

But Ferré was ambivalent. Fomento supporters, fearing an ideological, pro-statehood assault, saw instead that he took no action against Bootstrap and took several actions in its favor. In 1971, he proposed a bill extending the tax exemption until 1983. He dutifully signed the tax exemption decrees, more in his first three years than his predecessor in four.[9]

A critical test for Ferré came when Congress considered an increase in the federal minimum wage. Muñoz and Moscoso had always fought in Congress against its automatic application to the island. Congress had agreed to allow special treatment, giving island industries the opportunity to prove that they could not afford the minimum wage increases.

Ferré and the NPP leadership had strongly opposed the special treatment, attacking Muñoz and the PDP for using low wages as another industrial incentive. Full application of the federal minimum wage was touted as another benefit of statehood. So the NPP leadership and the statehood militants were surprised and dismayed when in 1971 Ferré and his resident commissioner in Washington, Jorge Cordova Díaz, made a critical pro-Fomento decision: they asked Congress to retain Puerto Rico's minimum wage flexibility.[10]

When Ferré surprisingly lost the 1972 election, it was seen by the young statehood militants as the result of not having fulfilled his campaign promise to drive relentlessly for statehood and his ambiguity as to tax exemption. Years later, they were again disappointed when Ferré came to Fomento's aid once more by joining Governor Rafael Hernández Colón in defending Section 936 before Congress and a Republican administration.

But in 1972, Moscoso and the Fomento supporters breathed a sigh of relief. Fomento was weakened but essentially intact. Bootstrap had survived four years of a pro-statehood government.

The Oil Crisis

Moscoso and his wife, Gloria, were visiting their daughter and husband in Brazil after the 1972 election when he was surprised by a telephone call from Muñoz. Moscoso knew how hard it had been to say no to Muñoz, but this time he did. Muñoz was pleading that he accept the new governor's request that he return to Fomento. Moscoso flatly declined.

Moscoso, who had just turned sixty-two, had returned to Puerto Rico in 1964 after President Kennedy's assassination and President Lyndon B. Johnson made it clear he did not fit into the new administration. Kennedy had named Moscoso ambassador to Venezuela and then asked him to organize and head the Alliance for Progress. Back on the island, he was determined not to reenter government. Resisting efforts by his admirers to run for governor that year, instead he first joined a local bank and then the petrochemical giant on the south coast, the Commonwealth Oil Refinery Company, where he felt that he was in fact continuing his vocation of job creation. The expanding petrochemical complex expected to create forty thousand new jobs. For the first time in island history, there was the hope that Puerto Rico would finally end its high unemployment rate.[11]

For the new governor, Hernández Colón, getting Moscoso to return was vital. He was intent on carrying out the transition of the Popular Democratic Party to a new generation that had failed and divided the party under Governor Sánchez Vilella. He would bring young professionals and politicians to his new administration but also old Muñoz hands, none more important than Moscoso. And, of course, who better to recharge the Fomento program?

Moscoso had many reasons to tell Muñoz no. But he could not. He agreed to return, for although Bootstrap had survived, it was not safe. The vulnerability of Bootstrap that concerned Moscoso when Ferré was elected was dramatically exposed by an event halfway around the world. Ten months into the new administration, on October 6, 1973, Egypt and Syria attacked Israel. What became known as the Yom Kippur War led to an Arab oil embargo, which hit Puerto Rico like a category 5 hurricane. The island's economy, which had grown by 7.3 percent in 1973, plunged.

Puerto Rico depended totally on imported oil for its energy. But even more devastating was the effect on the giant petrochemical industry that depended on the cost differential between domestic and imported oil. Puerto Rico had gotten President Johnson to give the island special quotas to import the much cheaper foreign oil. With tax exemption, this created an exceptionally powerful incentive. The oil embargo inverted the cost advantage.

Unemployment rose to Great Depression levels, 22.9 percent in 1976.[12] For the first time, the government suffered a decline in tax revenues. The government budget incurred a deficit; the debt leaped by 24.8 percent in 1974 and by 36.6 percent the following year.[13] Puerto Rico was in danger of losing its credit.[14]

Bootstrap came to a screeching halt: 24,000 manufacturing and 34,000 nonmanufacturing jobs were lost. Within a few years, the petrochemical industry collapsed. On the island's southern coast, west of Ponce, Moscoso's dream of the industry that would finally end Puerto Rico's intractable unemployment would become a graveyard of rusting refineries and chimney stacks that still exists today.

Governor Hernández Colón put in place an emergency austerity program. He froze government salary increases, cut cabinet members' salaries, and imposed eleven temporary tax increases. By 1976, Puerto Rico began to pull out of the crisis.

Then Puerto Rico had a stroke of luck. In 1976, the governor, Moscoso, Resident Commissioner Jaime Benítez, and Treasury Secretary Salvador Casellas convinced Congress to improve Puerto Rico's federal tax exemption incentives. Industries on the island, while exempt from local and federal taxes, were subject to full taxation when repatriating the profits to the mainland. The new incentive, Section 936 of the Internal Revenue Code, gave the industries a tax credit by exempting the repatriation of profits to the mainland. It also exempted interest and benefits that those profits earned if they were invested in Puerto Rico. Puerto Rico, in turn, would charge a 10 percent toll-gate tax to the repatriated profits.

Moscoso knew that this had the potential of not only overcoming the 1974–75 crisis and the collapse of the island's petrochemical industry but also giving the Fomento program a far more powerful boost. Exuberant, he made a bold prediction to Governor Hernández Colón regarding his adversary in the 1976 elections, San Juan mayor Carlos Romero Barceló: "If through the years Mr. Romero Barceló has had a hard time combating the tax exemption, the main pillar of the industrialization program, now he will find it impossible."[15]

But on election day, Hernández Colón, Moscoso, and the Popular Democratic Party were stunned. They expected that the economic recovery and promise of Section 936 would reward them with reelection. Many believed that the PDP defeat in 1968 was an aberration due to the Muñoz–Sánchez Villela division. Now, with this display of what they believed was good government, their willingness to take the politically painful but successful austerity measures, it would be back to normal in island politics and the PDP hegemony would be restored. They were wrong. And as Moscoso would soon learn, his glowing, bold prediction would prove dead wrong.

Carlos Romero Barceló

As much as Ferré, founder of the New Progressive Party, was admired, the young professionals who had joined him in forming the New Progressive Party believed that as governor he had acted the same as the old Statehood Republican Party leaders: concrete steps toward statehood had not been taken. There had been a lot of talk about statehood but no action.

If Ferré's victory in 1968 was a political watershed marking the end of Muñoz-PDP hegemony, the election of Carlos Romero Barceló in 1976 was a watershed event in the statehood movement. Romero Barceló was from one of the island's principal political families and grandson of the island's leader in the 1920s and 1930s, Antonio Barceló. Part of the island's political folklore was the bitter battle that took place in the late 1930s between the young Muñoz and Barceló.

Barceló had replaced Muñoz's father, Muñoz Rivera, after his death in 1916, as the leader of the Liberal Party. He had nurtured and often defended the rebellious, prodigal son. But after the surprise Liberal Party defeat in 1936, Barceló blamed young Muñoz, deeply hurt by what he considered a personal betrayal. Two years later, the seventy-year-old Barceló died.

When his grandson was elected in 1976, he had the reputation of being a tough, straight-talking, no-nonsense political street fighter. It was part of the political folklore that he was driven by a historical score to settle. Unlike the gentlemanly and at times seemingly ambiguous Ferré, Romero Barceló made clear that he was uncompromising in his drive toward statehood. As he had demonstrated in his 1965 testimony before the U.S.–Puerto Rico Status Commission, his style was to go for the jugular. And he was convinced that the jugular was the Muñoz-PDP-commonwealth policy of tax exemption and the Fomento program.

In 1973, Romero Barceló wrote the ninety-one-page campaign pamphlet, *Statehood Is for the Poor*, which became his political and ideological testament and the foundation of his lifelong crusade against tax exemption and Fomento. The pamphlet's argument was evident in its title. Contrary to the image of statehood as the ideology of the rich elite, the crusty old businesspeople who acted like they were ashamed of being Puerto Rican, it was the Muñoz-commonwealth-Fomento "conspiracy" that was devised precisely to benefit the rich at the expense of the poor.

This added a vital new element to the statehood argument. Of course, statehood was a matter of Puerto Rican political rights, of Puerto Rican dignity, of the century-old battle against "colonialism." Ferré had expanded the statehood campaign by emphasizing the economic benefits, the increase in federal funds, and the security and prosperity of becoming a state in the world's most powerful, prosperous nation.

But Romero Barceló focused the attack on tax exemption. He insisted that the use of tax exemption as an investment incentive was more than bad tax and economic policy. It was a scam on Puerto Ricans, especially the poor. The PDP had effectively bribed investors by giving them full local tax exemption and, just as important, exempting them from paying the federal minimum wage. In return, investors, reaping inordinately high profits, economically sustained the PDP in power in order to maintain the scam.

Statehood, he argued, made the scam impossible: investors would pay their taxes to the federal and local governments and would pay the federal minimum wage. Puerto Ricans, especially the poor, would not only receive the benefits of additional federal welfare programs and other federal funds, but the benefits of the new and greater island government services, now made possible by the great increase in tax revenue.

Tax exemption was at the root of the support for commonwealth and opposition to statehood, Romero Barceló argued: the Puerto Rican rich, emphasizing that Ferré was "the exception,"[16] benefited from not paying federal taxes, and, of course, so did the American industrialists. Romero Barceló's frontal attack on Fomento took the statehood campaign to a new level.

Referring to a number of island industrialists who published political ads defending Fomento and commonwealth status during the 1967 plebiscite, Romero Barceló asked why the "economic interests put their faith and their money year after year in the political party that defends Commonwealth status and opposes statehood. . . . [N]ot because statehood is bad for Puerto Rico and for the immense majority of poor Puerto Ricans. But because statehood is bad for their pockets."[17]

The attack on Fomento was a departure from Ferré's attitude that tax exemption and Fomento were "necessary evils"—that Puerto Rico in fact needed Fomento's economic development to make statehood economically viable. Back during the Ferré administration, San Juan mayor Romero Barceló's militancy against tax exemption and Fomento worried the governor. One of his closest advisers, Pedro Rivera Casiano, came up with an idea: if anyone could convince Romero Barceló to let up, it was Puerto Rico's master salesman, Moscoso himself. Romero Barceló declined to meet with Moscoso, insisting it was a waste of time. But after Ferré himself called, he relented.

They met for two hours. Moscoso did not impress, much less convince, Romero Barceló. But Romero Barceló's intense and emotional condemnation of tax exemption impressed Moscoso. It was evident that if Romero Barceló ever got the opportunity, he would simply eliminate it.

In 1978, Romero Barceló tried. Two years after being elected governor, he sent a bill to the NPP-controlled legislature to effectively repeal the tax exemption law. Alarmed, Moscoso, the private sector, economists, and others testified before the legislature that this would have a disastrous effect on manufacturing and on the entire economy. But the critical opposition came from within the Romero Barceló administration. The head of Fomento, the attorney Manuel Dubón, finally convinced him to reduce the exemption but not eliminate it.

Romero Barceló was narrowly reelected in 1980, after a recount winning by 3,000 votes, or 0.2 percent. With the PDP controlling the legislature, Fomento seemed safe from any new threat. Four years later, when Hernández Colón returned to power, defeating Romero Barceló, the Fomento program had again survived but this time seriously damaged.

But the statehood surge was only temporarily interrupted. It would resurface in the next decade and resurrect the crusade against the Fomento program and tax exemption.

Romero Barceló's pamphlet, *Statehood Is for the Poor*, charted a new path to statehood. The purpose of the book was to radically change the historical perception of statehood as the "status of the rich for the rich" and commonwealth as "the status of the poor."[18] Attack tax exemption, destroy Fomento, and destroy commonwealth status, and the road would be open to statehood. It was the path the New Progressive Party and the statehood movement would take in the next half century.

Romero Barceló, elected resident commissioner in Congress in 1992, went for the jugular. Aided by hostility in the U.S. Treasury Department and in Congress, he set out to kill Section 936.

CHAPTER THREE

The Demise of Section 936

In 2018, the U.S. Financial Oversight and Management Board for Puerto Rico, PROMESA, described the existing condition of Puerto Rico.

The people of Puerto Rico need and deserve plentiful good jobs, a dynamic and prosperous economy, affordable and reliable electricity, and an efficient and responsive public sector—but have not had any of these things for more than a decade. Instead, since 2005, the number of people living under the poverty level has increased, the economy has shrunk, electricity has remained expensive and unreliable, labor market regulation has remained burdensome—hindering job creation for the people—and the public sector has provided declining levels of service at a high cost to citizens. These problems predate Hurricanes Maria and Irma and will continue to plague Puerto Rico long after it recovers from the storms. . . .

Puerto Rico has been mired in an economic and demographic downward spiral for over a decade. The economy is $16 billion smaller in real terms and the population nearly a half million smaller (largely due to outmigration) than it was in 2005. . . . [T]oday, over 40% of the population lives below the poverty line, over 40% are dependent on Medicare or healthcare. Over 10% of the population has left or is projected to leave the island in the next five years to seek a better life elsewhere. . . . Meanwhile, the consolidated Commonwealth's outstanding debt and pension liabilities have grown to over $120 billion, with more than $70 billion in financial debt and more than $50 billion in pension liabilities—an amount almost twice the size of Puerto Rico's economy.[1]

What happened?

May 8, 1956, was a big day for Operation Bootstrap. Governor Luis Muñoz Marín was on hand to inaugurate the 400th Fomento plant. But this was not just another plant. For Teodoro Moscoso, for Walter K. Joelson, a German-born, Swiss-educated Fomento economist, and for the Puerto Rican Jerry Maldonado, the Puerto Rican economy had entered a new era.

This was a General Electric plant. Moscoso and his promoters had been knocking on GE's doors for over five years. It was vital to achieve Fomento's first promotion of a blue chip company, to enter the big leagues of American manufacturing. When Moscoso asked Joelson to make one more attempt in 1952, the Fomento staff was convinced that it was hopeless. But he succeeded. And there they were that sunny morning under the blazing sun at Palmer, about twenty miles from San Juan, at the base of the beautiful El Yunque rain forest, where a run-down 88,000-square-foot industrial building had been converted into a modern plant for 190 Puerto Rican workers to produce circuit breakers.

Jerry Maldonado, who had begun as a Fomento promoter in 1952 earning $250 a month and had been assigned to shepherd the project, was named plant manager. When he left the company in the early 1960s, the plant had a thousand workers. Ten years later, Joelson went on to become GE's chief economist.

And it went well for GE in Puerto Rico. Three decades later, it had twenty-one plants in Puerto Rico employing 11,300 people. Ignacio Rivera was area manager of GE from 1978 to 1983. The enormous success of GE, he said in August 2018, was based on two factors. The first was the stability and high productivity of the Puerto Rican workforce. Unlike in other areas where there was high labor turnover, the Puerto Rican workers, mostly women, stayed for a lifetime. The second factor was tax exemption. The Puerto Rican operation, Rivera said, generated as much as 5 percent of worldwide GE profits.

This changed with the loss of Section 936. Industry continued to be exempt from federal and local taxes but lost the 936 exemption on profits repatriated to the mainland. A private practicing attorney in San Juan in 2018, Rivera said, "The loss of 936 was a major tragedy for Puerto Rico. It was the error that killed Puerto Rico, much more than Hurricane Maria. We will recover from Maria. But our economy will not recover from the loss of jobs as a result of losing 936."

"It was not just the loss of jobs," Rivera continued. "GE had $450 million in 936 funds deposited in island banks. And especially the effect of the plant closing in the towns around the island that depended so much on the revenues: today all these towns—San German, Humacao, Fajardo, Ponce, Arecibo, Arroyo, Patillas, Vieques—are in dire economic crisis. And think of the hundreds of Puerto Rican engineers and other technicians and specialists that were highly-trained and became highly proficient in the GE plants having to leave the island and that you will find today around the world. This has been another tragic loss for Puerto Rico."[2]

That this would be the effect of repealing Section 936 has been evident and amply reported for years. As a September 26, 2017, CNBC story put it, Puerto Rico's "fiscal mess has its roots in the repeal of a controversial corporate tax break that helped spark an exodus from the island that sent its economy into reverse. . . . In 1996 President Bill Clinton signed the law that would phase out Section 936 over 10 years. Plant closures and jobs lost followed."[3]

The question is, why? Why did Congress and President Clinton eliminate Section 936? It was, after all, evident how vital 936 was to the island economy. Although by 1974 the Hernández Colón administration's austerity measures had begun to pull the island out of the Yom Kippur War crisis, it was evident that it was approval of 936 that reignited the Bootstrap economic growth.

Since the beginning—the July 25, 1898, American invasion—Puerto Rico's economic situation has been at the core of the always complicated, confusing struggle to fix the political relationship of the island to the United States. How to link one of the poorest economies to the biggest economy in the world? Free trade was vital for the island's survival. To Secretary of War Elihu Root in 1899, it was just as evident that Puerto Rico could not be subject to U.S. taxes. As military governor, George Davis, testified before Congress, Puerto Rico must keep its tax revenue in order to survive.[4] Congress agreed: the 1900 Foraker Act establishing civil government exempted Puerto Rico from all federal taxes, and after the 1913 constitutional amendment, to include federal income tax.

In the 1950–52 insular constitutional process that led to the creation of the commonwealth, Governor Muñoz and others focused on the success of Bootstrap to emphasize how essential these concessions were. The concessions were retained in the new Puerto Rico Federal Relations Act governing the new relationship between Puerto Rico and the United States.

But the Fomento program had an Achilles heel. Profits repatriated to the mainland were subject to full federal taxation. Moscoso and Fomento found a way to avoid this. In the 1920s, Congress approved Section 931 of the Internal Revenue Code to give U.S. investment in the Philippines a tax benefit enjoyed by competing European investors, mostly those from Germany. It allowed U.S. industries to repatriate their profits to the mainland tax-free once they liquidated their operations. Section 931 was extended to Puerto Rico but lay dormant until Bootstrap, when business and Fomento lawyers devised legal means to "liquidate" a corporation while continuing its operations and benefiting from the 931 exemption.

But 931 was the target of congressional leaders determined to close loopholes. In 1962, a congressional committee considering tax reforms decided to eliminate it. Alarmed, Governor Muñoz rushed to the U.S. Senate. Capitalizing on his popularity in Congress and his influence in the Kennedy administration, he persuaded the Senate to retain it.

In 1974, back at Fomento under the new Hernández Colón administration, Moscoso received an urgent call from Resident Commissioner Jaime Benitez. The flamboyant former president of the University of Puerto

Rico, a veteran of decades of battles, mostly against radical independentista university students, was furious. Without informing him, the House Ways and Means Committee had again voted to eliminate 931. He called committee chair Wilbur Mills and after expressing his outrage convinced him to give the island government an opportunity to testify and try to convince the committee to reinstate the benefit.

A few days later, Governor Hernández Colón, Moscoso, Benítez, and the young lawyer and treasury secretary Salvador Casellas testified that there could be no worse moment to deny Puerto Rico this critical tax incentive. Eliminating 931, they argued, would kill Bootstrap, which was already being battered by the oil embargo. Mills and the committee were convinced: he acknowledged that this was a case where eliminating a tax loophole would cause a greater problem.

Mills suggested that Moscoso and Casellas meet with the Internal Revenue Taxation Joint Committee adviser, Lawrence Woodworth, a tax expert who was unaware of Puerto Rico's status conflicts. To Moscoso's and Casellas's surprise, unlike Treasury Department officials, Woodworth was receptive to the idea of tax exemption as an investment incentive. A year later, he and the Puerto Ricans came up with a substitute to 931, Section 936.

Puerto Rico's tax exemption incentive, for the first time, was complete. U.S. investments now could repatriate their profits tax-free without the restrictions of 931. It quickly proved to be the most powerful incentive in Fomento history. It not only helped pull the island out of its economic decline, but spurred Bootstrap as never before. By the 1990s, pharmaceutical and high-tech electronics industries replaced and surpassed the petrochemical industry. Puerto Rico went on to become one of the world's leading producers of medicines, medical devices, and other pharmaceutical products. The housing and infrastructure construction industries boomed, taking advantage of the $9 billion in 936 funds that were deposited in private banking and financial institutions and in the Government Development Bank.[5]

But from the beginning the U.S. Treasury Department and congressional leaders opposed 936, as they had 931, as an ineffectual "loophole." In part to appease the U.S. Treasury, Congress required that it be periodically scrutinized to ensure that 936 was in fact creating the thousands of jobs that Puerto Rico desperately needed. In the following years, the Treasury Department and the critics insisted that the "cost" to the U.S. Treasury in tax revenue lost, what it called deferred tax revenue, did not justify the number of jobs being created.

Fomento was caught in a paradox. As 936 attracted more industries, particularly high-profit pharmaceuticals, the perceived deferred tax revenue increased. What to Puerto Rico was celebrated as the success of 936 was perceived by the U.S. Treasury as its loss. In each of its reports, the Treasury Department reinforced its objection that the rapidly expanding tax-free benefits to the industries far outweighed the benefits to Puerto Rico. The fourth report in February 1983 emphasized that the top 936 corporations, while paying their employees an average of $20,122 a year, were getting per job $168,270 in tax benefits.[6] Wouldn't it be, Treasury officials asked, more cost-effective for the United States to simply give Puerto Rico an outright federal grant to create jobs?

Decades earlier, Fomento's top economist, Hu Barton, had confessed to a newspaper reporter, "Let's face it. For all the good that Fomento is doing in Puerto Rico, in the end, its success is based on *greed*."[7] Obviously, Puerto Rico's motive for offering tax exemption was to reduce its poverty and unemployment. Just as obviously, the investor's motive for coming to Puerto Rico was high profits. The greater the expectation of profit, the greater the greed, the greater the success of Fomento, and the greater the success of the historical battle against poverty and unemployment.

Barton's avowal of the economic reality now came to haunt Puerto Rico. The government could not refute the critics of 936 in Washington: many 936 corporations were making huge tax-free profits. Critics pointed at a bottling company that made huge profits while employing few workers. The government and several 936 corporations admitted that there were abuses that should be corrected but that they were the exception.

Puerto Rico was caught in an old battle, between the supply side economists who argued that the lower the taxes, the greater the creation of jobs and the benefit to the working class, and the demand side economists who insisted that this was "trickle-down economics" that benefited the rich. But the only way for Puerto Rico to defend 936 was to essentially change the subject: see 936 not as a tax revenue issue, as the U.S. Treasury did, but as an economic development tool. Harp on the essential argument that Congress approved it not to benefit the pharmaceuticals and other 936 industries but to benefit jobs-starved Puerto Rico. So to eliminate it would hurt Puerto Rico much more than the industries. And in the end, it would *not* benefit the U.S. Treasury. Treasury was making a big mistake in its calculations of how much tax revenue it would receive by eliminating 936: the expected tax revenue windfall would not happen. There was, 936 advocates argued, no such thing as deferred tax revenue since once 936 was eliminated many corporations would simply seek other tax shelters or locations. So if there are no winners, only losers, why do something that will devastate Puerto Rico?

But for many in Puerto Rico the battle for 936 had another dimension. Many critics pointed out that it was bad for the economy to depend so much on a tax concession that Congress could eliminate at any time. As Ferré had insisted, Puerto Rico should not depend on a "tax gimmick" that created an artificial and thus fundamentally unstable economy. But the 936 advocates answered, what was the alternative? The real choice, they insisted, was between private productive jobs and increasing dependence on federal welfare funds that of course Congress could reduce or eliminate at any time. What, then, is the economy that Puerto Rico wants for itself, jobs or welfare?

The Losing Battle

As the years passed, the battle for Section 936 became increasingly difficult. It was increasingly trapped in the paradox that the more it succeeded, the harder it was to defend.

In 1983, it seemed that the battle was lost. President Ronald Reagan and Treasury Secretary James Baker announced that they were in favor of eliminating 936. Hernández Colón, after returning to the governorship in 1985, decided to use a different and imaginative strategy to save it. Taking an idea of the Washington attorney Richard Copaken, he reverted to the old concept of Puerto Rico as the "showcase of democracy" — the democratic, free-market alternative to the Cuban Revolution. Copaken proposed that the save 936 strategy be linked to the "Reagan Doctrine" intended to prevent "another Cuba" in the Caribbean and Central America. On February 24, 1982, President Reagan warned in a speech before the

Organization of American States, "If we do not act properly in defense of freedom, new Cubas will arise from the ruins of today's conflicts. We will face more totalitarian regimes tied militarily to the Soviet Union, more regimes exporting subversion, more regimes so incompetent that their citizens" will be driven to migrate in large numbers to the United States, as had occurred in Cuba.[8]

Reagan announced the Caribbean Basin Initiative, which entailed economic and military aid to Caribbean and Central American countries. Hernández Colón proposed to Reagan that Puerto Rico would extend the Fomento program by promoting the establishment of 936 satellite plants in the Caribbean and Central America if his administration dropped its intention to kill 936. It worked. In a Miami speech, Vice President George H. W. Bush announced that the government had dropped its anti-936 proposal.

In the following years, Hernández Colón and his administration dedicated themselves to fulfilling this commitment. By the early 1990s, he and the Fomento administrator, Antonio Colorado, had promoted fifty-eight twin plants of operations in Puerto Rico throughout the Caribbean and Central America; more than $1 billion in 936 funds had been used in infrastructure development.

Another battle was won. Section 936 was saved. But again it proved only a reprieve. In Puerto Rico the drive to eliminate 936 became a battle cry in the never-ending political status war.

Governor Pedro Rosselló

In 1992, the statehood surge returned. New Progressive Party candidate Pedro Rosselló won the governorship that year and was reelected overwhelmingly in 1996, becoming the first governor to get over a million votes and the first pro-statehood candidate to get more than 50 percent of the vote.

Rosselló was from a well-to-do family of professionals. He was a brilliant university student, earning degrees from Notre Dame and Yale and receiving an MD from Harvard as a pediatric surgeon. Handsome, athletic, and a tennis champion, he also had an interest in politics. He ran and lost the election for resident commissioner in 1988. Four years later, he defeated the supporters of former governor Romero Barceló, who considered running again for the governorship. In the elections, demonstrating his charisma, projecting a can-do, no-nonsense personality, he convincingly defeated Muñoz's daughter, Victoria Muñoz, the Popular Democratic Party candidate.

Rosselló came to power as an activist determined to change Puerto Rico, to carry out a reform program as ambitious as Muñoz's in 1940; he wanted to "reinvent government." His massive spending on social programs and infrastructure during his two terms in office became crucial to the Puerto Rican economy.

In the beginning, Rosselló's views on Section 936 seemed to be similar to those of Ferré. He understood that federal tax exemption was incompatible with statehood, but like Ferré, he accepted that it was vital to the island economy and had to continue until Puerto Rico and Congress came up with an alternative.

In the 1992 contest against Romero Barceló for the NPP gubernatorial nomination, Section 936 was a big political issue. Romero continued his opposition to the tax exemption incentive, now strongly attacking 936. Rosselló campaigned in favor of 936 and after winning the nomination personally included his support for it in the NPP platform:

> As part of our commitment to increase the flow of direct capital investment from the United States, our position with respect to tax exemption is the following:
> a) While Puerto Rico maintains the current relationship with the United States, we support in the most energetic form possible the permanence of the existing tax incentives under section 936 of the Federal Internal Revenue Code.
> b) Seek of the United States Congress that it continues similar tax benefits, under the existing status as under statehood, until the Puerto Rico economy reaches levels comparable to the other states.

Bootstrap advocates, again wondering what the NPP's return to power would mean to the Fomento program, had reason to be relieved and pleased. The new governor and his party were committed to the commonwealth economic policies and programs until Puerto Rico reached the same economic level as the U.S. mainland. The future of Section 936 again seemed safe.

Romero Barceló was elected the island's resident commissioner in Congress, and in spite of the NPP endorsement of 936, he carried out his anti–tax exemption crusade. Once in Washington, he got strong support. In his first budget, the new president, Bill Clinton, proposed eliminating Section 936. As part of the Deficit Reduction Act, the Treasury Department again insisted that closing this loophole would add billions in tax revenue. Clinton had announced his plan to enact major health reform. For members of Congress and other critics who accused the U.S. pharmaceutical industry of grossly overpricing medical products and profiting excessively, there was no better proof than what they had been denouncing for years: the "obscene 936 profits" of the drug makers in Puerto Rico.[9]

Arkansas senator David Pryor presented a bill on February 15, 1993, to eliminate 936. Pryor accused the pharmaceutical industry of effectively getting away with murder in Puerto Rico with the "mother of all loopholes"[10]—echoing the Treasury Department's criticism that the industries were creating relatively few jobs. As chairman of the Senate Aging Committee, Pryor had become the leading critic of the industry in Congress.

Pryor was widely seen as Clinton's political mentor. A leader in Arkansas politics since the 1960s, as state governor he named Clinton the state's attorney general. In 1979, he was elected senator and Clinton succeeded him as governor. Pryor recognized how important 936 was to the island economy and proposed a substitute, a five-year phase-in of a wage credit of up to $8,000. As Treasury officials and other critics had long argued, he believed that what Puerto Rico needed were other incentives that actually created many more thousands of jobs.

Resident Commissioner Romero Barceló immediately supported the Pryor bill. The party leadership followed him, seeking to eliminate what had always been considered an obstacle to statehood. Rosselló's vice-governor, Secretary of State Baltasar Corrada del Río, joined Romero in Washington to lobby against 936.

The mood in Puerto Rico's NPP-controlled legislature turned against the incentive. When the island's Pharmaceutical Industry Association testified before the Senate that eliminating 936 would result not only in plants leaving the island and thousands of lost jobs but also in preventing "billions" of potential new investments and thousands of potential jobs, the reaction of the NPP senators, according to the industrialists, "bordered on hostility."[11]

The powerful Puerto Rico Manufacturer's Association, opponent of the Fomento program in the past, now led the private sector battle to save 936. It lobbied more than fifty members of Congress, warning that eliminating the incentive would cause "an economic debacle."[12] As to the wage credit alternative, the private sector argued it was not in fact a substitute. Years of Boostrap had convinced Fomento that what attracted investments were not credits based on income. The other lesson was that what made the Fomento program work and 936 such a powerful incentive was precisely that Puerto Rico offered tax benefits that no state could match. Wage credits, tax exemption based on wages paid, as the often mentioned "enterprise zones" designed to promote job creation in areas of high poverty, were available to all states and denied the island what had always been the crux of the Bootstrap program, its competitive advantage.

Meanwhile, it was not clear in Washington where Governor Rosselló stood in the battle over 936. Congress was receiving a mixed message from the island. While Romero Barceló and the political leadership pushed to finally eliminate it, Rosselló's closest adviser, former campaign manager, and current chief of staff, Álvaro Cifuentes, supported 936, assuring members of Congress that this was the official position. In 1993, he had dismayed party leaders by telling the press that his priority was not statehood but good government.

The mixed message confused and dismayed the senators and representatives who through the years had supported Puerto Rico in the unpopular and difficult fight for Section 936. The Democrat from New York, Charles Rangel, chair of the Ways and Means Committee, had led the battle for 936: being a liberal, his support was critical. Now he expressed his "bewilderment and disillusionment by the abysmal division that exists in the Puerto Rico political leadership, and in other sectors, that has resulted in the loss of a single voice for the welfare of Puerto Rico."[13]

As Cifuentes countered Romero Barceló's anti-936 campaign in Washington, Rosselló faced within his party leadership the revival of the old accusation against the defunct Statehood Republican Party, an accusation made against Ferré himself. Rosselló's position on 936 would determine if he was, after all, a "true statehooder," or, like the old guard, all talk but no action. Rosselló seemed to waver, sometimes appearing to side with the 936 advocates, sometimes with the pro-statehood, anti-936 forces.

The criticism of not being a true statehooder stung. In November 1993, Rosselló's government held a second status plebiscite. Given their margin of victory in the 1992 elections, the largest for the NPP thus far, and the opposition's demoralization, the governor and his party leaders were certain the plebiscite would likewise produce a big statehood victory. Shockingly, statehood lost: commonwealth won with 48.4 percent; statehood got 46.2 percent. Obviously there was something confusing here: how could the pro-statehood party defeat the pro-commonwealth party in 1992 and statehood lose just a year later? One thing seemed clear to many NPP leaders: Rosselló's inconsistency in defending statehood and on 936 had "confused" and depressed the statehood movement.

In 1995, Rosselló decided to publicly reconcile with Romero Barceló. Up to that point it was generally perceived in Puerto Rico that he and Romero Barceló had not ceased seeing each other as rivals. But in February he made a highly publicized visit to Romero Barceló at his Capitol office to "make peace." Later that year, he campaigned for Romero Barceló in a primary election to lead the local Democratic Party. But again the NPP was surprised to lose to the PDP-backed candidate, the educator Celeste Benítez, who vigorously defended Section 936.

Rosselló had suffered two political defeats. He decided to end any doubt as to his attitude toward 936. He joined the Pryor and Romero Barceló campaign to eliminate 936, attacking it as corporate welfare. The anti-936 campaign escalated. When the governors of New York, New Jersey, and Connecticut, defending firms in their states that had plants in Puerto Rico, wrote a letter to Congress supporting 936, Romero sent them a four-page rebuttal. Reverting to his 1973 attack, Romero described 936 as a form of "South African apartheid," accusing anyone who defended it as "an enemy of Puerto Rico."[14] For Romero Barceló, to oppose statehood was to support keeping Puerto Ricans "second-class citizens." And as he had argued in his 1973 pamphlet, *Statehood Is for the Poor*, support for the federal tax exemption denied the Puerto Rican poor the federal funds and other economic benefits of statehood.

Now, for the first time with the government not aggressively supporting but aggressively against 936, the growing feeling among 936 supporters in Puerto Rico and Washington was that this time the program would
be killed.

Was 936 Doomed Anyway?

Was Section 936 doomed anyway, no matter what the government of
Puerto Rico did? Was it no longer possible to overcome the cumulative
effect of the constant opposition of members of Congress, the Treasury,
cabinet members, and the president?

Yet, in May 1993, it survived another call for its elimination when the
Senate Finance Committee decided to retain it with reductions in the tax
benefits. In the next three years, the Manufacturers Association along
with other Puerto Rican private sector organizations stepped up the fight
for 936, sending tens of thousands of letters to members of Congress and
making hundreds of visits to members and their staffs and to administration officials. But there was the growing sense that the battle now seemed
futile. The Puerto Rico–USA Foundation, the trade organization organized by the pharmaceutical industry to lobby for 936, as well as individual corporations, also began to believe that the fight was hopeless. The
936 firms, comprising pharmaceuticals and electronics and other industries, began to diverge in their strategies since eliminating the incentive
would affect them differently. Several pharmaceuticals engaged in their
own negotiations with Congress for an orderly ten-year phase-out.

The pharmaceutical industry had to face the reality that now seemed all
too obvious: without strong, consistent support from the Puerto Rican
government they could not, and in fact never could, credibly defend 936
in Congress. The reality had always been that there was only one credible
defense: 936 was not approved to benefit the pharmaceuticals but to
benefit Puerto Rico. But it was demonstrably true that it gave these industries enormous tax benefits and that after two decades, far from solving the
island's terrible unemployment, it was still three times higher than on the
mainland. The opposition was simply too strong.

In addition, the battle for 936 always had to overcome the negative image of the American pharmaceutical industry in Congress and American public opinion—an image, as Senator Pryor had portrayed in his crusade, of an exceptionally greedy industry willing to sacrifice the public good for excessive profits. This was the image that several years later, in 2001, the British novelist John Le Carré depicted in his best-selling *The Constant Gardener*, which became a 2005 Hollywood movie, portraying Big Pharma as more than madly greed driven but as criminal and even murderous.

As exaggerated as this was, it dramatizes how difficult it was to defend 936, to communicate that to defend 936 was *not* to defend Big Pharma. There were many nonpharmaceutical companies that were creating thousands of jobs. The government and private sector groups had attempted to communicate to Congress that while the pharmaceuticals were investing big money, it was GE, Westinghouse, Playtex, and Baxter that were creating jobs in many small towns throughout the island and were especially civic-minded.

It was, they argued, a critically important mistake to lump together all the 936 corporations as there were huge differences among them. In 1975, for instance, the pharmaceuticals' 936 tax benefits averaged $35,000, while the nonpharmaceuticals were receiving less than $3,000 per employee. In 1987, the pharmaceuticals received 56 percent of all 936 benefits and created 18,000 jobs, while the nonpharmaceuticals created 83,000 jobs. The pharmaceuticals were receiving three to four times greater tax benefits than the electronics and electric equipment industry.[15]

From the beginning of 936, the government of Puerto Rico had argued that Congress should not make the terrible mistake of hurting Puerto Rico in order to hurt the pharmaceuticals. Through the years, because it was the government fighting for 936, the argument—don't kill the job-creating nonpharma industries because the pharmaceuticals are not creating enough jobs—had credibility.

But once Governor Rosselló joined Resident Commissioner Romero Barceló in supporting Senator Pryor's bill, the message to Congress changed fundamentally: it was no longer eliminate the "abuses" and "excesses" but eliminate 936 itself. The argument that eliminating it would hurt Puerto Rico much more than the pharmaceuticals lost the credibility that had saved it in the past.

Puerto Rican media reported that after President Clinton signed the law eliminating 936, Governor Rosselló was "euphoric." A few months later, he had another reason to celebrate; he won reelection overwhelmingly. To the surprise of many, the anti-936 campaign did not hurt him politically.

In the following years, as Puerto Rico began to feel the effects of the elimination of Section 936, the position of the New Progressive Party leaders changed. No longer celebrating the removal of the "obstacle to statehood," they now argued that it was unfair and inaccurate to blame them for its demise. Section 936 was doomed anyway. But from the beginning, Romero Barceló never hesitated to take credit. In 1995, when he began to see his lifelong crusade coming to fruition, he said, "When I began I was alone in this. . . . [E]verybody criticized [me] calling me the enemy of the workers[;] now it is an immense joy for me to see that it is moving toward a program of more stable development."[16]

The Effect of Losing Section 936

The phase-out of Section 936 in 1996 is nearly unanimously recognized as having triggered Puerto Rico's economic crisis. The importance of 936 had been evident. The Puerto Rican economy depended on manufacturing generating 46 percent of the island's GDP. A study conducted by two City University of New York professors, Zadia Feliciano and Andrew Green, for the National Bureau of Economic Research, a private nonprofit research organization, reported that 936 firms contributed 82.3 percent of manufacturing production in 1987.[17]

According to the U.S. Internal Revenue Service, in 1995, before the ten-year phase-out of 936, there were 440 companies reporting $40 billion in gross income, and manufacturing firms were earning $2.7 billion while creating over 100,000 jobs. When the phase-out ended in 2005, the number of 936 companies had declined to 157, with $18 billion in gross income.

In August 2017, the National Bureau of Economic Research study reported that manufacturing jobs declined from 163,605 in 1997 to 83,834 in 2012. The total number of industrial plants declined from 2,092 to

1,852.[18] By March 2018, the number had declined to 70,000. Without adding the government's multiplier effect of indirect jobs, Puerto Rico suffered a loss of 102,000 direct jobs. While manufacturing jobs accounted for 16.4 percent of all employment, by 2000, it had dropped to 13.7 percent. As of March 2018, it stood at 8.2 percent.

Several pharmaceutical corporations converted to Controlled Foreign Corporation status and remained on the island, several carried out big expansions, and others left. In 1995, there were 332 operations on the island receiving a total of $3.7 billion in 936 tax credits. By 2003, there were 124 operations receiving $1.1 billion. GE reduced the number of its plants in Puerto Rico from twenty-two to nine. The nonpharmaceutical industries declined from 264 plants to 114, and their tax credit went from $932 million to $384 million.[19]

In 1996, Section 936 deposits in the island banks and financial institutions began to decline, from $15 billion in the 1990s to $6.8 billion in 2000. After 2006, they became extinct. A big part of the crisis found in the Government Development Bank in 2001 was due precisely to the withdrawal of over a billion dollars in Section 936 deposits. But the totality of the effect, while impossible to quantify and at the beginning invisible to the public, was much greater.

By the 1990s, almost all the Section 936 plant executives and managers were Puerto Rican. They had become the true promoters of the island's industrialization, to a large extent doing what Moscoso and Fomento had done decades earlier. Within their corporations, they fought to bring the fabrication of new products and new plants to the island. Now they lost what had been for them, as for Fomento, the principal weapon.

The pharmaceutical Wyeth had to make a big decision: where it would produce its new product, Embrel. A 158-year-old, $23 billion company acquired by Pfizer in 2009, Wyeth had a big Section 936 operation in Puerto Rico. Its two 936 manufacturing plants and marketing offices employed about three thousand workers.[20] Now it had to decide where to build a $2 billion high-tech biochemical plant to produce the new product. It had three options: Puerto Rico, Singapore, and Ireland. At its Philadelphia corporate headquarters, executives had assumed that Puerto Rico was a slam-dunk for two reasons: proximity to the main market—the U.S. mainland—and Section 936.

In 1993, the company's corporate leaders had begun to have doubts about the future of 936. Administrations changed from Republican to Democratic in Washington and from pro-commonwealth to pro-statehood in Puerto Rico. Section 936 had been under attack in the past, but with the island government now withdrawing its support, it was obvious to Wyeth's management, and to other 936 corporations, that a sea change was occurring. As the chief tax officer told a Puerto Rican general manager, "The fate of 936 is already decided."[21] The Puerto Rican management fought hard but lost. Wyeth built the plant in Ireland.

At about the same time, several 936 corporations decided to get together to build a big industrial park in Dorado to house industry suppliers. The plans called for a $2 billion investment. Once they perceived that 936 was doomed, they killed the project.

When the president of the Pharmaceutical Industry Association, Wyeth's general manager, Héctor Cabrera, testified before the island's Senate in 1993, he found that the New Progressive Party senators did not believe that 936 industries, which had invested so much in Puerto Rico, would leave. Cabrera tried to explain that this way of viewing the effect of eliminating 936 was mistaken. The amount invested in a plant was not the key factor. It was whether that plant could attract the manufacture of new products to replace the ones that would lose their patent protection and begin to wind down. And without the power of Section 936, he testified, Puerto Rico would not be able to compete with other sites for new products.

It is, of course, impossible to quantify the potential investments and jobs the island lost. According to the Pharmaceutical Industry Association, there were $5 billion in new product investments in line for Puerto Rico that went elsewhere when the island lost 936.[22]

A decade earlier, in 1996, the U.S. Treasury assured Congress that closing the 936 "loophole" would bring a $10.6 billion windfall in additional tax revenue. But on September 18, 2006, the *Congressional Quarterly*, in an article on the effect of eliminating 936, reported that the expected tax windfall was not taking place. Some 936 corporations, converting to Controlled Foreign Corporation status, paid federal taxes only when they repatriated income to the mainland. Others, like Wyeth, Pfizer, Bristol-Myers, and Abbot Laboratories, started operations in Ireland. Others, like Merck, invested $100 million in Singapore. "It is possible," the article concluded, "that Treasury hasn't collected a single dollar from the repeal of Section

936."[23] The warnings of the 936 defenders proved right: the repeal did not benefit the United States; instead it benefited Ireland and Singapore.[24]

In 2003, Puerto Rico, again under a Popular Democratic Party administration, now led by Governor Sila Calderón, made a new effort to get Congress to approve a substitute to 936. She and her administration convinced Senators John Breaux (D-LA) and Rick Santorum (R-PA) to introduce Section 956, essentially restoring the 936 incentive.

The 936 corporations, through the Puerto Rico–USA Foundation, lobbied in favor. But again, the NPP opposed the incentive. Now former governor Rosselló lobbied against it. Senate Finance Committee chair Charles Grassley (R-IA) and the ranking Democrat, Max Baucus (D-MT), came out against it, and the 956 bill was withdrawn.

The foundation's executive director who led the campaign for Section 956, Peter Holmes, wrote an article in the *San Juan Star* explaining why the bill failed. Grassley and Baucus, he wrote, initially did not oppose the bill on its merits. They were convinced that it would not represent a significant cost to the Treasury Department and were pleased by the "anti–runaway plant" provision that addressed the old accusation that Fomento was unfairly luring existing industries and jobs from the mainland. Although "the proposal has nothing to do with the political status debate," Holmes wrote, the "statehood lobby's opposition" convinced the senators that approving the bill would embroil the Senate in the island's "political status quagmire."[25] For the statehood lobby, supporting 956 meant opposing statehood. Holmes ended his article by expressing amazement that any Puerto Rican would believe that impeding the island's economic development would favor their political status. As the 2006 article in the *Congressional Quarterly* on Section 956 repeatedly pointed out, the big problem for getting Congress to approve any federal tax exemption for Puerto Rico was the relentless opposition of Puerto Rico's pro-statehood movement.

In 2011, however, a new NPP governor, Luis Fortuño, and the resident commissioner, Pedro Pierluisi, breaking with their party's traditional opposition to any federal tax incentive incompatible with statehood, launched a new effort to get Congress to approve a substitute to 936.

On September 11, 2011, Pierluisi introduced the Puerto Rico Investment Promotion Act to give island industries a similar federal tax exemption and include safeguards against what had been perceived as abuses under 936. Again strongly supported by the island's private sector and the then-minority Popular Democratic Party, Section 933A seemed to have a good chance at congressional approval. But again top NPP legislative leaders came out against the bill, effectively overruling the governor and Pierluisi. The bill died in Congress.

Still another effort was made in 2014, after the election of PDP candidate Alejandro García Padilla. And again there was hope of success. On November 13, 2014, former governor Rafael Hernández Colón met with House Speaker Paul Ryan to plead for new legislation restoring a 936-like tax incentive. This was a mission of vital importance not only to Puerto Rico but also Hernández Colón. Getting Congress to approve Section 936 in 1976 was one of the highlights of his term as governor, and defending Section 936 from presidential and congressional opposition had marked his two subsequent terms in office. This time Hernández Colón believed that he had irrefutable proof that it was precisely the repeal of 936 that had plunged Puerto Rico into its worst economic and fiscal crisis since the Great Depression. Ryan reacted positively and asked Hernández to come back with a proposal.

On September 17, 2015, the former governor delivered the proposal to House Ways and Means Committee chair Kevin Bryan, who also reacted positively. But Congress was now focused on Puerto Rico's debt crisis. Six weeks earlier, on June 29, 2015, Governor García Padilla had announced that Puerto Rico was unable to pay its $72 billion debt. When Congress created the PROMESA Fiscal Board, the drive to revive the 936 tax incentive was directed to the Congressional Task Force created with the PROMESA Fiscal Board to come up with the "economic development tools" the island needed to pull out of the crisis.

The Puerto Rican government's report to the Task Force declared, "Contrary to popular belief the large debt accumulated by Puerto Rico is not the cause of the economic crisis but is rather one symptom of a crisis brought about by the collapse of economic growth. Economic experts and bondholders agree that the root cause of the rapid erosion of Puerto Rico's debt is the collapse of economic growth that followed the elimination of Section 936 of the US Tax Code." The report went on to state that Puerto Rico had lost 100,100 nonfarm jobs and that while the U.S. GNP grew by 12.1 percent from 2005 to 2014, Puerto Rico's declined by 12.6 percent and Puerto Rico had lost half of its manufacturing jobs, from 160,000 in 1995 to fewer than 80,000 in 2014. Without "tax incentives for continued industrial development," the report declared, "the current courageous efforts to stabilize the government's finances will be doomed to eventual failure."[26]

According to Juan Eugenio Hernández Mayoral, head of the Puerto Rican Government Office in Washington, who was present at the promising meetings with Ryan and Bryan, although the Congressional Task Force eventually included Hernández Colón's proposal in its report to Congress, it got lost in the magnitude and complexity of dealing with Puerto Rico's monstrous debt crisis. That year, 2016, the pro-statehood New Progressive Party was reelected to power. Another effort to revive 936 failed.

Who Was Responsible

As Puerto Rico sank deeper into the economic and fiscal crisis that began in 2006, many in the media and Washington began to wonder who was responsible. Most observers point the finger at Congress and President Clinton for having deprived Puerto Rico of its principal economic growth incentive without an alternative. So, in the end, was Congress responsible for what some economists and others consider the worst mistake in the 120-year history of the U.S.–Puerto Rican relationship?

In spite of persistent opposition—from the U.S. Treasury, from several presidents, from members of Congress—the government of Puerto Rico fought to save Section 936 and succeeded. It was when the government of Puerto Rico turned against 936 that Congress finally killed it.

University of Puerto Rico professor Félix Córdova Iturregui, in his book *La eliminación de la Sección 936*, addressed the question of why President Clinton and Congress, acknowledging that it would cripple the Puerto Rican economy, proceeded to kill Section 936 without an alternative. The thesis of the book is that the drive in Puerto Rico against 936 was never about economics; it was about politics and status ideology: "Among those who aligned themselves politically against Section 936, there was an illusion that was gaining strength. With the elimination of this mechanism or tax system beneficial to big multinations, they gave commonwealth status the deathblow."[27] This was the road map to statehood Romero Barceló spelled out in 1973 in *Statehood Is for the Poor*.

Representative Charles Rangel put it succinctly in November 1995: "All of this is because of the status question. I will not be the one that will have to respond to the Puerto Ricans for the high unemployment they will suffer when all of this ends."[28]

Section 936 was the victim of Puerto Rico's status politics, of the ideological contest within the statehood movement. Since the election of Governor Ferré in 1968, there had been two essential ideological currents. One of them accepted the 1964 Status Commission conclusion that achieving statehood would take time and that Puerto Rico needed to continue growing economically to make it viable. This was Ferré's position and that of subsequent statehood moderates such as Governor Fortuño and Resident Commissioner Pierluisi. They accepted, and sometimes supported, the Fomento tax exemption program and what made it possible: commonwealth status.

The other current, the "statehood now" camp, held that this is a matter of Puerto Rico's fundamental rights and fundamental dignity, which are not negotiable or subject to economic conditions or time frames. In this view, statehood consisted precisely in opposing and defeating any program that was not compatible, beginning with federal tax exemption. As Romero Barceló had insisted in 1973, the road to statehood required the destruction of the Fomento program and of commonwealth status. After the mid-1990s, it was this current, under the leadership of Resident Commissioner Romero Barceló and Governor Rosselló, that prevailed. When in power—Romero from 1977 to 1984, Rosselló from 1993 to 2000—they were convinced that the island's economy had to be restructured to pave the way to statehood. The result was the demise of Section 936, the end of Operation Bootstrap, and the beginning of Puerto Rico's economic and fiscal crisis.

CHAPTER FOUR

The Turning Point

A month after President Clinton signed the law killing Section 936, in August 1996, one of Puerto Rico's leading economists, Eliezer Curet Cuevas, made a dire prediction: "The consequences for the economy of Puerto Rico will be an enormous loss of direct and indirect jobs and an even greater loss in productivity. As the working-age population will inexorably continue to grow in the next decade, Puerto Rico will experience a state of economic crisis, social tensions, and personal suffering that will shake the fiber of our society."[1]

Curet Cuevas, a veteran economist, had joined the Pedro Rosselló campaign in 1992, writing the New Progressive Party's platform on the economy. After the election, he became Governor Rosselló's chief economist as the secretary of organization and governmental policy. But before the end of Rosselló's first year in office, he resigned, convinced that the governor and his party were leading the island to an economic and fiscal crisis.

In the election year 1996, he published a tell-all book describing a litany of bad economic and fiscal policies and actions, none more damaging than getting Congress to eliminate Section 936. Having served in numerous capacities in past administrations and in the legislature under both parties, he believed that he had a good understanding not only of the island's economy but also of its politics. And he was certain that Rosselló would pay heavily in the election for his mistakes. Predicting a crushing defeat, he wrote, "In the year 1996 the NPP ship is sinking. Rosselló finds himself with the water at his neck. The extraordinary political advantage he had at the beginning of 1993 has evaporated."[2]

Curet Cuevas was wrong. Rosselló was reelected in a landslide. How could Curet Cuevas, while accurately predicting the consequences of the governor's economic policies, have so badly miscalculated Puerto Rican voters? Indeed, why had voters ignored, not only the warnings in his book and of other economists, but also the massive campaigns in favor of 936 by the private sector, the 936 corporations, the labor unions, and the opposition Popular Democratic Party? Had they effectively *rewarded* Rosselló?

Curet Cuevas had clearly miscalculated Rosselló the politician. Rosselló had conducted an unusual campaign. In the past political rallies were attended by thousands of people most of whom had been bused to the events and fed sandwiches by their local leaders. Baked under the blistering sun or soaked under the drenching rains of the tropical island, they withstood the politicians' endless speeches. But Rosselló, energetic and athletic, converted the rallies into vibrant, fun entertainment. And he was the star performer. Dancing to the tune of the 1996 Spanish hit song, "La Macarena," Rosselló worked the crowds differently. Thousands, including many young people, who were usually relatively absent at these rallies, turned them into rock concert frenzy, as they cried out, "Baila, Pedro, baila," "Dance, Pedro, dance." At the end of the campaign, Rosselló called on his followers to set the world record for the largest crowd dancing "La Macarena" at the same place and time at his closing rally.

The PDP had gone into the campaign believing, as did Curet Cuevas, that the loss of Section 936 would be a big, perhaps decisive factor. A poll published in the island's main newspaper, *El Nuevo Día*, a year earlier, in August 1995, showed Rosselló tied with the PDP candidate, San Juan mayor Héctor Luis Acevedo.[3] But the PDP's traditional campaign was no match. Days before the election, the same newspaper's poll had

Rosselló winning by 400,000 votes, or 16 percent, a margin not seen since Muñoz's hegemony.

Curet Cuevas understood that in all elections, in Puerto Rico and throughout the world, the decisive factor was the economy. As a professional economist, he felt secure in his sophisticated analysis of the future effects of Rosselló's policies. However, in the 1996 election year the economy seemed to be booming: big new social programs, giant public works projects, and unprecedented government spending and borrowing.

Health Reform

Governor Rosselló's biggest project, like that of President Bill Clinton in Washington, was health reform. The plan was to totally change Puerto Rico's government-run health care system—through the years denounced by the Medical Association and others as "socialized medicine." The old system would be replaced with a private sector, universal health insurance structure that would guarantee good medical services to all Puerto Ricans regardless of income.

During the 1992 campaign, the team drawing up the reform, including Curet Cuevas, emphasized the complexity of the project and the magnitude of the cost. They wrote into the party program that Rosselló, a successful pediatric surgeon, would proceed cautiously, carefully implementing the change in a step-by-step trial-and-error process. The government would first set up a pilot project in one of the smaller municipalities and, as it gained experience, would make the necessary adjustments to gradually extend the reform to the entire island.

To resolve the critical cost issue, the government would sell the government-run municipal hospitals and clinics to the private sector. The income from the sales plus the big savings from not providing health care services directly to the population would help finance the reform. And the governor expected that a good part of the financing would also come from Clinton's health reform.

But after the elections, Curet Cuevas and the reform team saw the new governor abandoning the trial-and-error approach. When the government began to distribute the new health reform insurance cards for free in the experimental Fajardo area, to no one's surprise, the positive feedback to the "Rosselló card" triggered political pressure from the other seventy-seven municipalities to extend the reform as quickly as possible.

Dismayed, Curet Cuevas wrote in his book that when he and others witnessed the governor yielding to political pressure, they warned that he was endangering the reform. When the Medical Association and other medical groups joined the warnings, Rosselló became more insistent, even hostile. His medical colleagues, he said, should finally accept that the reform is not for them but for the Puerto Rican poor. Instead of slowing down its implementation, Curet Cuevas wrote, he told the media he ordered it accelerated to even more.[4]

Meanwhile, the financing strategy faced serious problems. The government was able to privatize only part of the public health system, nine of the twelve public hospitals and most of the diagnostic and treatment clinics. It found itself financing *both* health systems, a good part of the old and the new. Then bad news came from Washington. On September 26, 1994, a year after President Clinton announced his health reform in a message to Congress and named his wife, Hillary, to construct it, it was pronounced dead in Congress.

By now it was evident that the initial financing plan was not going to happen. Rosselló was urged by economists and sectors of the medical profession to do the same as Washington: give up the reform, or at least slow it down. But with the 1996 elections approaching, the political momentum was too strong, and the drive was to distribute the Rosselló card as soon as possible everywhere in Puerto Rico.

The cost of the reform skyrocketed. Before the reform, in 1993, the government spent $900 million providing health services to 2.1 million inhabitants. By the early 2000s, the cost was $3 billion. To cover the deficits, Rosselló recurred to borrowing.

Since the Muñoz-Tugwell days, as in many U.S. states, the government fiscal policy was not to borrow to cover operational costs and budget deficits. The policy, in some states the law, was to borrow only for infrastructure — roads, bridges, and aqueducts — which was seen as an economic investment that would generate the growth and revenue to pay for itself. Previous island administrations had at times violated this policy, for instance, incurring short-term debt to fill budget gaps in the Health Department.

But Rosselló began to systematically borrow to finance the massive health reform and other big programs, in large part from the Government Development Bank. Curet Cuevas and others were alarmed. As he did in regard to losing Section 936, he made another dire prediction in his book: "To the degree that the [Health] Reform is extended to the entire island and the fiscal impact grows, eventually the financial load on the Government Development Bank and the government deficit will be of such magnitude that it will endanger the continuation of the health insurance program and the fiscal stability of the government itself."[5]

But the warning of Curet Cuevas and other "prophets of doom" contradicted the perceived reality. Thousands of Puerto Ricans received the free Rosselló card, most from the governor himself. Thousands were employed in the other giant projects. It seemed that Puerto Rico was enjoying an unprecedented economic boom.

The Urban Train

The biggest public works project in Puerto Rican history was the Tren Urbano, or Urban Train. Like everywhere else, one of the prices Puerto Ricans paid for the rapid economic development was the "tapón"—the traffic bottleneck. By the 1970s, a journalist calculated that a typical Puerto Rican driving to San Juan from one of the sprawling neighborhoods in Caguas, Bayamón, or Carolina to work, to a shopping center on weekends, to Old San Juan at night, or to the beaches on Sunday would spend about a month a year trapped in crawling, bumper-to-bumper traffic. In an adult lifetime, he wrote, this was comparable to a four-and-a-half-year prison term.

Operation Bootstrap had set off the migration of Puerto Ricans from the countryside to the San Juan metropolitan area—its population growing from 338,537 in 1940 to 1.2 million in 1990—and the explosive growth in vehicles. The government's road-building program, in large part financed by the U.S. government, could not keep up. From 1970 to 2000, total road miles grew from 4,428 to 14,400, a 200 percent increase. But the number of vehicles grew by 350 percent. By 1990, there were 1.6 million vehicles on the island, whose total population was 3.5 million.

The need for a mass transportation system, recognized for decades, was now urgent.

Puerto Rico, in fact, had a rail system that was begun in the nineteenth century under the Spanish regime that was vital for transporting people and agricultural products around the island. In San Juan there was a twenty-mile street tramway network, a trolley, that transported over ten million people a year. Although Puerto Rico prided itself on rivaling the modern electric streetcar systems in New York and Toronto, by the 1950s, as agriculture, especially sugar, declined and as industrial and commercial land development grew and the government embarked on more road construction, both the train and the trolleys were abandoned.

In 1967, the government contracted with two private engineering companies that came up with a proposed double-track rail system that would cost $281 million. Two lines, with a total of thirty-seven stations, would crisscross east-west and north-south, with the transfer station in Hato Rey. In 1971, there was another proposal, this one from the island Planning Board and the U.S. government.

As evident as it was that the San Juan area urgently needed a rapid transit system, there were doubts that it was economically viable. It was not clear that it had the needed population densities. Even more critical was the so-called origin-destination factor. Would the system take commuters faster and closer to their destinations than their own vehicles?

In 1991, Governor Hernández Colón decided to proceed with an eighteen-station light-rail system at a cost of $612 million.[6] The following year, a final design was approved that only covered part of the San Juan metropolitan area and did not extend to Old San Juan. In 1993, Governor Rosselló, with the approval of the Federal Transportation Administration, decided to go forward with Phase 1: one 10.7-mile line with sixteen stations serving San Juan, Bayamón, and Guaynabo.

When construction began in 1997, the cost had almost doubled from the original Hernández Colón project to $13 billion. Ignoring the growing alarm signals of cost overruns and numerous delays, Rosselló added two new stations. Although most of the system was elevated, the additions required a 1.1-mile tunnel to one of the new stations at the University of Puerto Rico at Río Piedras. There were conflicts and claims, at one point totaling $350 million, between the contractors and the government. And throughout there was growing criticism that the ballooning cost was in large part the result of Rosselló's insistence on building a much too extravagant system whose custom-built trains and stations were described by one critic as "pharaonic."[7]

Still in government, Curet Cuevas, as he had done with the health reform, warned that the numbers simply did not add up. Even if the train reached the optimistic goal of 100,000 passengers a day, it would incur enormous losses.[8]

In 2001, Secretary of Transportation and Public Works José Izquierdo Encarnación took over the Urban Train project under the new PDP governor, Sila María Calderón. Izquierdo Encarnación was convinced that the system could not work because it did not meet the critical origin and destination factor. It needed the feeder system, integrated into the Metropolitan Bus system, taking passengers to their destinations, for instance, those working in Old San Juan. But "after Puerto Rico went into a recession in 2006," he wrote, "the budget for public transportation went into a downward spiral, thus preventing the development of a feeder system." Critically underfunded from the beginning, Izquierdo Encarnación concluded that the only source of the desperately needed additional financing had to come from additional taxes, precisely what neither party was willing to impose. The enormous cost and operating loss of the Urban Train, although not nearly as big as that of the three times larger health reform, according to Izquierdo Encarnación, who went on to serve as secretary of state from 2002 to 2005, "ruined the Puerto Rico Highway and Transportation Authority."[9]

According to the U.S. Department of Transportation, when the Urban Train was inaugurated in December 2004, the cost had doubled again, to $2.25 billion: $828.8 million in federal grants, $637.8 million in Puerto Rico bonds, a $300 million Transportation Infrastructure Finance and Innovation (U.S. Department of Transportation) loan, and $483 million from other sources.

A year after its 2004 inauguration, there were fewer than 25,000 daily passengers, many of them enjoying student and senior discounts. The many spaces for shops and other businesses at the train stations remained empty. By 2016, the Tren Urbano was losing $85 million a year. The annual number of passengers had dropped to 6.3 million a year, a fraction of the original estimate of 40 million a year. As with the health reform, Rosselló relied on Government Development Bank credit to fill its operational deficits. By 2016, the train's total debt was $6.9 billion.

The Coliseum and Other Projects

The Urban Train reflected the enthusiasm and optimism generated by the Rosselló administration. The ingrained attitude at the close of the millennium in Puerto Rico—that its economic growth, regardless of the bumps along the way and of the "doomsday economists," was unstoppable—got a powerful boost from Rosselló's fundamental attitude, as described by Curet Cuevas: "If we should, we can!" Another example was the drive to make Puerto Rico the site of the 2004 Olympics.

One of the peculiarities of the island's relationship to the United States is that since 1948 Puerto Rico has had its own Olympics Committee and participates as a separate nation in the Olympics. Like so much else in island politics, this was another issue in the status conflict, statehood advocates insisting that if the island became a state it would find a way to retain its Olympics standing.

When Rosselló was elected in 1992, he decided to go forward with the petition for the 2004 Olympics that had been made under the previous administration. He also decided to proceed with building a sports and entertainment coliseum. The government began construction at the San Juan sports complex next to the Hiram Bithorn baseball stadium, Pedrín Zorrilla Mini-Coliseum, and Roberto Clemente Coliseum, at a cost of $62 million. Problems arose quickly. The cost ballooned to $108 million; then Puerto Rico lost its bid to host the Olympics.

As he had done after President Clinton's health reform collapsed, Governor Rosselló decided not only to go ahead, but to greatly increase the scope and cost of the project. The site was transferred to the Milla de Oro (Golden Mile), near the financial district of Hato Rey. The Coliseum was expanded by adding four thousand seats, space for an ice rink, and luxury corporate suites. The cost increased to $220 million.

In 2001, the new administration of Governor Calderón found that the Coliseum was only 43 percent complete, sixteen months behind schedule. The contractor faced critical financial problems, and the new site was too small for the necessary parking spaces. Once again, the Government Development Bank was used to bail out the Coliseum with $145 million in financing. When the Coliseum was finally inaugurated on September 4, 2004, the bank had financed $300 million.[10] Although popular with fans and entertainers, the Coliseum became still another economic drain on the government.

The Spending Binge

When the Calderón administration took over in 2001, the phase-out of Section 936 had five years to go, and the economy had still not begun to feel the effects. Government revenues were growing rapidly, but they were being overtaken by the spending binge. During 1994–2000, the government accumulated a budget deficit of $3 billion: total revenue of $42.9 billion and total spending of $45.9 billion.[11] The growing gap was filled by massive borrowing.

The total government debt, which had increased steadily from $119 million in 1950 to $12.9 billion in 1991, during the Rosselló administration, grew to $22.8 billion in 2000.[12] The critical difference was the unprecedented magnitude of the new infrastructure projects. Just as critical was that now, unlike in prior governments, debt was being used to cover a growing part of the government's operational deficits.

On January 7, 2002, Governor Calderón, in her second year in office, received a chilling personal letter from the president of the Government Development Bank, Juan Agosto Alicea: "We knew before the elections that Puerto Rico's [economic] situation was difficult. We never imagined that it was bankrupt."[13]

The governor had convinced Agosto to return to the government after a long career in public and in private accounting. Prior his tenure at the Government Development Bank, he had served as treasury secretary under Hernández Colón and in the private sector had headed the accounting firm Peat Marwick's office in Puerto Rico. The island media referred to him as the "Super Secretary." He had a reputation for being a nonpartisan economic and fiscal troubleshooter. In his 2011 memoirs,

Crisis: Al borde de la quiebra, he wrote that he was stunned to find what had happened to the Government Development Bank. It had an outstanding debt of $2.4 billion and assets of only $1.4 billion.[14]

Used to financing Rosselló's big projects — the health reform, the Urban Train, the Coliseum, an $800 million "super aqueduct" to pipe water into the San Juan area — now the bank had 140 outstanding loans to one client. And it was a "client" that could not pay: the government of Puerto Rico.

The Rosselló economic bubble, Agosto informed Calderón in his letter, had burst. "The economic bonanza ended in 2000," he wrote, "and the recession has begun."[15]

The economist Curet Cuevas had seen it coming in 1996. "One thing is certain," he wrote at the end of his book, "the Rosselló administration is financing its actions and programs based on irresponsibly compromising the economic future of the Puerto Rico economy beyond its capacity to pay."[16]

Puerto Rico was digging itself into a hole it could not climb out of. The economic and fiscal crisis had begun.

CHAPTER FIVE

The Breakdown of
the Public Corporations

Rexford Tugwell's core belief was that good government was possible only through government administration as free as possible of the scourge of partisan politics. He was delighted to be named governor of Puerto Rico in 1941 by President Roosevelt. But he had witnessed firsthand the destructiveness of island partisan politics: he was a participant in Roosevelt's effort to extend the New Deal to the island and saw its undermining and eventual failure in what Interior Secretary Harold Ickes had described to him as a political "barrel of snakes."[1]

How, then, with all his government and academic experience, could Tugwell, a congenital skeptic, believe that he would succeed in Puerto Rico? He did. His five years in office were by far the most successful of any American governor. And the key was the government-owned public corporation. The idea was that essential functions and services were carried out by government agencies that ultimately responded to the democratically elected politicians but that were autonomous enough to be run by apolitical administrators, were self-sustaining, and did not depend on government funds and were thus free of political interference. It was used throughout the world, especially when a massive nationalization of key industries — telephones, railroads, airlines, fossil fuels — took place in Europe after World War II. For a critic of laissez-faire capitalism like Tugwell, it was what made representational democracy *work*, especially in overpoliticized places like Puerto Rico.

For the public, public corporations are indistinguishable from all the other government agencies. The difference is that they are allowed to be run independently as private enterprises. The boards, whose members are chosen by the governor, name the executives, not necessarily but usually with the governor's approval, but they and their staff are allowed to operate free of political interference. Most important, public corporations are expected to operate with the efficiency to generate enough income to cover or exceed their own costs. They are empowered to issue bonds to finance their infrastructure programs under the supervision of the Government Development Bank. They are expected to not be a drain on the government budget or affect the government debt limit. They are also free of public employee limitations and regulations. Paying competitive salaries and labor benefits, they are expected to attract the best professional talent on the island regardless of party affiliation.

It seemed clear to Tugwell why what the British historian Raymond Carr was to call the American "colonial experiment" had not worked. It was not that the Americans did not try. It was mostly, Tugwell believed, due to American incompetence. Americans, without colonial experience, had created a structure that was a mixture of colonialism and self-government; it had an appointed American governor and a Puerto Rican elected legislature, a recipe for conflict.

Some of the governors were inept political appointees, among the worst named by Roosevelt himself, seeing the governorship as a year or so of living on a beautiful Caribbean island, in a grand Spanish fortress, La Fortaleza, as a reward for political contributions. There were several capable and talented governors, and some did make progress. But in the end they were thwarted by the island politicians who controlled the legislature and saw the role of government as their parties' employment agency.

The idea was that American "tutelage" would gradually instill in Puerto Rico political leaders the culture and institutions of democratic representational government. But island leaders saw no reason for being "tutored" and resented it. For the status-obsessed leaders, cooperation with the American governor was seen as unpatriotic acquiescence to the island's colonial status.

The reality, Tugwell found, was that "American rule" was an overstatement. Although the governor of Puerto Rico represented the most powerful nation in world history, named by and responding to the "leader of the free world," in fact, Tugwell wrote in *The Stricken Land*, "nowhere in the civilized world is there an executive with so little power." Puerto Rican politicians, he wrote, while endlessly whining about the abuse and indignity of "American colonialism," in fact had effectively decapitated the American governor. Four decades of "confused colonialism," he wrote, had left the American governor powerless, "a shell of authority [that] was empty."[2]

Tugwell strongly believed that the "colonial experiment" should end, that Puerto Rico should govern itself and in the long run would become a U.S. state. But to succeed, he was determined not be another American enjoying the Puerto Rican weather and the beauty of its landscape, sending glowing reports to Congress and the president. As he describes it in his memoirs, *The Stricken Land*, he and his family also relished Puerto Rico's scenic beauty. Whenever he could he would escape from La Fortaleza in San Juan to the spectacular beauty of the governor's "summer home" in the central mountain area of Jájome. "For Jájome," he wrote, "has appealed to my pessimistic mood. Up there I was like a Scotsman on a misty headland."[3] But he was determined not to be another "empty shell," to exercise *American rule*, real power, to *govern*.

Tugwell and Muñoz

But there was a problem. To govern, he had to confront the new political leader, elected president of the Senate in 1941, Luis Muñoz Marín. Tugwell knew him well. They had worked together to bring the New Deal to the island in the 1930s. Muñoz had played a big role in getting him named governor. After the 1940 elections, he convinced Tugwell to become University of Puerto Rico chancellor. But Tugwell wanted the governorship, and for a short time, he was both chancellor and governor, causing a firestorm of criticism in the island newspapers and marking the beginning of a four-year war with the media.

And Tugwell knew that Muñoz was unlike the other politicos. The problem was that Muñoz had a peculiar idea—that the 1940 election had given *him* and his Popular Democratic Party a mandate to govern—not just, as in the past, to run the legislature and manipulate the budget for partisan purposes, but to exercise the power to govern.

In fact, it was not clear that Muñoz had won the 1940 election, much less that he had received any mandate. The Republican coalition had received more votes and elected the resident commissioner. Muñoz won control of the Senate; only later did he also control the House.

Yet on February 11, 1940, having sworn in as Senate president, Muñoz proclaimed, "The governor of Puerto Rico is [the president's] representative. Within the principles of democracy in the person of the governor reside the democratic principles of the president and the democratic principles of the people of Puerto Rico."[4] Muñoz was saying not only that he had a mandate but also that it extended to the governor and to the president himself.

Was this typical Puerto Rican political bombast? Did Muñoz really believe the governor and the president himself were subject to "the democratic principles of the people of Puerto Rico"? Did he really believe that Tugwell and the president were obligated to carry out his radical reforms? As much as Tugwell and the president sympathized with the reforms, the elections had not changed the power structure or the island's political status. If Muñoz believed it, he, Tugwell, was headed toward big trouble in Puerto Rico. Big trouble with Muñoz.

Muñoz, of course, understood that the island's political status and power structure had not changed. But he was dead serious. As much as Tugwell was determined not to be another "empty shell," Muñoz was determined to carry out the people's mandate and exercise the power of government.

Tugwell was a different governor and Muñoz a different Puerto Rican leader. The question was, would they work together? They had one thing in their favor: they spoke the same language. Communicating with island politicos had always been a big problem for American governors: most did not speak Spanish. Few island leaders spoke English. Tugwell did not speak Spanish, but he had bonded with Muñoz in the 1930s in large part because Muñoz spoke and wrote good American English, having been brought up and educated both in the United States and on the island. And they spoke the same political language: as Muñoz wrote in *La historia del Partido Popular Democrático*, precisely in late 1941 when Tugwell arrived, what made his party different was that it was the first in island history whose top leadership, beginning with himself, "is from the generation most subject to American democratic influence."[5]

They shared the same view of capitalism: "the profit motive" was the bane of civilization, creating the consumer-driven society that is the source of human conflict and unhappiness. Democratic socialism, anchored by powerful government planning—as Tugwell put it, *cooperation, not competition*—is the source of human happiness. As Muñoz put it later in life, "Capitalism is efficient but immoral, socialism is moral but inefficient."[6]

And it was important to Tugwell that he felt he could count on Muñoz in the world conflict against fascism. He wasn't sure about other island politicians, writing in *The Stricken Land* that he suspected that conservative Statehood Republican Party leaders, some of whom expressed admiration for the Spanish dictator Francisco Franco, were fascist sympathizers that could not be trusted.

They both wanted the same thing: a profound economic and social democratic revolution in Puerto Rico. But did Muñoz understand that a real revolution is not made with *pronunciamientos* (pronouncements)? Or with changing one government for another? To actually change the lives of the Puerto Ricans, it had to be an *administrative* revolution. And did he understand that for there to be an administrative revolution, there had to be a revolution in Puerto Rico's political culture? This meant a radically depoliticized public administration. It meant Muñoz and the PDP would have to yield political power to autonomous government entities. It meant public corporations.

Tugwell and Muñoz created nineteen public corporations. Before Tugwell arrived, Muñoz had already created several. They became the core of what the Harvard historian Charles T. Goodsell called "the administration of a revolution," the title of his 1965 history of Tugwell's five-year governorship. The administrative revolution, as Goodsell described it, led to radical improvement in the lives of all Puerto Ricans, turning four decades of American failure into the "economic miracle."[7]

But within the reality of Puerto Rican politics, how much public corporation independence would be tolerated? Did Moscoso's Puerto Rico Industrial Development Company, PRIDCO, and the Government Development Bank (GDB), go too far? By the late 1940s, the Fomento head was criticized, including by his brother-in-law and Muñoz's right-hand man, Roberto Sánchez Vilella, as being a loose cannon that had to be reined in. Moscoso sent angry memos insisting that the only way it could succeed was precisely if left free to be run as a private enterprise. Moscoso acknowledged that of course he and Fomento were part of the Puerto Rican government, but at the same time he had built in his agency a sense of their own identity, the staff proudly wearing lapel buttons that identified them as Fomento employees, a kind of badge of honor that marked them as part of an elite. To impose on them the uniformity of government rules and norms, he argued, would kill this spirit. Bootstrap was beginning Puerto Rico's economic takeoff, and PRIDCO, its independence protected by Moscoso, was a model public corporation. For the GDB, the battle for independence would prove crucial in the following decades.

Luchetti and the Battle for Public Power

In contrast to Moscoso, who sought visibility and put up billboards throughout the island announcing, "This is a Fomento plant," and seemed to be always engaged in public controversy, the veteran engineer Antonio Luchetti was nearly invisible. But he played a critical role in the island's economic growth. He led the public corporation that more directly than any other imbued in Puerto Ricans the sense of "revolution."

Nothing was more radical for a Puerto Rican in San Juan or in a tin-roofed wooden shack in the central mountains than the act of pulling a string and turning on a lightbulb. Luchetti had organized and led the Puerto Rico Water Resources Authority, the precursor to the Puerto Rico Electric Power Authority. And it filled Tugwell with satisfaction that he had created the islandwide electric power monopoly that became the pride of Puerto Rico.

Luchetti, after graduating from Cornell University in 1910, came to work for the island government running the private hydroelectric plants that supplied the sugar mills with energy. Under different governors and political parties, he relentlessly went about extending the government power grid. When Tugwell arrived, the San Juan area and the much smaller Mayagüez area were served by private power companies.

Tugwell was determined to take over both companies. The fact that they resisted fiercely was for Tugwell still another example of capitalist greed taking precedence over the public good. The San Juan authority was owned by a Canadian, Lord Beaverbrook. Using his personal relationship with President Roosevelt, Tugwell got him to use his wartime powers to expropriate the utilities. The battle continued, however, as federal courts annulled the takeover. It was not until December 1943, two years after having created the Puerto Rico Water Resources Authority, that Tugwell and Luchetti achieved their goal of a single power monopoly.

By the 1950s, as the lights went on in all of Puerto Rico, as Goodsell describes it, Luchetti's power authority was recognized as the "most prestigious and efficient component of the insular government."[8]

The public corporations were only part of the extraordinary growth of the island government during the Tugwell years. He and Muñoz created a total of forty-one new agencies, the number of executive public employees grew from 15,579 to 21,000, and the budget grew from $47 million to $112.9 million, a 140 percent increase.

The great question that Tugwell had asked himself was answered: Puerto Rico had indeed broken out of the political culture that had defeated the attempts at good government and stifled the economy. And he had reason to feel vindicated in his essential conviction. What had been denounced as his socialist experiment in Puerto Rico had worked. While Muñoz and Moscoso took credit around the world for the remarkable economic take-off, they knew that the key was the success of the public corporations.

The Power of the Public Corporation Unions

As Moscoso, Luchetti, and other public corporation heads battled for their independence, battles *within* the corporations gradually shifted the power structure. In the 1951 Constitutional Convention, Muñoz and the other delegates extended to all public corporation workers the right to unionize and engage in collective bargaining, the same right given to all private sector workers. But they were not given the right to strike. The public corporations were all unionized, including supervisory personnel. The fundamental rationale was evident. As the constitutional delegates declared, since public corporations are meant to function as private entities, its personnel should have the same union rights as private sector workers.

But there was a vital difference. These corporations were all monopolies, which not only delivered indispensable services, like electric power and drinking water, but also ran vital entities like the docks and the airports. This gave these unions a power much greater than those in the private sector.

The nature of collective bargaining is fundamentally different. In the private sector, national and local unions succeeded in organizing the hotels, the garment industry, and newspapers and other media. Union power consisted of the threat to disrupt and paralyze the operation—the use of pickets, the threat of a strike. But if a strike closed a hotel or a newspaper, although the public may well be inconvenienced, there are alternatives.

In public corporation bargaining, threatening to disrupt or interrupt a vital service becomes a political crisis. Although this was prohibited, the unions used the threat of strike and occasionally walked out, paralyzing vital services. Several unions, such as those in the electric power and water and sewerage agencies, achieved great power. As the public corporations grew, the negotiating power was used not only to negotiate salaries and benefits far beyond those in the central government but also to steadily increase the ability to effectively control the agency's operations.

At the same time there was a critical political shift within the labor movement. In the 1940s, Muñoz and the Popular Democratic Party had wide influence in the local and national unions, an important factor in the Fomento program. Many union leaders were also PDP leaders. When the Teamsters made a big push in the 1960s to organize the tourism industries, particularly the hotels with casinos, and communications industries, Muñoz backed U.S. organized labor in its conflicts with the union.

But by the early 1970s, local labor leaders were accusing Muñoz and the U.S. labor unions as being too close. They sought to break the bonds between them. The political and ideological influence in the local unions shifted away from the PDP toward the radical independence movement. Several leaders were influenced by Fidel Castro's 1959 Cuban Revolution.

The self-proclaimed Marxist-Leninist Puerto Rican Socialist Party believed that it would not waste time in the ideological status fight or engage in suicidal acts of violence that resulted in instilling even more fear of independence but instead would mobilize the growing labor class that Bootstrap was rapidly creating. The PSP's secretary general in 1983, Carlos Gallisá, was a labor lawyer who had begun his career at Fomento.

The PSP's goal was to penetrate and control the powerful public corporation unions. None was more powerful than those in the Puerto Rico Electric Power Authority. The biggest union, the 4,800-member Electrical Industry and Irrigation Workers Union (UTIER), was headed by the PSP candidate for governor in 1980, Luis Lausell Hernández. He got only 5,224 votes, or 0.3 percent, in the elections. But he and other PSP leaders, like the veteran Pedro Grant, head of the Movimiento Obrero Unido (MOU; United Workers Movement), became the most powerful labor leaders in Puerto Rico.

This seemed like a contradictory phenomenon. The vast majority of the union members in the public corporations, as in large private sector unions, such as the island's largest daily newspaper, *El Mundo*, voted for the pro-statehood or pro-commonwealth party. They not only opposed independence and "socialism," but many feared it. Yet they voted the PSP leaders into union leadership. It was, in fact, no contradiction. Many union members trusted that the PSP guaranteed the militancy and, if necessary, intimidation and even acts of violence that would result in the best collective bargaining labor benefits.

The union leaders had another key benefit. They often negotiated with former union members who became part of the agency's management and now benefited directly from the higher salaries and benefits negotiated. These management negotiators, aside from the political pressure to reach an agreement and avoid a strike or other crisis, had a strong personal incentive to give in to union demands.

All this undermined the essential independence of the public corporation from partisan political interference. Faced with a threatened shutdown in a vital service, the Tugwell theory of autonomous public corporations broke down. On the one hand, political leaders believed they were forced to interfere to avoid political damage; on the other, the union's ultimate power came precisely from that interference.

In the 1970s, political leaders had reason to fear the growing union powers. Governor Hernández Colón decided to confront one of the electric power unions that had declared a strike and had begun to bring down power lines and sabotage power plants. He mobilized the National Guard and ended the sabotage and then the strike. But when he was unexpectedly defeated in his bid for reelection, he and others were convinced that the ugly labor conflict, as much as anything else, cost him the election.

Returning to the governorship in 1985, Hernández Colón let his cabinet know that he had learned his lesson and would not repeat the same mistake. His cabinet got the message: no more public corporation labor union confrontations. He would always decide, they understood, in favor of "labor peace."

As management lost power to the unions, the public corporations began to deteriorate. The economic effect became increasingly evident.

Private sector studies on Puerto Rico's competitiveness began to highlight that what had been one of the island's strengths was becoming a major impediment to economic development. The cost of electric power in Puerto Rico was always higher than on the mainland, as it was an island a thousand miles from the coast and depended mostly on imported petroleum. But through the years, the gap increased: by 2011, the cost of a kilowatt-hour, 27.9 cents, was two and a half times that on the mainland, 9.9 cents. A significant factor was growing inefficiencies: massive overstaffing compared to mainland power utilities and exorbitant labor salaries and benefits.

In 2018, the World Bank's Ease of Doing Business Report gave PREPA a low ranking, 69. The deterioration had many causes. In addition to being plagued by weak management, it suffered from increasing political interference as the political parties began to alternate in power, greatly politicizing government actions and decisions. As a 2018 GAO report, "Puerto Rico: Factors Contributing to the Debt Crisis and Potential Federal Actions to Address Them," points out, "PREPA did not update or improve its electrical generation and transmission system, which hampered their performance and led to increased production cost."[9]

The September 20, 2017, Hurricane Maria, which left Puerto Rico without power for months, some sectors for over a year, exposed the degree of deterioration of what had been celebrated as a model of the public corporation — the pride of Puerto Rico.

The Aqueduct and Sewerage Authority

As much as the power authority, the Aqueduct and Sewerage Authority (AAA) was a vital part of the "revolution" that became real when a Puerto Rican turned on a faucet and there was safe drinking water.

In 1943, the island's health commissioner testified before a congressional committee that 30 percent of the water in the urban areas was contaminated, 100 percent in the rural areas. Two years later, Tugwell and Muñoz created the Aqueduct and Sewerage Authority. By the 1970s it had become a giant, supplying 98 percent of the island's drinking water and operating sixty water treatment plants. Among its 5,000 employees, 3,700 were unionized.[10]

In 1974, the biggest union, the Aqueduct Independent Union (UIA), declared an illegal strike. When eleven union leaders violated a court order to return to work, they were imprisoned. Ten days later, Governor Hernández Colón pardoned them.

When Governor Rosselló came to power in 1993, determined to "reinvent government," he decided that the solution to the problem of public corporations was to privatize them. In 1995, the French firm Vivendi, then the world's largest operator of water companies, took over. It didn't work. Seven years later, in 2002, Governor Calderón decided not to renew the contract. The government absorbed its accumulated $990.5 million deficit.

The contract was awarded to another French water company, Suez, the world's second largest. In the negotiations, headed by GDB president Juan Agosto Alicea, the new firm, convinced that the agency had been grossly mismanaged and that Vivendi had not been able to improve it, was confident that it had the management skills to turn it around. It would reduce the massive "water theft" and the loss of 54 percent of water that never reached consumers. It projected that this would generate $100 million in revenue. The firm also set out to reduce the agency's bloated workforce, cutting 550 jobs by offering early retirement in the first six months.

But Suez, also known as the Ondeo Company, found that it had been unrealistically optimistic. It was unable to reduce the water theft and loss and by the end of December 2002 had run up an $82.2 million operational deficit. In August 2013, Suez executives from Paris told the government to either amend the contract or it would pull out of Puerto Rico. In November they asked for a $125 million "refund" to recover the company's losses and a $27 million increase in the contract fees. Governor Calderón gave up: on January 15, 2004, the contract was rescinded.

The Authority returned to government hands. It was evident that as part of the government the public corporation had been run into the ground by mismanagement and debt. Now, privatization had not worked: the two biggest water companies in the world had tried and failed.

In 2002, Governor Calderón had convinced Agosto Alicea to leave the Government Development Bank to lead the transition from Vivendi to Suez. Now she asked him to stay and run the water authority. Agosto Alicea quickly discovered what the essential problem was. It was not whether the government or a private company ran it; it was the power of the unions. Even with his long experience in government, he was surprised to see how much power they exerted. The real problem, he candidly told the press, was that the union ran the agency, so that the person who actually ran it was not him, Agosto Alicea, but the president of the UIA, Hector René Lugo, one of the leaders jailed in the 1974 strike. He was not, he insisted, exaggerating.

Lugo, like other public corporation labor leaders, was an expert at using political intervention in his favor. He made sure to negotiate new contracts during election years. He knew that the political pressure to reach an agreement and avoid a politically fatal strike gave him a decisive advantage in negotiations. Lugo negotiated contracts that diminished management's authority. One example, according to Agosto Alicea, became evident when Lugo pushed to give drivers the same privilege as commercial airline pilots, who have the right to refuse to fly an aircraft they determined was unsafe. So, on occasion, enough drivers found "defects" in their vehicles to effectively paralyze the agency. Another example was that management could not transfer a union member without union approval. Agosto Alicea found that a plant in Caguas was closed, but the unionized plant manager refused to be transferred to another plant. For several months, the manager went to the closed plant, receiving his full salary while doing nothing.

It was not even necessary to spell out the union's powers in the contract. Soon after taking over, Agosto Alicea convened an employee meeting, and a union member insisted that he could not call the meeting without union approval. When Agosto Alicea asked to see where that rule appeared in the union contract, the union member shouted, "Ese es el uso y costumbre"— "That is the way it is always done"—a phrase used often by union leaders that has the force of a contract.

But Lugo's real power was in extracting economic benefits and sometimes outright payoffs. In 2000, Lugo knew how anxious Governor Rosselló was to inaugurate one of his big projects, the "Super Aqueduct," before the elections. Lugo protested that a private firm was contracted to maintain it. Aware of the governor's political interest, the Aqueducts and Sewerage Authority (AAA) board quickly agreed to pay the union $1.2 million over five years.[11] The union withdrew its protest, and the project's inauguration went on as planned.

The union extracted from the AAA $1.9 million a year to maintain the union's "vacation centers" around the island, hotel and recreational facilities that Agosto Alicea found were lucrative businesses run by the union leaders.[12] The union contract also called for full salaries and benefits to twenty union officials who were not required to work at the AAA, since they were on what was called "union sabbatical," supposedly doing union work. The cost to the AAA was $1 million a year.[13] In 2004, the union won a court case dating from 1998, when it sued for payment of vacations accumulated in excess of sixty days, not only for unionized employees, but also for retired employees. The AAA had to pay $24 million to the union and $4.8 million to its lawyers.

What infuriated Agosto Alicea was that the union leaders on "union sabbatical" were included in the judgment, among them Lugo, who received $268,899, his wife, $43,549, and the union vice president, $84,846. Although the courts later rescinded the lawyer's fee, he testified in another case that Lugo had given him a "gift" of $246,000 in gratitude.[14]

The union insisted that it was negotiating benefits and powers that existed in the United States and elsewhere. But Agosto Alicea was determined to push back. In 2004, again an election year, the agency negotiated a new contract with the union. This time, Agosto Alicea decided, it would be different. After five sessions during which nothing was agreed, he and the board, convinced that again Lugo would stall to get closer to the elections, decided to play hard ball. They informed the union that the agency was suspending the $500,000 union dues deductions, the "union sabbaticals," and the payment for the "vacation centers."

The agency braced itself for another strike, but then the Puerto Rico Insurance Commissioner accused the union of misusing for the benefit of the union leaders $12 million of the $45 million the AAA had paid for health insurance. Lugo was ordered to return the $12 million and resign as head of the health plan.

On October 4, 2004, a month before the elections, the union went on strike. The AAA board had begun to establish its own health plan for the workers. The union came back that it would not negotiate until the board desisted. The Popular Democratic Party's candidate for governor, Aníbal Acevedo Vilá, fearing that the strike would cost him the election, called Agosto Alicea to plead that he settle it. Agosto Alicea and the board resisted the pressure. Contrary to what Lugo and the union leadership expected, this time the strike did not hurt the PDP: Acevedo Vilá was elected. The strike lasted eighty-four days, ending on December 27, after the November elections.

Later that year, the United States indicted Lugo and ten other UIA members for conspiring to use $15 million in health plan funds for their own benefit and of money laundering. They were convicted in the Federal Court for the District of Puerto Rico and sentenced to prison.

From being considered the best water utility in the United States in 1970, as Agosto Alicea recorded in his 2011 memoir, "thirty years later, in 2000, it was considered one of the worst, probably the worst."[15]

The breakdown of the public corporations, originally intended to be economically self-sufficient, was a big component of the debt crisis. In 2014, they had run up a debt of $27.6 billion, 40.5 percent of the government's total debt. The Puerto Rico Electric Power Authority had the biggest share, $9.4 billion; the Puerto Rico Highway and Transportation Authority, which was financing the huge losses of the Urban Train, $5 billion; the Puerto Rico Aqueduct and Water Authority, $4.7 billion.

But none was more important to the island's economic growth or contributed as much to the debt crisis as the deterioration and eventual demise of the Government Development Bank.

CHAPTER SIX

The Demise of the Government Development Bank

There are not many open spaces in San Juan. But there is one in Santurce, in the Spanish past an upscale San Juan suburb, now a mixed bag of expensive condominiums, restaurants, and commercial areas, along with rundown communities, many populated by Dominican immigrants. Across the avenue from the Puerto Rico Art Museum, there is the Puerto Rico Government Center: tall, modern, metal and stone sculptures, flanked by two attractive, brownstone nineteen-story buildings that house many government offices.

Between the buildings, behind a very tall futuristic metal sculpture, there is an eye-catching four-story building. Because of its central location and the space surrounding it, it makes a statement that among all the government agencies, it is unique, it is important. The sculpture symbolizes that Puerto Rico's future resides in this building. On top, in big blue letters, is written the words, Banco Gubernamental de Fomento para Puerto Rico.

Despite its significance, since this agency was founded on May 13, 1942, very few Puerto Ricans knew what it was or what it did. In fact, as the story of Puerto Rico's economic decline began with the demise of Section 936, the story of the fiscal crisis centers on the demise of the Government Development Bank.

February 4, 2014, is described by economists as Puerto Rico's "day of infamy." Standard & Poor's announced it had degraded Puerto Rican bonds to junk status. But this was not the island's first such event. Puerto Rico had lost its credit in 1973 when it suffered its worst economic downturn since the Great Depression. Losing its access to the bond market, Puerto Rico could no longer borrow to carry out its infrastructure program. Treasury Secretary Salvador Casellas had no funds to meet the payroll for the first time since 1935.

The Yom Kippur War and the Arab and Venezuelan petroleum boycott increased the price of oil by 400 percent. Puerto Rico's economy, for two decades propelled by Operation Bootstrap's success, came to a screeching halt and began to decline. Unemployment and the interest rate shot up. Six island banks were on the verge of collapse. Again the Government Development Bank was critical. The governor convinced Moscoso's old right-hand man, Guillermo Rodríguez, who had become a successful businessman and major patron of the arts, to return to government and take over the bank. Associated with Bootstrap Puerto Rico, Rodríguez restored Wall Street confidence and the government's credit.

Hernández Colón also got the Yale economist James Tobin, later a Nobel laureate, to head a committee that in 1975 outlined a program of fiscal policies to avoid overextended debt and budget deficits. The Tobin Report played a crucial role in restoring the island's credibility and its recovery. Its essential point was that the island should not expect to return to the accustomed rapid growth after the crisis and that deep and difficult reforms were needed. "The government spending tendencies, the deficits in the government enterprises, the public debt and the productions costs could not be sustained even with favorable economic conditions in the exterior," the report stated. Tobin recommended an "austerity program" extending several years that included reducing the growth in public spending, increasing taxes and other revenue, and freezing government salaries, including rolling back some of the legislated labor benefits.[1]

The Tobin Report recognized and applauded the fact that Hernández Colón had already begun to carry out an austerity program. But it also recognized the political cost: "Drastic adjustments are needed, especially painful, because they involve the postponement of expectations profoundly rooted in the island's economic and political life during an era of rapid industrial growth and abundant external financing."[2]

In the early 1970s, Governor Ferré had convinced Congress to extend the food stamp program to Puerto Rico, but concerned about the cost, the administration had not implemented it. Now, Governor Hernández Colón carried out a crash program to do so, injecting $350 million into the economy. In 1976, the approval of Section 936 not only revived the Fomento program but also gave it an unprecedented boost. In 1977, Puerto Rico regained its borrowing credit. The Government Development Bank sold $350 million in government bonds, the largest issue in island history.

But the austerity program had its political effect. From 1973 to 1975, Hernández Colón increased tax revenue by 45 percent.[3] One of them, a temporary income tax surcharge dubbed by a local newspaper "La Vampirita," the Little Vampire, was picked up by the opposition party to great effect. Months before the elections, when Treasury informed Hernández Colón of a budgetary surplus, he resisted great pressure to use it for a promised government salary increase.

Hernández Colón and his administration earned the accolades of economists and others for what was considered an example of how to put partisan politics aside to pull an economy out of an abrupt and violent nosedive. But he lost the election in 1976.

The 2016 announcement that the government of Puerto Rico was bankrupt and could not pay its debts was news that made the front pages throughout the United States and the world as "the biggest government financial collapse in United States history."[4] It seemed unfathomable. With a per capita income one-half that of the poorest state, Mississippi, in 2017, Puerto Rico's debt per capita was eleven times higher than that of the United States as a whole, and four and a half times highter than the average of the ten most indebted states. Debt service was 28.1 percent of government revenues, compared to the average of 8.8 percent for the ten states with the highest debt. The amount of debt to personal income was

102.6 percent, compared to the 3 percent national average. The debt to GDP ratio was 55.1 percent; the U.S. average was 2.6 percent.[5]

How could this small island in the Caribbean—one-twelfth the size of Cuba, one-fourth that of the Dominican Republic—run up such a huge debt? When one adds the pensions to the government's debt, it amounted to $124 billion. No factor was more important than the misuse of the one government agency that seemed immune to political interference, the Government Development Bank.

The Invisible Bank

The GDB was born, according to its founder, Teodoro Moscoso, by accident. In 1942, when Moscoso convinced Senator Muñoz and Governor Tugwell to create the agency to promote new industries that became Fomento, the obvious question was who would finance them. The idea of attracting private investment seemed unrealistic. The few Puerto Ricans with wealth were risk-averse, investing only in import businesses, agriculture, sugar, and rum. American investments in the midst of World War II were obviously out of the question. If Moscoso and his new agency were going to build factories, somehow the government would have to finance them totally.

Since Muñoz came to power in 1941 and Tugwell became governor the following year, there was an unceasing drumbeat of opposition in Puerto Rico and Washington claiming that their goal was to socialize the island economy. The enormous expansion of the island government and the nineteen public corporations that took over vital public services were denounced as overwhelming poof.

In Washington, members of Congress and others were influenced by a chart, published in the English-language *World Journal* on October 28, 1942, titled, "Chart to illustrate some recent changes in the Government of Puerto Rico indicating (1) concentration of authority, (2) control of free commercial enterprise,(3) large scale commercial undertaken by the island government." This was seen in Washington, as in Puerto Rico, as proof, Tugwell wrote in his memoirs, that "a Mussolini-like regime existed in Puerto Rico."[6]

The plan to create Fomento was a particular target. Although Tugwell gave it little importance, convinced that industrializing the island was not possible, critics saw the new agency as part of the socialist, anti–private sector conspiracy. Moscoso was stunned when Muñoz informed him that the opposition had succeeded in blocking his Fomento bill. Enough members of the majority Popular Democratic Party, not comfortable with the idea of industrialization, had joined the conservative Republican coalition opposition.

As Moscoso recalled decades later, he got an idea. Why not send another bill creating a Fomento bank and appoint top businesspeople, including bankers, to its board of directors? Wouldn't this quiet the alarmed private sector? As he spoke, a Tugwell lawyer sat on the windowsill of Muñoz's office with a notepad and drafted the bill creating the bank and authorizing the governor to write its charter and name the board. After Moscoso convinced a leading banker, Rafael Carrión, president of Banco Popular, to agree to sit on the board, he convinced Muñoz to resubmit the Development Company bill alongside the new Government Development Bank bill. It worked. Almost entirely unreported by the media and unnoticed by the public, both bills were passed.[7]

Tugwell confessed in his 1946 memoirs that he paid little attention to the Moscoso bills. After the GDB was created, he wrote, he understood that its purpose was to somehow provide Moscoso's Development Company with financing, but he admitted that he had little idea how it was going to do so.[8]

Moscoso's ploy had worked in the legislature but not in Washington. Although Tugwell and the Puerto Rican public had given the bank such little importance, the tiny agency became a weapon in the unrelenting hostility to him on the part of conservative members of Congress. On May 30, 1943, a congressional committee arrived in Puerto Rico to investigate what was happening on the island under Tugwell. As Washington friends warned Tugwell, the committee's goal was to "clean up the Puerto Rico Reds."[9] The committee's main task was to determine, in the words of its chairman, the veteran Democratic representative from Missouri, Charles Jasper Bell, if the Government Development Bank and the Development Company were "part of a general plan by the [Tugwell] government to take over business." According to the carefully selected witnesses, such as one of Puerto Rico's largest sugar producers, Antonio Roig, it would take only five years "to destroy all private business."[10]

This was, of course, a continuation of the old campaign against "Red Rex" Tugwell that had driven him from Washington in 1934. Puerto

Rico's resident commissioner in Congress, Bolívar Pagan, leader of the anti-Muñoz coalition, strongly supported by the island's major newspaper, *El Mundo*, and its *World Herald*, fueled the new campaign against Tugwell.

Now these two new agencies, with less than half a dozen employees together, had become a tool in a much bigger game. Tugwell wrote in his memoirs that he was convinced that the target was not only him but President Roosevelt himself; it was part of conservatives' campaign to prevent him from running for a fourth term.

Meanwhile, in Puerto Rico the GDB's purpose remained a mystery. "The brief law that created it in 1942," Charles T. Goodsell wrote in *Administration of a Revolution*, "said almost nothing about what it was supposed to do, except for engaging in general banking business."[11] When Tugwell got around to writing the charter, it was a generalized "declaration of purpose." A year later, the GDB issued its first loan to the Water Resources Authority, later named the Electric Power Authority. In 1947, it financed a four-hundred-unit low-cost housing project. But still, for three years, Goodsell wrote, the government did not decide "what really to use it for." It had a full-time management staff of one.[12]

In 1945, it again became a target, this time of the influential Puerto Rico Manufacturer's Association. The association's executive secretary, Vicente León, although a founding member of the Popular Democratic Party, attacked the bank and Fomento for "discriminating" against local business. The bank, he insisted, should be used to provide financing for firms that could not get it from private banks.[13]

Rafael Buscaglia, treasury secretary and GDB president, responded, writing to León on February 23, 1945, that "the Bank is not a self-help, welfare institution, but a commercial institution that wants to further Puerto Rico's economic development through prudent and judicious banking practices." He warned that if the bank abandoned its conservative practices, providing loans to government and private entities that had a high probability of nonpayment, it would "not last long."[14]

His warning proved prophetic. A half century later the economically stricken government used the bank precisely as a "self-help, welfare institution," or as the former president of the GDB, Juan Agosto Alicea, put it, "the government's ATM machine."[15]

The Indispensable Bank

After a new charter was enacted on September 23, 1948, the question as to the GDB's purpose was answered: while it would continue to provide financing to specific government projects, its primary mission was to serve as the government's fiscal agent, responsible for selling government bonds in the U.S. municipal bond market. The bank issued its first General Obligations bonds to finance public works projects, guaranteed by the government's tax revenue.

By 1950, Moscoso's industrialization was in full gear. The tax exemption law had been approved. The economy, finally, had begun to take off: per capita income, $121 in 1940, had doubled to $279 in 1950. The bank's small staff began to play a central role in the island's "democratic revolution." The General Obligation bonds financed massive growth in infrastructure: roads, electric power, aqueducts and sewerage, airports, and luxurious tourist hotels like the 1949, $7.2 million Caribe Hilton, which was bitterly attacked by Fomento critics and the media as "Moscoso's folly" but instead launched the island's tourism industry and was the first Hilton outside the mainland. By the mid-1950s, the GDB began facilitating the private financing of projects ranging from giant shopping centers to the restoration of homes and retail businesses in Old San Juan. Bonds made this possible. By 1956, the bank had issued over $1 billion in bonds, 20 percent of the island's GDP. By the late 1960s, with Fomento attracting large investments in heavy industry, the island became a center of petrochemical production. The bank made possible the construction of forty-seven petrochemical and related plants along the island's southern coast.

Still the GDB seemed like an anomaly: it did not appear to be part of the government. At its small offices in San Juan, men in dark business suits and well-dressed women silently went about their business. Some were Americans — white, tall — and even the Puerto Ricans looked like they came from Wall Street.

Few knew that it existed, much less how much the island was now depending on it. Muñoz, as much as Moscoso and Fomento's administrators, knew how vital it was to protect the island's credit, and this depended on protecting the bank, ensuring it stayed vigorously off-limits to political and partisan interference. Further, it required that the government heed Buscaglia's admonition at the beginning: it must not be misused, and it must safeguard its own and Puerto Rico's reputation for fiscal responsibility.

Trust

Muñoz and Moscoso knew that the core of the industrialization program rested on one word: trust. Investors were being asked to trust an island that just a few years earlier was seen as "hopeless," the woebegone "poorhouse of the Caribbean," and to trust a government that recently had been investigated by congressional committees as Tugwell's socialist experiment.

As much as Moscoso's aggressive and creative public relations, run by David Ogilvy and his agency, succeeding in changing the island's image and as much as Muñoz and Moscoso themselves generated positive publicity throughout the United States—in 1949, a nine-page spread on Fomento in *LIFE* magazine, followed by Muñoz appearing twice on the cover of *Time*—the trust had to be created and *sustained*, especially its face on Wall Street, by the Government Development Bank.

That Puerto Rico would continue to be fiscally responsible seemed to be mandated by Puerto Rico's 1952 constitutionally fixed debt limit: of particular interest to investors, payment of the principal and interest of the debt could not exceed 15 percent of the average government revenue in the previous two years. It also mandated a balanced budget and that in the event of budget deficits, the government had to pay off its debt before incurring other expenditures. That Puerto Rico would live by its own constitution was the foundation of the trust.

There also had to be confidence in the continuity of Puerto Rico's relationship to the United States. Because of Puerto Rico's commonwealth status, unlike all other U.S. municipal bonds, Puerto Rico's had triple tax exemption: federal, state, and local. Just as the island's federal tax exemption gave it a powerful competitive advantage in attracting industrial investment, the triple tax exemption gave the island a competitive advantage in the bond market. As Puerto Rico vastly increased its borrowing, the GDB had to pay particular attention to the public corporations. It was critical to ensure that the autonomous agencies did not violate the government's conservative fiscal norms. The Puerto Rico Aqueduct and Sewer Authority, the Puerto Rico Electric Power Authority, and the Puerto Rico Ports Authority and other corporations had now borrowed hundreds of millions through municipal bonds. The GDB's oversight was especially important: this was "extraconstitutional" borrowing, not restricted by the constitutional debt limit. It was the bank's task to ensure that the credit agencies, mostly Moody's and Standard & Poor's, gave the corporation's debt the excellent ratings they gave to government General Obligation bonds.

No one, especially Tugwell, believed that Puerto Rico would achieve such a positive reputation in the bond market or that its economy generated such trust on Wall Street. Now this small island, this small economy, had a degree of trust that seemed to give it unlimited borrowing power. At the same time this placed an added responsibility on the government, beginning with the GDB, to exercise prudent *self-restraint*.

Puerto Ricans had reason to be proud. Confidence in the island's credit was based ultimately on confidence in Puerto Rico's economy and its leaders. This Puerto Rican government had taken the hard measures to overcome the 1973 oil crisis, proving the economic development program was fundamentally sound. And again, in the early 1980s, it recovered from another recession that afflicted the United States during the Reagan administration. As much as the island depended on conditions on the mainland — the post–World War II industrial boom — and on Americans — from Tugwell to Tobin — the Puerto Ricans themselves did it.

When Hernández Colón returned to power in 1985, it seemed Puerto Rico was back on track. Like Muñoz in 1940, he promised a status politics hiatus. He dedicated his term in office to the economy, to jobs. It worked. As a candidate for reelection, he ran ads celebrating his creation of 178,000 new jobs, enough to create a human chain from the northern capital of San Juan to the southern city of Ponce and back.

By 1987, the Government Development Bank had become a giant in the bond market. That year it issued a $1.6 billion General Obligation bond sale, the second largest in U.S. municipal bond market history. The government pointed out that it had a minimal effect on increasing the government debt since it was in large part to refinance previous bond issues, generating for the government big savings by paying substantially lower interest rates.

For the first time, the GDB asked for a credit rating. Standard & Poor's and Thompson Bankwatch rated it as "Excellent," a rating the bank shared with only eight other financial institutions in the world.

Descent into Debt

Puerto Rico's gradual slide into $70 billion in debt took place over a twenty-year period under four governors, two from each political party. By the 1970s, as the Muñoz generation of administrators retired and new administrations began to govern, some began to question whether the government's policies were *too* conservative. Puerto Rico started to drift away from those policies and to change its virtually sacrosanct attitude toward the GDB.

As the pressure for more spending on infrastructure and services increased, the government found ways to increase its legal capacity to borrow. It began to create, through the GDB, new public corporations free of the constitutional debt limit, each with its own borrowing capacity. In 1972, it created the Municipal Financing Agency to borrow for the island's seventy-eight municipal governments.

During the Arab oil embargo of 1973–75, the Hernández Colón administration created the Administration for the Financing of Health Services to cover the Health Department's annual deficit. In 1974, it also created the Tax Revenue and Anticipatory Notes Agency, known as TRANS, allowing the government to borrow on its accounts receivable—money owed to the government. And two years later, the administration created the Puerto Rico Development Funds agency, financed by selling government savings bonds to the public. Then, in 1977, under the Romero Barceló administration, the government created the Puerto Rico Industrial, Tourism, Educational, Medical, and Environmental Financing Authority, or AFICA.

The creation of new public corporations, some of them specifically to borrow hundreds of millions of dollars, meant that the holy grail of fiscal responsibility, the constitutional debt limit, in fact was circumvented, albeit legally. Nor did the constitutionally mandated balanced budget preclude increasing budget deficits. It was obvious that "balanced budget" meant that expenditure did not exceed income. Borrowing to cover deficits, some economists argued, was in spirit, if not in deed, "unconstitutional."

But government officials and their lawyers believed they had also found a way to circumvent the constitutional balanced budget mandate. The 2018 Government Accountability Office (GAO) report to Congress declares, "In 1974, Puerto Rico's Attorney General issued a broad interpretation of the balanced budget clause in Puerto Rico's Constitution that allowed Puerto Rico to borrow funds . . . to balance its budget."[16]

The Hernández Colón administration justified its decision by pointing out that it allowed only borrowing guaranteed by the government's accounts receivable. Since it did not authorize issuing bonds to cover deficits, it was argued, it did not contribute to the debt.

But the doors were opened. As the GAO report states, subsequent administrations did issue bonds to cover budget deficits: "In the following years, Puerto Rico's Government made decisions that contributed to the accumulation of unsustainable debt despite constitutional controls to prevent that occurrence. . . . Puerto Rico's government chose to use bonds to balance the budget. According to ratings agency officials and experts in state and local government, states rarely issued debt to fund operations, and many states prohibited this practice."[17]

Puerto Rico, drifting away from its critical self-restraint, was drifting toward the debt crisis.

Political Interference

Of all the government decisions and policies—at the time imperceptible and apparently innocuous—none was more important than the change in the attitude toward the Government Development Bank. Since its first president, Rafael Buscaglia, there had been recognition that because the bank was different, it had to be treated differently. It could not be treated as another public corporation. Tugwell's ideal was that it would have administrative autonomy. As government entities delivering vital public services, public corporations are ultimately responsible to the elected officials: absolute nonpolitical interference was not possible. But the goal for the bank was precisely to achieve that to the extent possible.

In the early 1970s, the GDB yielded to political pressure. Governor Luis A. Ferré asked it to approve a $100 million loan to rescue the island's sinking sugar industry. The board declined, like many others, not having much confidence in the future of the industry. The GDB was subject to strong political pressure from Ferré through his treasury secretary, the board's president. The board finally gave in and approved the loan.

But the GDB also resisted political pressure. In late 1985, its board was surprised to learn that Governor Hernández Colón, during a trip to Tokyo, announced what the media called "samurai bonds," the first bonds issued outside the United States. The board did not think it was a good idea. Its president, the young lawyer José Ramón González, who later became a member of the PROMESA Fiscal Board, pointed out that with the exchange rate, Puerto Rico would lose $12 million. The board, with the support of Treasury Secretary Agosto Alicea, disapproved the bond issue. The governor accepted the decision.

As Curet Cuevas described it in his 2003 book, the GDB's independence broke down totally during the Rosselló administration. Treating the bank as another government agency, the governor simply ordered the bank's president to approve lines of credit. Curet Cuevas wrote, "The process for issuing extra-constitutional debt transpired between the Governor and the president of the GDB. . . . [I]t became a process where the Governor instructed the extension of a determined line of credit to this or that agency or department for a specified amount. The GDB president would approve it without that agency's judgment or capacity to repay and without providing for the source of funds to pay assumed obligations."[18] The result, Curet Cuevas continued, was that "these decisions, essentially by one man[,] . . . [had] the consequence of authorizing the investment of multi-million-dollar public funds that were not economically viable."[19] By 2001, Puerto Rico was well on its way to the debt crisis.

The president of the Government Development Bank, Agosto Alicea, under the new Calderón administration, found that that the "extraconstitutional debt" had climbed to $5,898 billion, *surpassing* the constitutional debt of $5,575 billion.[20] Most of it, $2.3 billion, had gone to finance Rosselló's health reform.[21] Another big chunk, $1.2 billion, went to the Water and Sewerage Authority.[22] The rest went to other big projects, like the Coliseum.

But Agosto Alicea found that the bank's crisis was even worse. There was what he called "a secret debt" of $2.4 billion. In the bank's bookkeeping, the loans to the government agencies were recorded as "collectable debt" when in fact, Agosto Alicea wrote, the bank "knew that the agencies did not have the resources to pay off their debt."[23] According to Agosto Alicea, the bank was effectively bankrupt. It had assets of $1.7 billion but a debt of $2.4 billion. It lent 140 percent of its assets' worth to one client, the Puerto Rican government, which could not pay it back.

Agosto Alicea and Governor Calderón went on to refinance the GDB debt, reestablishing its liquidity with an annual legislative appropriation of $225 million a year to pay off the "secret debt" in thirty years. "We have saved the Bank from bankruptcy," Agosto Alicea wrote to the governor, but by "worsening the general fund deficit."[24] Puerto Rico was at a crossroad. Agosto Alicea told the governor that the new administration had two alternatives: "try to survive temporarily with the hope that the recession will end, repeating the economic bonanza and the increase in revenue"; or undertake "a profound restructuring of the government, reducing operational costs . . . especially in Education and Health." He ended, "I recognize that this decision is very difficult and drastic."[25]

Two PDP Administrations

Calderón, Puerto Rico's first woman governor, had a different background from Rosselló. The young former governor had ascended to office at the age of forty-two, with little government experience, determined to carry out big reforms and projects, an optimist willing to take risks. Calderón was fifty-eight, a government veteran, having served as Governor Hernández Colón's chief of staff, the secretary of state, and mayor of San Juan. She saw herself as an administrator, not a politician: as the "daughter of Bootstrap." Her father, an industrialist, had worked for Moscoso in Fomento. From one of the island's elite families, she had chosen a life of government service and was considered an expert in public administration and economic development. She was known, at times criticized, for her forceful, no-nonsense, driving, apolitical style that in some ways emulated Moscoso.

After taking office, Calderón found herself having to prove that it was true: she was not another politico. She was confronted by the reality of the government crisis she had inherited. Treasury Secretary Agosto Alicea informed her that he was unable to meet the February government payroll. She called an emergency meeting of her cabinet. As Agosto Alicea recalled, Calderón — unfazed, confident — coolly warned her cabinet not to publicly attack the Rosselló administration. We were elected, she said, not to engage in the usual political attacks but to solve problems. She had decided not to attack the Rosselló administration for having left the $2.4 billion debt he incurred for his big projects but instead to quietly proceed to refinance it. This was precisely the nonpartisan decision that Agosto Alicea and other administrators in her cabinet expected of her.

And this was an example of the Bootstrap spirit that she wanted to personify: the can-do drive of not looking back but continuing to plow ahead. What was Bootstrap all about if not precisely the conviction, the confidence, that Puerto Rico would always overcome killer hurricanes, bad government, and even monstrous debt?

But she had come to office with a goal: to finish what Bootstrap had started, attacking the pockets of extreme poverty throughout the island, the forgotten and isolated communities. It was an expensive project. She decided to ignore the warnings about the vulnerable condition of the government's finances, and in particular of the Government Development Bank. In the essential optimism of the Bootstrap spirit, she decided to go ahead, financing the project by extracting a $500 million GDB loan to pay for part of the $1.4 billion "isolated community" project.

In 2003, she decided not to run for reelection the following year. Meanwhile, the political pressure to use the GDB to fill budget deficits resurfaced. Preparing her last, 2004–5 government budget, she faced a $500 million deficit. The big problem was that she had promised public employees four $100 a month salary increases and now lacked the funds for the last increase. She knew that Hernández Colón's defeat in 1976 was in large part due to his decision to forgo government salary increases. But now she faced irresistible pressure to proceed with the raises. Resident commissioner Aníbal Acevedo Vilá, the Popular Democratic Party's gubernatorial candidate in 2004, had been Hernández's Colón's aide and also knew firsthand the political cost. He warned Calderón that if she did not give the raises, "we will lose the elections."[26] She gave in and went forward with the salary increase. The decision helped Acevedo Vilá win in 2004 but left him with a $550 million budget deficit when he took office.

During her governorship, Calderón incurred $13 billion in debt. Half of it went to completing the Rosselló's administration giant projects, the other half to cover the budget deficits. The slide toward crisis continued. In 2006, GDB president Alfredo Salazar warned Governor Acevedo Vilá that it was time for Puerto Rico to face reality: "The time for theory and fantasy is over."[27] The veteran economist Fernando Zacalán predicted "the worst recession in fifty years."[28]

Acevedo Vilá was willing to take action that had always been avoided as politically toxic. Yielding to the now-irresistible pressure to increase revenue, he proposed a 7 percent sales tax. But he had some political cover. He shared power with the New Progressive Party, which controlled the legislature, and he believed that he could share the blame. After much haggling, the tax was approved, both parties vigorously blaming the other.

In the 1960s, Puerto Rico's experience with shared government — NPP governor Ferré and the PDP under Hernández Colón controlling the Senate — had worked well. No longer. Now the war between Acevedo Vilá and the legislature was continuous. Unable to agree on the government budget, there was a government shutdown.

The issue that had always divided the Popular Democratic and New Progressive Parties — tax exemption — resurfaced. The existing tax exemption law, Law 137, was about to expire. The PDP governor, with the support of the private sector, launched a campaign to extend it. There were 1,473 tax exempt manufacturing operations on the island, creating a total of 387,000 direct and indirect jobs. Fomento was currently negotiating plant expansions and new operations with 24 tax exempt firms.[29] But the House, led by NPP Speaker José Aponte, resisted. He refused to meet with alarmed private sector representatives, including delegations from the Pharmaceutical Industry Association and the Manufacturer's Association. Finally, on May 28, 2008, Aponte relented; he and the NPP agreed to extend the tax exemption program for five years.

But the damage had been done. By 2006 the phase-out of Section 936 was complete. In the United States the housing bubble burst. By September 2008, the United States and much of the developed world were in the

Great Recession. As Acevedo Vilá approached his campaign for reelection, he had still another serious setback: he was formally accused by the U.S. Attorney in San Juan of misusing campaign funds. A year later he was exonerated. But Acevedo Vilá and the PDP were again defeated in the 2008 elections.

Two Popular Democratic Party administrations, fully supporting the Fomento program, tax exemption, did not arrest the decline. Governor Calderón had dedicated much of her administration to resolving the government fiscal crisis, especially in the GDB. She understood what Agosto Alicea had described as the "difficult and drastic" measures that were required. Governor Acevedo Vilá, unabashedly a politico, had taken the politically toxic bitter pill of imposing a sales tax.

But the reality of what was happening to the island economy had not sunk in. As the Tobin Report had warned in 1975, after the years of Bootstrap growth, it was painful to face the reality of having to forgo expectations. In spite of the warnings of economists and other naysayers, some argued that austerity would make the crisis worse, that somehow with increased spending and debt the economy would hit bottom and rebound.

It did not seem to matter what party was in power. The economy continued to decline for there was no bottom.

Luis Fortuño

In 2008, the New Progressive Party returned to power, for the sixth time in the past ten elections. Again it elected a professional who, like Calderón, had wide government experience but did not see himself as a politico. In the NPP primaries, Luis Fortuño had defeated former governor Rosselló, who was trying to return to the governorship, with 60 percent of the vote.

Fortuño campaigned with the promise that he and his administration would finally face the reality that difficult and drastic actions could no longer be avoided. Involved in the statehood movement throughout his life, he had introduced statehood bills in Congress as resident commissioner. But in the campaign, he assured the private sector that his priority was to pull the island out of the economic and fiscal crisis and he would put the "statehood ideal on the back burner."[30]

Fortuño knew the Fomento program well. He had served in the Rosselló administration, first as head of tourism and then as head of Fomento as secretary of economic development and commerce. In the private sector he had been a corporate lawyer. In 2004 he was elected NPP resident commissioner in Congress.

Fortuño won the 2008 election by 220,000 votes, the biggest margin since Puerto Rico began electing its governors in 1948. Active in national Republican organizations on the mainland, he was a fiscal conservative who believed in cutting taxes. His campaign slogan had been that a "dollar in the consumer's pocket is much better than a dollar in the government's pocket."

Two months after his inauguration, on March 3, 2009, he announced that he intended to cut government spending by $2 billion. Although he had promised in the campaign not to cut government jobs, it was widely reported that the budget cut meant eliminating thirty thousand jobs. This haunted him throughout his governorship, sparking labor strikes and protests and unrelenting attacks from the opposition parties.

Fortuño attempted to reduce the giant government debt. Two years earlier, the government had created COFINA, the Puerto Rico Sales Tax Financing Corporation. Fortuño made two changes in the sales tax law. One of them increased from 1 to 2.75 percent the revenue earmarked for the COFINA fund that was used to pay off the government's debt. But the other change provoked sharp criticism from economists and the private sector: it authorized the use of COFINA funds to cover budget deficits.

Fortuño had denounced the Acevedo Vilá administration's $3.2 billion budget deficit when he took office. Now he was criticized for authorizing even more borrowing to cover deficits, according to economists, in violation of the constitutional balanced budget clause. Although Fortuño went on to cut some taxes, under pressure for more government income to cut the deficits and pay off the debt, by the end of his governorship he had added fifteen new sources of government revenue.

An important and controversial law was Law 154, which imposed a 4 percent tax on the island's tax exempt industries. Knowing that it would ignite a firestorm of criticism, including from corporate lawyers like himself, that it undermined the essential trust in the government's word, violating the government's own tax exemption decrees, Fortuño and the legislature approved the bill over a weekend without public hearings.

The private sector was outraged. It could not understand that Fortuño, former head of Fomento, seen as the ally of the private sector, had approved what now seemed a final blow to investor confidence in Puerto Rico. Many believed that Teodoro Moscoso, who had fought so hard for maintaining the integrity and credibility of the tax exemption program and had so vigorously fought against imposing the 10 percent "toll gate tax" on the new Section 936 industries, would be turning in his grave.

But the governor was convinced that he had no alternative: this was another drastic measure to head off the government's descent into insolvency. The law raised $1.9 billion in additional tax revenue in 2012, in addition to the $1.4 billion all island manufacturing contributed to the treasury.[31] Of this, the pharmaceuticals paid $891 million.[32] In any case, Fortuño pointed out, the American-based industries got a U.S Treasury Department credit for the 4 percent tax. But even so, the private sector organizations replied, again the industrial climate was damaged and again there was insecurity over how long the credit would be retained by Congress.

Determined to find some means to revive the economy, in 2012, Fortuño went against his party's statehood orthodoxy when he approved Laws 20 and 22, offering tax exemption to enterprises and individuals that relocated to Puerto Rico and provided export services. It was severely criticized by leaders of all the parties as excessively generous while creating a small number of jobs.

But the harshest criticism came from former governor Carlos Romero Barceló, who urged Fortuño to instead increase the taxes on businesses. Eight years later, in a June 9, 2019, article, he accused Fortuño of betraying statehood: "He opened the doors to the enemies of statehood. He opened the doors and invited them to come here, giving them benefits to oppose statehood."[33]

Fortuño lost his bid for reelection. His attempts to tackle the crisis could not overcome the political resistance from his own party as much as from the opposition. Although his announced reduction of public employees amounted to only 12,500 individuals, it cost him the election.

Nothing seemed to deter Puerto Rico's economic decline. Since 2006, the year the ten-year phase-out of Section 936 expired, the economy declined by over 11 percent, from a GNP of $53 billion in 2005 to $47.7

billion in 2016.[34] And nothing seemed to slow the debt's growth. Despite the promises of every new governor and attempts to fulfill them, from 2000 to 2012, the debt grew from $26 billion to $70 billion, an average of $3.75 billion a year.

When Fortuño left office, the government debt had increased by $11 billion. The most stinging criticism of his administration came from the eighty-six-year-old elder statesman of his own party, Romero Barceló, who described him as Puerto Rico's "worst governor."[35] Fortuño learned, as had Hernández Colón in 1976, how unforgiving was Puerto Rican politics.

The 2018 GAO Report

Puerto Rico was in a perfect storm. It had effectively lost control of its economy.

The fifty-seven-page 2018 GAO report to Congress described in detail how the Puerto Rican government sank the island into unpayable debt by circumventing the constitutional limits and safeguards. The "main factor contributing to the debt crisis" was that the government of Puerto Rico had operated with growing budget deficits every year since 2002. Budget spending is determined by the revenue the government expects in the next fiscal year. But the government purposely overstated the revenue estimate, which in turn inflated spending authorizations and produced inevitable deficits. At times, agencies would overspend illegally beyond the *inflated* estimates. From 2002 to 2014, the government overestimated revenues in eight of thirteen years, for example, in 2008 by 10 percent and in 2009 by 19 percent. For nine years, the government overspent beyond the already inflated authorization an average of 5.6 percent, or $459 million a year.

Second, from 2000 to 2017, of the twenty largest bond issues, totaling $31 billion, thirteen were used *exclusively* to fund operations or repay or refinance existing debt. COFINA, created to pay off the debt, was used to continue to increase it. By 2009, after raising the sales tax, the COFINA bonds were used to finance government operations.

Other factors listed by the GAO were out-migration, especially of working people; the "regulatory challenges of doing business in Puerto Rico," which included not only the government permitting process but also the many legislated labor benefits that do not exist on the mainland; the application of federal minimum wages; the high cost of importing goods and energy; and the struggles in the banking and housing industries.[36]

The GAO emphasized, once again, the impact of losing Section 936. It pointed out that the economic recession began with the ending of Section 936, the sharp decline in 936 operations on the island during the ten-year phase-out period, from 440 down to 157, and the loss of the $9 billion to $10 billion deposited by the 936 companies in the island's financial institutions between 1984 and 1991 — capital used for Puerto Rico's economic development.

The GAO report offered a litany of Puerto Rico's bad policy decisions that inexorably led to the perfect storm. There were many, by different governments and different parties. But there is one policy decision whose negative impact cannot be overstated: the decision of the Romero Barceló–Rosselló administration to ask Congress to eliminate Section 936. That was the decision that changed the *structure* of the island economy. As bad as it got in the past — and the 1973–74 oil crisis was bad — there was always Fomento. Revive the Bootstrap program, crank up Puerto Rico's engine of growth, and the economy would resuscitate. Now there was no engine, no Bootstrap.

On Sunday, May 1, 2016, in a ten-minute TV address, Governor García Padilla, who defeated Fortuño in 2012, announced that the Government Development Bank would default on a $422 million bond payment. Bloomberg News reported, "This will likely trigger a restructuring . . . which would be the largest ever in the tax-exempt market."[37] Puerto Rico was bankrupt: it could not pay its debt, the interest or the principal. García Padilla did not run for reelection in 2016, becoming the fourth governor in a row to serve only one term.

On April 28, 2017, the new governor, Ricardo Rosselló, son of Pedro Rosselló, submitted to the PROMESA Fiscal Board the "Government Development Bank Fiscal Plan." Describing the history "of fiscal mismanagement and irresponsible . . . out of control [government] spending," it concluded that it would carry out "an orderly winding down" of the bank's operations.[38]

Without credit, without the ability to borrow, obviously the bank had lost its historical function. The government began to dismantle it. The Financial Advisory and Fiscal Agency Authority (AAFAF), created by the previous administration to restructure the island's debt, took over the GDB's functions.

June 30, 2017, was another watershed date in the Puerto Rican economy. The government notified the Fiscal Board that the Government Development Bank would cease operations. From 204 employees in January 2017, it was down to six by March 2018.[39]

No longer politically untouchable, no longer sacrosanct, ignoring Buscaglia's admonition that the bank must be "prudent and judicious" to survive, the misuse and demise of the Government Development Bank was a major cause of the economic and fiscal crisis.

A curious visitor to the Puerto Rico Government Center decided to walk up the stairs of the GDB building. The front of the building and the grounds needed maintenance. What had started as the "invisible bank" seventy-seven years earlier had grown into this attractive building in the center of the Santurce government complex. But it was now strangely silent inside, despite its still-impressive sign in front of the building. It was, like Tugwell's colonial governors, an "empty shell."

The visitor approached a guard sitting behind a desk and asked, "Is the bank open?"

The guard answered, "What bank?"

CHAPTER SEVEN

"That Is Nuts"

Puerto Rico's Labor Policy

In mid-April 2018, *The Economist* published a long article on Puerto Rico's economic and fiscal crisis. The magazine reported, "Puerto Ricans enjoy among the most generous protection of any American worker, including mandatory holidays and severance pay. They also have the highest unemployment rate in the country (it was 10.6 percent before Maria) and are losing workers to states such as Florida and Texas that have few state-level labor laws. *That is nuts.*"[1]

In October, the Fiscal Board reported, "California offers workers more protection and benefits than most states. . . . [I]t offers 24 hours, 3 days, of paid sick leave, while Puerto Rico's guarantees of a yearly Christmas bonus, severance pay, 27 days of paid time off, maternity leave are far beyond those required by any mainland state."[2]

On July 26, 2019, the *Wall Street Journal* editorial commenting on the resignation of Governor Ricardo Rosselló stated, "Puerto Rico's main problem is democratic socialism, and Mr. Rosselló is typical of a political class that buys votes with handouts. For decades high taxes and inflexible labor laws have depressed investment and incentives to work. Private workers are guaranteed $600 Christmas bonuses, 15 days of vacation and ironclad job protections."

If it was "nuts" that this small island in the Caribbean had created the biggest per capita debt in the United States, it would seem equally nuts that with unemployment more than three times that of the United States and a labor participation rate of 37 percent, near the bottom in the world, compared to 60 percent in the United States, Puerto Rico would mandate the nation's highest labor benefits.[3]

In 1975, a letter from Volkswagen to Moscoso hurt. Moscoso was long accustomed to celebrating the agonizingly few industrial promotion efforts that had succeeded, accepting the reality that the vast majority failed. He had personally led the effort to bring a new Volkswagen assembly plant to Puerto Rico. It would have been a Bootstrap game changer, and he felt that this was one effort that would succeed. It did not.

What struck him when he got the crushing news that Volkswagen would not locate a plant on the island was the reason that seemed to have mostly influenced Volkswagen: labor costs. The German firm cited the mandatory Christmas bonus, holidays, vacations, sick leave, and other legislated days off.

Moscoso decided to send the letter to Governor Hernández Colón and his administration and party leaders. He knew that he was entering a political minefield. Throughout, he and Fomento had had to fight the perception that Bootstrap was anti-labor, as Romero Barceló and other opposition leaders alleged, that is, that Fomento denied workers fair salaries and benefits as an investment incentive.

Moscoso was not surprised: distribution of the letter had no effect on the political leadership. On the contrary, the following year, 1976, the government approved still another labor benefit, Law 80, requiring "just cause" to discharge an employee and placing the burden of proving that cause on the employer. Four decades later, when Puerto Rico was in the depths of the economic and fiscal crisis, this law became the center of a battle between the island government and the Fiscal Board over how to pull out of the crisis.

It was true that from the beginning of Bootstrap, especially when it was attracting a large number of labor-intensive industries, Moscoso fought for what he saw as a rational labor policy. Of course labor costs would go up, but he and Fomento pushed back against the ever-growing pressure for more and more generous labor benefits, making the island less and less competitive. And as hard as it had been to win the battle for tax exemption since the days of Rexford Tugwell, this was harder.

In Fomento, it had always been evident that in industrial promotion, offering tax exemption is worthless as an incentive unless the investor does the simple arithmetic of cost and income and comes up with a good profit. The bigger the profit, the bigger the value of the exemption and the bigger the incentive.

The principal reason economists, beginning with Tugwell himself, did not believe that Fomento could succeed was precisely that the arithmetic did not add up: even with low labor costs, the other operating costs were so high that Puerto Rico was simply not competitive. Just about everything—electric power, water, communication—cost more than on the mainland. Federal law mandated that all shipping to and from the island, offshore states and possessions, and the mainland had to be via U.S. transport ships, which were among the most expensive in the world.

So for Fomento is was important not to lose the competitive edge of significantly lower labor costs. But Fomento economists, knowing that salaries and benefits had to increase, warned Moscoso that at some point they would reach mainland levels, obviously ending the incentive. The need to slow it down was a particularly hard message for the Popular Democratic Party.

A Devilish Paradox

Muñoz and the party were faced with what had always been a devilish paradox everywhere: Is the priority to raise the wages and benefits of the working class or to create jobs for the unemployed? Or is it possible to achieve both?

In the United States since the first New Deal law, economists and others have disagreed on the effect of the minimum wage: Does it help or hurt workers, and does it help or hinder economic growth? One side has insisted that of course it helps workers and of course putting more money into the hands of consumers helps economic growth. The other side insists that it has the unintended consequence of discouraging job creation, especially for young workers and minorities attempting to enter the labor market. In Puerto Rico, Fomento and economists used another argument: since Puerto Rico imports almost all of what it consumes, it is growth in productivity, not consumption, that will most benefit the economy.

In 1933, the federal minimum wage of 25 cents an hour, a cornerstone of the New Deal, was applied to Puerto Rico. It had a disastrous effect on the island economy, devastating one of the very few "industries," the thousands of women sewing garments and hats in their homes. The Roosevelt administration acknowledged that applying the world's most advanced economy's minimum wage in one of the most undeveloped economies made no sense. By 1940, Congress amended the law to exempt Puerto Rico from automatic wage increases, establishing a "flexible" system that permitted a federal wage committee to set a lower minimum wage for those industries on the island that proved they could not pay the new minimum wage.

Yet when Muñoz and the PDP came to power in 1941 one of their first reform laws was to create the Minimum Wage Board. This seemed to be a contradiction: Muñoz strongly opposed the federal minimum wage. The priority, he explained, was to create jobs, and in order to do so increases in labor costs must be kept to a minimum. The "flexible system" was vital to continue to attract labor-intensive garment factories.

Muñoz, as uncomfortable as it was for him personally and politically, carried on the battle each time Congress set about increasing the minimum wage. As an old socialist, he had to explain how a politician that considered himself Puerto Rico's true labor leader would battle the island's unions and in the United States especially the powerful International Ladies Garment Workers Union (ILGWU). He had to convince Democrats in Congress, including Senator John F. Kennedy, who complained to Muñoz that Fomento was using unfair tactics to lure Massachusetts textile industries and jobs to the island with the promise of lower salaries, a criticism made by others of the Fomento program.

At an ILGWU convention in 1956, directing his remarks at union president, David Dubinsky, the most influential labor leader in minimum wage legislation, Muñoz argued, "We are on the same side." He said, "I want to tell you most emphatically that a low wage policy is not part of Operation Bootstrap." The policy, he went on, was to raise wages as fast as possible to reach the mainland level, but given Puerto Rico's much higher unemployment, if it grew too fast, it would kill jobs.[4]

Once elected, Governor Ferré found himself in a similar situation. Ferré had opposed the flexible system. The statehood movement touted full application of the federal minimum wage as one of the benefits of statehood. But when Congress approved a new increase, Ferré and the NPP resident commissioner, Jorge Córdova Díaz, surprised everyone by defending the flexible system and opposing the full application of a new minimum wage. Ferré and Córdova Díaz were convinced that Moscoso and the Fomento economists were right: it would cost the island thousands of jobs. And how could hurting the economy advance the statehood goal?

Ferré lost in 1972. Postelection polls showed that although his loyalty to statehood was questioned by some leaders, his decision did not cost him statehood votes: 96 percent of those in favor of statehood voted for him. In fact, he gained 133,000 votes. But the young statehood militants were determined to continue to fight for the full federal minimum wage. In 1998, Governor Rosselló approved legislation that automatically applied it to the island. For Fomento supporters, having lost Section 936 in 1966, this was the other blow in the pincer attack against Bootstrap.

The Christmas Bonus

One reason Ferré's defeat was so surprising was that he *had* increased labor benefits. The signature benefit was the mandatory Christmas bonus for public and private employees, beginning at 2 percent of their annual salary in 1969 and gradually increasing to 4 percent by 1971. He had been proposing it since the 1940s, when he started his political career. Ferré promoted it as member of the 1951 constitutional convention and later introduced legislation to enact it as a minority representative in the legislature from 1953 to 1956. The PDP legislature did not approve it.

During the Muñoz-PDP hegemony it was assumed that it was not necessary to pander to organized labor: the PDP could oppose Ferré's

Christmas bonus and the full application of the federal minimum wage and still win big. But after the PDP lost in 1968, it reversed itself. The PDP-controlled Senate approved Ferré's Christmas bonus. The new party leadership saw that the PDP could no longer afford to oppose politically attractive labor benefits.

The return to the two-party system meant that Fomento lost much of its influence over political decisions. The days when Moscoso felt confident he could convince Muñoz to get his party to take action that was good economically but bad politically were gone. Fomento could no longer slow down rising labor costs. Both parties, uncertain about the next election, had begun to return to the old politics where partisan reality trumped economic reality. And while the parties continued and intensified their conflict over status, they agreed on labor policy, indeed at times competing over which offered greater benefits.

Through the years, the Christmas bonus has been cited as an example of the island's inane labor policies. It was cited in the 1976 Tobin Report, the 2018 GAO report, and repeatedly by the PROMESA Fiscal Board. But with unanimous political support, it was untouchable.

Unionization of All Public Employees

The most important labor policy decision occurred on February 25, 1998. Governor Rosselló signed Law 45, which authorized all public employees to unionize and engage in collective bargaining. Its impact was felt not only in the island economy, but in the very functioning of the government itself.

Again, the PDP reversed its historical position and supported unionization. In 1951, Muñoz and the PDP had opposed extending the right to unionize and collective bargaining to employees in the central government. The question had been hotly debated at the constitutional convention.

Leading the battle against public employee unionization was the president of the Bill of Rights Committee, the flamboyant chancellor of the University of Puerto Rico, Jaime Benítez. On December 14, 1951, he issued a long report describing labor rights that included equal pay for equal work, a "reasonable minimum salary," an eight-hour workday, and the right to unionize, picket, and strike. But he went on to explain in detail why the right to unionize and strike was not extended to public employees. The underlying reason, he wrote, is the difference between a public and a private sector employee. For public employees, service has precedence: their priority is their "inescapable responsibility to the citizen. To interrupt those services signifies a temporary paralysis of the responsibilities of government. The constitutional regime cannot tolerate the contradiction of giving a small minority the right to suspend the execution of the laws. . . . Collective bargaining is not justified since the salaries and working conditions of public employees is not set in contracts but in law."[5]

But through the years, the question remained: Why extend the right to unionization to one category of government employees and deny it to all others? As the powerful public corporation unions negotiated salaries and benefits far higher than those in the central government, there was a growing accusation of unfairness.

In Fomento itself the argument seemed irrefutable. The Economic Development Administration (EDA) was a department of the central government, running not only Bootstrap but also tourism and the airports and other government functions. There were, as in most other government agencies, "associations" that carried out some union functions, but they could not engage in collective bargaining. The employees in the Industrial Development Company, a public corporation within EDA in charge of financing and building industrial buildings, could. A unionized secretary in PRIDCO earned more and received better benefits than an EDA secretary, although they did identical work.

Combating the argument of unfairness, those opposed to unionization, almost all of whom were in the private sector, argued that the mistake was the original decision at the constitutional convention. Labor unions in any part of government, they argued, made no sense. In the private sector workers clearly have the right to engage in collective bargaining to essentially determine their share of the company's profits. But as Benítez had pointed out, the purpose of government is service, not profits. In government, the "owners" are not investors but "the people." The power of the unions is precisely over "the people."

The experience of having allowed unionization in the public corporations, the opponents argued, had given unions the power to hold the people hostage in negotiations, contributing greatly to the deterioration of the corporations, to the entire government, and to the economy. The experience, in fact, had proven that once unionized, contrary to Benitez's premise, public employees did indeed put their labor benefits above their "inescapable responsibilities to the citizen."

Back in Rosselló's first term, in 1995, his first attempt to enact a unionization law surprisingly provoked the opposition of one of the New Progressive Party leaders, House Speaker Zaida Hernández. The proposal, she said, would have the effect of taking from the legislature the power to authorize and control government spending—the power to approve the government budget, which in the end is the power to govern. How, she asked, will the administration and the legislature proceed to decrease bloated government spending, decrease government waste and inefficiency, and increase worker productivity? She warned, prophetically, that this would have a negative effect on Puerto Rico's bond classifications and the island's credit.[6]

In part because of her objections, the 1995 unionization bill failed. But Rosselló tried again in 1998, and with the support of the PDP, it became law. Seven years later her warning that the law would tie up future governments proved correct. After Aníbal Acevedo Vilá narrowly defeated Pedro Rosselló for governor in 2004, his administration was at one point negotiating thirty-three collective bargaining contracts with government unions.

As Speaker Hernández had foreseen, what seemed like another labor benefit was a shift in the power to govern. In 2004, the new head of the Aqueduct and Sewerage Authority found that the unions virtually controlled it. When the education secretary tried to increase the number of students per classroom, the union said no. As one union leader put it, "working conditions" negotiated in the contract included determining "the number of art and physical education teachers."[7] Now the unions would achieve power within the entire central government.

On October 27, 2018, *The Economist* ran a report on the decline of California: "How a Prosperous State (the Fifth Highest Economy in the World) Ended up with America's Highest Poverty Rate." The experience in California also seemed to confirm Speaker Hernández's fear. In 2009, the veteran California-based journalist and columnist, Steven Greenhut, wrote a book titled, *Plunder! How Public Employee Unions Are Raiding*

Treasuries, Controlling our Lives, and Bankrupting the Nation, in which he argues that the state was "ruined," driven to bankruptcy, in large part because of the political power of government unions: "the public servants have truly become the public's masters."[8]

The Battle for Labor Reform

After the 1973–74 oil crisis, the Tobin Report, pointing out that a serious structural problem in the island economy was that labor costs were growing faster than productivity, called for sweeping labor reform. "The government," the report stated, "should carry out a global revision of all legislation that raises labor costs, including the great number of holidays with mandatory pay, vacations and sick leave, the Christmas bonus, overtime, and free time."[9]

Forty-three years later, in 2018, the PROMESA Fiscal Board came to the same conclusion and again called on the island government to carry out wide reforms. But there was a big difference: the Tobin Report consisted of recommendations that the then-governor mostly followed. PROMESA, created by the U.S. government in June 2016, although with the power to require the island government to take actions and follow policies, has faced a wall of opposition by the island government and the political leadership.

On February 5, 2018, the Fiscal Board sent Governor Ricardo Rosselló a letter reiterating what the GAO and other reports had emphasized, that labor costs made Puerto Rico noncompetitive compared to many states: "No mainland states require either severance pay or the payment of a Christmas Bonus. . . . [N]o state requires that employers provide vacation pay. Only nine of the fifty mainland states require any paid sick leave, and none of the nine . . . require as much as does Puerto Rico."[10]

The board, determined from the beginning to avoid the island's political minefields, was asking the new governor to do what none had dared in the past: take away what the unions and workers described as "acquired rights." The board's demand set off political fireworks, none as explosive as repealing what the NPP considered one of its signature achievements, Governor Ferré's Christmas bonus.

At first Governor Rosselló agreed. In 2017, he had taken the first steps toward labor reform. After receiving the Fiscal Board's letter on March 21, 2018, he announced that he was proposing a reduction in the mandatory vacation and sick leave from fifteen to seven days and also called for the repeal of Law 80, which restricts employers' rights to dismiss workers and provides benefits for unjust dismissals. Surprisingly, he proposed eliminating the mandatory Christmas bonus for private sector employees. To dramatize how big a step this was for him politically, in making the announcement, Rosselló was flanked by party leaders, including Senate president Thomas Rivera Schatz, a tough political leader known for his independence, and House Speaker Carlos "Johnny" Mendez, as well as by private sector leaders who had long been clamoring for the reforms.

This seemed to be a major victory for the Fiscal Board in its mission to restore the island's competitive edge. And, importantly, it seemed to be a breakthrough in the relationship between the Fiscal Board and the Puerto Rican government. From the beginning, the board had to combat the accusation that it was "anti–Puerto Rican," that its real mission was to pay off the American bondholders, ensuring that they would get back a good part of the $70 billion debt, and that it was willing to sacrifice Puerto Rico, particularly the suffering working class. Now it seemed that Rosselló had overcome the hostility.

Rosselló's attitude toward the board was ambiguous: he was caught between the evident need to work with it and the political imperative to attack it. He had to prove that he was on the side of the Puerto Ricans, of the workers. He insisted that the board was the result of the island's colonial status: if the island had been a state, Congress would not have been able to usurp the powers of its government. But at the same time, the reality was that the economy was sinking, and Rosselló needed the board, and the federal government it represents, to rescue the island.

On the one hand, Rosselló declared that he would cooperate with the board but not on fiscal matters: while the board can "recommend," it had no authority to impose policy. The board responded that Congress explicitly gave it the power to do so. Now the question was whether the governor's acceptance of labor reform finally put Puerto Rico on the path to making the painful sacrifices—as it did in the 1973–74 oil crisis—needed to pull out of the economic and fiscal crisis.

It seemed it was. With the party's political leadership at his side in his March press conference, it seemed that the young governor had his party solidly behind him.

But it was not. The day after Rosselló's announcement, the political backlash began. Rosselló again seemed determined to stand fast, reiterating that the reform's purpose was not to hurt the labor class but precisely to remove obstacles to economic growth and job creation. He rebutted the argument that the reform would drive even more workers to migrate to the United States. Why would they migrate to the United States, he asked, where none of these benefits exist?

The attacks escalated. It was absurd, critics claimed, to compare the benefits here to those in the United States. Workers in Puerto Rico need much more protection because they earn one-third less than workers on the mainland. A Puerto Rican losing his job here, unlike in the United States, with such low unemployment, would most likely not find another.

Rosselló's surprising announcement of sweeping labor reform lasted only days. He began backtracking, claiming that he only announced it because the board required him to. Then, on March 22, political reality kicked in. The New Progressive Party's elder statesman, the eighty-five-year-old former governor Carlos Romero Barceló, had a dire warning for the thirty-nine-year-old governor. The labor reform, he said, would cost him the election in 2020. Romero recalled that he had opposed Governor Luis Fortuño's reduction of public employees, predicting that it would cost him the 2012 election. And, he reminded the governor, it did.

On March 29, the governor announced that he had changed his mind. He withdrew his labor reform proposal. He would not, he reiterated in news conferences and TV appearances, accept that the board dictate public policy to him. Instead of an armistice, he declared all-out war on the board.

On April 18, 2018, former governor García Padilla joined the battle, declaring that he was ready to fight shoulder to shoulder with his adversary Rosselló against the Fiscal Board's reduction in labor benefits. Once again, the Popular Democratic and New Progressive Parties were in lockstep in the labor reform war.

The Fiscal Board decided to retreat. Its five-year fiscal plan for Puerto Rico, released on October 23, 2018, declared, "There are some important reforms that are not included in this New Fiscal Plan because the political will to adopt them does not exist. Chief among them is labor reform, which is essential to truly unlocking growth and prosperity for the island and driving fiscal sustainability in the long term."[11]

Puerto Rico remained trapped by partisan politics.

The May 2018 GAO to report to Congress declared that the government of Puerto Rico had not released its audited financial statement since fiscal year 2014. It was therefore impossible to diagnose with precision the cause of the economic and fiscal crisis.

It was not until 2018 that Governor Rosselló released the 2015 financial statement. The accumulated government budget deficit, $49.2 billion in 2014, had leaped to $67 billion. The GAO was unable to audit the entire financial statement due to numerous omissions and errors.

But one thing was clear. In the 1970s, Governor Hernández Colón took tough, apolitical decisions to pull Puerto Rico out of the Yom Kippur War economic spiral. In the early 2000s, Governor Fortuño took tough, apolitical decisions to arrest the growing economic and fiscal crisis. Both were defeated in their reelection campaigns. Now it was evident that Puerto Rico had lost the will to take the tough and apolitical measures to pull the island out of what has become, as Governor García Padilla described it in the *New York Times,* Puerto Rico's "death spiral."[12]

The Perfect Storm

The perfect storm that engulfed Puerto Rico is the result of the convergence of seven factors:

1. The effects of losing Section 936.
2. The death of Operation Bootstrap, which meant losing the island's competitive advantage in attracting investment. In 2018, Puerto Rico was ranked 64 by the World Bank in its Ease of Doing Business Report, 58 spots lower than the United States. In other vital categories, such as getting construction permits, it was ranked 138; in registering property, 153.[13]

3. The two-party system after 1968 and status politics, which disrupted the continuity in economic policy. It held hard economic and fiscal decisions hostage to partisan politics, leaving Puerto Rico without the political will to make tough but vital decisions. No governor has served more than one term since the first Rosselló was re-elected in 1996.
4. The breakdown of public corporations that provide vital services, such as electric power and water, particularly the misuse of the Government Development Bank.
5. The 1993–2000 Rosselló spending and borrowing binge that led to explosive growth in the debt.
6. The litany of bad policy decisions and bad fiscal policies by both political parties.
7. The political status conflict: the policies and actions to remake the island economy to make it compatible with statehood.

The Fiscal Board, the private sector, and economists repeatedly point out that the key to pulling Puerto Rico out of its financial crisis is to remove the politically self-imposed obstacles to economic growth by making Puerto Rico *competitive* again. But removing obstacles in themselves will not reignite the economy. The loss of Section 936 changed the structure of the Puerto Rican economy. As bad as it got in the past, there was always Fomento: revive Operation Bootstrap, crank up Puerto Rico's engine of growth, and the economy would be resuscitated.

Now there was no engine. There was no Bootstrap.

CHAPTER EIGHT

Will Puerto Rico Become a State?

As Puerto Rico looks to the future, as it and the United States seek a way to pull the island out of its economic and fiscal crisis, and if political status and the economy are inexorably linked, the question is, will Puerto Rico become a state?

When the thirty-eight-year-old Ricardo Rosselló was elected governor in November 2016, he had no doubt that statehood was his mandate. Like his father, Pedro Rosselló, he had an impressive academic background: he graduated from MIT and obtained a PhD at the University of Michigan in biomedical engineering, then specializing in stem cell research. Also like his father, he was athletic and charismatic.

Yet it seemed to make little sense that Puerto Rico, in the depth of an economic and fiscal crisis, would elect a candidate with no experience in economic and fiscal matters, indeed with no government experience. He had, in fact, no administrative experience, having dedicated himself to laboratory research.

He had won the New Progressive Party nomination by defeating a candidate with wide experience in government, precisely in dealing with the economic crisis, NPP president and resident commissioner Pedro Pierluisi, who had served as Rosselló's father's attorney general and dedicated most of his efforts in Congress to reviving the island's economy. With Governor Alejandro García Padilla, of the rival political party, he successfully lobbied Congress to allow the island to file for bankruptcy, the law that created the PROMESA Fiscal Board.

But Pierluisi had a political handicap. For the NPP leadership and militants, statehood was the party's priority, and Pierluisi was not considered militant enough, as much as he tried to prove otherwise by promoting statehood in Congress. He had introduced a bill to hold another status plebiscite that was approved in the House but died in the Senate and later introduced another statehood bill following the 2012 plebiscite. Also, his willingness to work with the opposition on the island and in Washington and his support in Congress of economic measures seen by the militants as "incompatible" with statehood, such as a proposed substitute for Section 936, made him seem, at best, a statehood moderate.

This proved to be young Rosselló's decisive advantage. Throughout his adult life he had shown an interest in politics, participating in his father's campaigns and in national elections in favor of Democratic candidates. There was no doubt about his statehood militancy, having created an advocacy group demanding, "Statehood Now!" He also had the advantage in the NPP that he was the son of the former governor and party leader. Still, he narrowly beat Pierluisi in the primaries with 51 percent of the vote.

Now the new governor was of course faced with Puerto Rico's horrendous economic and fiscal crisis. But he was determined to accomplish what no other statehood leader had achieved in almost 120 years, beginning with José Celso Barbosa in 1898. What had dismayed the new generation of statehood leaders about the "old guard" was the insistence that statehood would be achieved sometime in the future. Party founder Luis A. Ferré himself at times said it would take ten years. He had signed the 1966 Status Commission Report that said that it would take from "from a minimum of 15 years to a much longer period."[1]

But in 1967, it was precisely the cries of "Statehood Now!" that had given birth to the New Progressive Party. A half century later, after three other pro-statehood governors, including his father, the reality that Rosselló faced was that Puerto Rico was no closer to statehood.

The Plebiscites

It was not for lack of trying. The first step obviously had to be Puerto Rico asking for statehood. Statehood lost the first plebiscite in 1967, with the pro-commonwealth referendum getting 60 percent of the vote. The statehood governors held five more plebiscites, two under his father, Pedro Rosselló.

Although legislated and implemented by his pro-statehood government, on November 14, 1993, commonwealth won the second plebiscite, 48 to 46 percent. Rosselló declared that he had made a mistake. He had allowed the commonwealth option to appear on the ballot, permitting each party to define the status options. Of course, he said, continuing as a colony was not a valid option. So he made another attempt on December 13, 1998.

He drafted the definition of *commonwealth*, framing it in explicitly colonial terms, knowing that its supporters would have difficulty voting for it. To further confuse them, he added a fourth option called "free association" or "sovereign commonwealth," whereby Puerto Rico became independent and associated with the United States through a treaty—an option discussed for many years in the island's status politics debate and now supported by a small fraction of the Popular Democratic Party leadership.

The governor's strategy seemed to work as the PDP leadership was undecided whether to participate. It seemed evident to it that the plebiscite was rigged to guarantee a pro-statehood vote. But the island's supreme court ruled that a fifth option, "none of the above," be added to the ballot. The PDP decided to participate, calling on its followers to vote for this option. Again, the statehood leadership was astonished: "none of the above" won, getting 50.5 percent of the vote, 4 percent more than statehood.

In 2012, under another pro-statehood governor, Luis Fortuño, a third attempt was made, this time as a separate vote in the 2012 general elections. It consisted of two questions. The first asked voters if they wanted to continue under the "present form of territorial status." Again the idea was to discourage a pro-commonwealth vote: the name "Estado Libre Asociado," Spanish for "commonwealth," did not appear on the ballot. The second asked voters to choose between statehood, independence, and "sovereign commonwealth."

Again the PDP was undecided, fearing that its voters would be confused. Some leaders advocated voting for "sovereign commonwealth" in order to stop the statehood movement. Finally the PDP urged voters to vote "Yes" on the first question and cast blank ballots on the second. This time the statehood leadership claimed victory: on the first question, 46 percent voted in favor of the "current territorial status"; 61 percent favored statehood on the second question. But the statehood opponents insisted that commonwealth voters had cast blank ballots, and there were 515,348 blank ballots on the second question. Adding them dropped the statehood vote to 44 percent.

Among the U.S. public and in Congress there was again confusion about whether in fact Puerto Rico had indeed expressed an indisputable demand for statehood. Pierluisi's statehood bill after the vote was ignored in Congress.

On June 4, 2017, the NPP tried again. In his 2016 campaign, Rosselló promised still another plebiscite. In the 2016 election, with five candidates for governor on the ballot, Rosselló won with only 41.7 percent, the lowest margin in history. Yet with Puerto Rico obviously focused on its economic and fiscal problems, the new governor interpreted this as a mandate to proceed with the plebiscite, the fourth under a pro-statehood party. This confounded many on the island, as in Washington. Five plebiscites since 1967 had effectively resolved nothing, so what was the point of another? The big news in the United States and around the world was the island's inability to pay its monstrous debt. And there were already signs in Congress of displeasure over what seemed to them incompetence, mismanagement, and signs of corruption in the island government. Rosselló was in office only five months. Why wasn't he concentrating totally on the crisis? And with the history of Congress failing to act on previous plebiscites, what was the likelihood that it would this time?

Through the years, members of Congress and others had made it clear that although U.S. policy has long been to grant Puerto Rico independence if it asked for it, Congress would not commit beforehand to any other plebiscite result. After Governor Hernández Colón failed in the early 1990s to get Congress to approve significant changes in Puerto Rico's commonwealth status, he wrote that of all the reasons, the most important was that Congress simply would not commit to statehood.[2]

But Rosselló believed he had a way: if he could not get a prior commitment, at least he could get congressional approval of the plebiscite process. In 2014, Congress had approved an appropriation of $2.5 million for "objective, nonpartisan voter education about, and a plebiscite on, options that would resolve Puerto Rico's future status." Rosselló submitted to the U.S. Justice Department the voter education materials and the ballot to be used on June 11, 2017, asking that the Justice Department endorse the release of the funds to Puerto Rico.

On April 13, Acting Deputy Attorney General Dana J. Boente replied, "The Department has determined that multiple considerations preclude it from notifying Congress that it approves of the plebiscite ballot and obligating funds." The ballot, she went on, contains statements that mislead and confuse the voters. It declares that statehood is "the only option that guarantees American citizenship by birth in Puerto Rico." This is "inaccurate," as "Puerto Ricans have an unconditional statutory right to birthright citizenship." She also objected to the description of "free association" on the ballot, misleading the voters into believing that it is a form of "enhanced commonwealth," whereas "a vote for Free Association is a vote for complete and unencumbered independence." The greatest objection, she said, is that the plebiscite excludes commonwealth status, based on the assertion that the voters rejected it in the 2012 elections. The Justice Department, she wrote, does not agree that they did, and a commonwealth option should be on the ballot.[3]

The letter was a serious blow to Rosselló and the statehood movement, but they decided to proceed with the plebiscite. This time they believed that they finally achieved their goal: not just a statehood victory, but an *overwhelming* victory. Statehood, they announced, got 97.18 percent of the vote. The U.S. media was skeptical that the statehood vote could have increased to such an extent when previously statehood and commonwealth support had been pretty even.

Although the opposition parties, led by the PDP, had urged their voters to boycott the plebiscite or cast blank ballots, the day before the plebiscite, the island's main newspaper's poll had predicted a 71 percent turnout. This was normal for the historically high voter participation in Puerto Rico. It was evident, however, that the boycott campaign worked: only 23 percent of the electorate voted, 1.2 million fewer than in the

2012 plebiscite. Rosselló and the NPP failed to get out even the statehood vote: only 503,000 voted for statehood, 332,000 fewer than in the 2012 plebiscite.

The Full-Press Drive for Statehood

"The road to statehood," the 1966 Status Commission reported, consists "of a sustained desire for statehood actively expressed over a period of time by a clear majority of the community."[4] A half century later, after five plebiscites, the statehood party had been elected seven times, and the statehood movement was determined it was time to put on a full-press drive. Certainly no letter from a Justice Department bureaucrat was going to stop them.

Citing the 97 percent pro-statehood vote, Rosselló launched what is called the "Tennessee Plan." Puerto Rico would send to Washington two "senators" and five "representatives"—Puerto Rico's congressional delegation as a state—to lobby for statehood. The governor named his father, Pedro Rosselló, to head what was called the Democracy Commission, along with former governor Romero Barceló. Senate president Thomas Rivera Schatz opened an office in Washington to assist in promoting statehood. No more delaying statehood for the future. Their mission in Washington, the governor announced, was to achieve statehood in five years.

But the drive for statehood was derailed. Two and a half months later, on September 20, Hurricane María devastated the island. The island government estimated reconstruction would cost $94.4 billion. The governor's attention was now focused on the tragedy, as it was in the United States and throughout the world.

An army of federal reconstruction and relief people, from FEMA, the Army Corps of Engineers and other government agencies, federal and private contractors, and civic groups and volunteers, descended on the island to provide relief and reconstruction. President Trump, House Speaker Paul Ryan, scores of members of Congress, state governors, and other U.S. leaders came, some repeatedly, to pledge support. New York governor Andrew Cuomo and his staff made repeated visits to the island, sending teams of technicians and equipment to repair the power system.

Yet Puerto Rico's recovery was agonizingly slow. There were growing reports in the United States of what appeared to be serious missteps and mismanagement by the government of Puerto Rico. The governor himself at times seemed confused, and he grossly miscalculated the time it would take to restore power, assuring the public it would be weeks. In fact, it would take nearly a year. He underestimated the fatalities by thousands. President Trump, who drew fire from mainland and island political leaders and the media for seeming to underestimate the number of deaths and the damage, returned the criticism, claiming that the island government was misusing billions of dollars in federal disaster funds.

Yet the governor and the NPP leadership saw an opportunity to convert the hurricane disaster and the controversy over U.S. relief into a tool to get the statehood drive back on track. Picking up on the many media reports that the U.S. government had been slow and negligent in comparison to its response to disasters in the states, Rosselló and Resident Commissioner González Colón insisted that this would not have been possible if Puerto Rico were not a U.S. colony, if it had been a state with two senators and five representatives in Congress.

The push for statehood took on another dimension, this time involving the PROMESA Fiscal Board. The government's January 24, 2018, proposed fiscal plan for Puerto Rico was meant to provide a road map for the island's emergence from the economic and fiscal crisis to economic growth. The first nine pages were a plea for statehood. "Puerto Rico's territorial status deprives its residents of the quality of life they deserve as U.S. citizens," the fiscal plan stated. "The delays in restoring the energy grid, among other recovery initiatives, are the most recent evidence that Puerto Rico's territorial status and lack of voting representation in Congress poses the greatest impediment to its sustainable economic development."[5]

On February 5, the Fiscal Board asked for a number of changes in the fiscal plan, including removing the opening section on statehood: "The Board is a non-political entity, and therefore cannot certify a fiscal plan that includes positions on the political status of Puerto Rico."[6] But for the governor and the New Progressive Party, as spelled out in the fiscal plan, statehood was the *solution* to the economic and fiscal crisis.

On October 5, 2018, Governor Rosselló; the president of the Senate, Thomas Rivera Schatz; the Speaker of the House, Carlos "Johnny" Méndez; Secretary of State Luis Rivera Marín; former governor Pedro Rosselló; and other political leaders and island business leaders traveled to Boulder, Colorado, to petition the Inter-American Human Rights Commission, an entity of the Organization of American States (OAS), to back their demand for statehood. On October 17, 2006, then-governor Pedro Rosselló had made the same petition.

The U.S. ambassador to the OAS, Carlos Trujillo, departing from the government's usual neutrality as to status, strongly disagreed. He urged the commission not to allow itself to be used to promote statehood. He said that it was not true that Puerto Rico expressed overwhelming support for statehood, since only 23 percent of eligible voters had voted in the last, 2017 plebiscite and that in fact Puerto Rico had favored commonwealth status in all the plebiscites.

In any case, Trujillo insisted, statehood for Puerto Rico was a "political domestic issue," and there was nothing in the OAS Human Rights Declaration that gave Puerto Rico the right to statehood. As the United States had always done, he rejected the claim that Puerto Rico was being discriminated against as a colony. There is nothing, he said, "discriminatory in the U.S. Constitution."[7]

The Republican Party, in fact, had moved away from its traditional position in its attitude toward statehood. Going back to Celso Barbosa in 1899, when he organized the island's Republican Party to seek statehood, the GOP platform included a pro-statehood plank.

A week earlier, President Trump came out against statehood. Asked about it in a radio interview, he answered that he was "absolutely" against it. His reason was not clear. "With a mayor of San Juan," he said, "as bad as she is and as incompetent as she is, Puerto Rico shouldn't be talking about statehood until they get some people who really know what they are doing."[8]

It seemed strange to Puerto Rico that his attitude on status depended on his running feud with San Juan mayor Carmen Yulín Cruz, who had criticized the U.S. response to Hurricane María. But he seemed to have a message for Puerto Rico: get your act together before you request coming into the union.

Mitch McConnell (R-KY), Senate majority leader, had made clear his opposition to statehood. When Resident Commissioner Jenniffer González Colón presented a new pro-statehood bill in the House after the 2017 plebiscite, he immediately pronounced it dead on arrival.

Now, on June 15, 2020, reacting to the House Democrats' announced intention to approve a Washington statehood bill, he said, "As long as I am the Republican majority leader, it will not happen."[9] On September 22, 2020, he spelled out why. In a speech in Kentucky, he said, "Know where the [Democrats] want to take us: statehood for D.C., statehood for Puerto Rico, pack the courts, increase taxes, over regulate the economy. . . . [T]his is a Democratic Party much more radical than what we have ever seen."[10]

Other Republicans joined in. Arizona Republican senator Martha McSally, for example, said, "They will make D.C. and Puerto Rico a state and have four new Democratic senators. We are never going to get the Senate back."[11]

Meanwhile, while island statehood advocates and leaders had long accused the GOP of only giving lip service to statehood, using it only to win the backing of Puerto Rico's delegates to the GOP convention, now mainland Puerto Rican liberals made the same accusation against the Democratic Party. Referring to Democratic presidential candidate Joe Biden's support for statehood at a Hispanic Heritage Month event in central Florida, they protested that instead of letting Puerto Ricans decide for themselves, the Democrats were promoting statehood for their own political purposes: to ensure two new Democrats in the Senate. As one Puerto Rican liberal put it, "White liberals must stop pushing Puerto Rico statehood for their own benefit. Let us decide."[12]

Is Statehood Economically Viable?

Going back to the beginning of the statehood movement in 1899, while many have pointed out the obstacles, there has always been a sense of inevitability that at some point Puerto Rico would become a state. Tugwell took it for granted. The long report on Puerto Rico in the April 14, 2018, *Economist* concluded, "It seems likely that Puerto Rico will become a state eventually."[13] Puerto Rico, the report concluded, will find a way to revive the economy: the island government knows what it needs to do, and the Fiscal Board will see to it that it is done.

In 1966, the Status Commission, which Muñoz and commonwealth supporters believed would finally prove that statehood was not economically viable, instead concluded that while the promise of immediate statehood was unrealistic, it was equally wrong to argue that it would never be viable economically. The statehood leaders who signed the report, Luis A. Ferré and Miguel Angel García Méndez, were delighted. They stated, "The final report of the Commission is a historic step forward in the inevitable advance toward statehood for Puerto Rico." They described as "an extraordinary achievement" the fact that the commission agreed that statehood was a "realistic possibility."[14]

But for the commonwealth advocates, the key was that the Status Commission also emphatically stated that of all the factors in the status issue, the "first is . . . [the] Commonwealth's continued success. . . . [T]he growth under [the] Commonwealth not only serves to validate its own position, but is essential also to make possible the realization of any other status without prohibitive hardships."[15]

If the future of statehood depended on the "success" of the commonwealth, the statehood movement was confronted with a dilemma. The new generation of statehood leaders was convinced that the road to statehood consisted in destroying the commonwealth. This is why it was seen as essential to eliminate the "big obstacle," Section 936. But with a per capita income one-third that of the United States and one-half that of the poorest state, Mississippi, how could making Puerto Rico poorer be a step toward statehood?

The unavoidable challenge for the statehood movement, as much as it wants to concentrate on "denied" political rights, has been to prove to Congress and the U.S. public that statehood *is* economically viable. There have been a number of attempts by the government and other entities to gauge the economic impact of statehood. One important issue is that the state of Puerto Rico, in issuing government bonds, would lose its unique triple tax exemption. How would this affect restoring the government's credit, which is essential to reviving the island's economic recovery?

But the biggest issue is what would replace Operation Bootstrap. While insisting on the future feasibility of statehood, the Status Commission reported that unless "appropriate substitutes for Puerto Rico's present special economic arrangements" — federal tax exemption under the commonwealth — were found, statehood would have "severe and probably disastrous consequences."[16] In addition to the Status Commission study, the General Accountability Office published in 1981 a 167-page report on the economic consequences of changing Puerto Rico's status, including an in-depth analysis of the consequences of losing the tax exemption incentive. Quoting the U.S. Department of Commerce, the report described tax exemption as "the *sine qua non* for attracting more United States investment capital." Changing the island's status to statehood, the report continued, "holds significant consequences for future development and could alter the island's attractiveness as a place for investment."[17]

In addition to losing the tax exemption incentive to attract investment, as Moody's pointed out in a November 4, 2020, report, "statehood could also make it more expensive to lure bond investors, with future commonwealth bonds losing their historic triple tax-exempt status."[18]

Statehood would require a *restructuring* of Puerto Rico's tax base. As in all the states, federal taxation would preempt local taxation, which was 10 to 30 percent higher than in the states. Statehood advocates point out that 80 percent of Puerto Rican workers earn too little to pay federal taxes, but the impact on the island taxpayers would be high. An analysis by veteran CPA Edgardo Sanabría found that if island taxes were not lowered, parents in their thirties, with one child, earning $65,000 would pay $2,858 in local taxes and $2,487 in federal taxes, an increase of 87 percent. A family earning $85,000 would have an increase of 88.56 percent.[19] Obviously, federal taxation would force Puerto Rico to greatly lower its rates to state levels, significantly decreasing tax revenues, the number of public employees, and government services.

Puerto Rico has had a foretaste of the political and economic effects of such a radical restructuring. The Fiscal Board, attempting to get the government to reduce the budget by making modest changes — consolidating agencies, eliminating duplication, and undertaking a relatively small reduction in personnel — has met fierce opposition from all the parties. Pro-statehood NPP Senate president Thomas Rivera Schatz referred to the Fiscal Board as "enemy number one of Puerto Rico"[20] — the American dictatorial entity out to cut University of Puerto Rico funds, eliminate cultural programs, and deny Puerto Ricans their hard-earned pensions. In the 2020 gubernatorial campaign, the principal accusation against NPP candidate Pedro Pierluisi was his perceived "friendly" relationship with the Fiscal Board.

Statehood advocates respond that a statehood enabling act would include government funding for the economic transition; the island could retain much of its industrialization through federal "enterprise zones" and other programs where the federal government provides incentives to assist high poverty and unemployment areas. Any loss to the economy due to federal taxation, they point out, would be compensated by the big increase in federal funds—big because of the island's high poverty and unemployment.

But independent economic studies find that there would be a net loss. In 2014, with Puerto Rico already in an economic and fiscal crisis, the GAO issued another report, again balancing the benefits of additional federal funds with what individuals and corporations would pay in federal taxes. As a state, there would be an increase in eleven of the twenty-nine federal programs on the island: many of the programs designed to promote economic growth and reduce unemployment already apply to the island. The report estimated, on the other hand, that Puerto Ricans would pay from $2.2 billion to $2.3 billion in federal income taxes. Emphasizing that it is difficult to estimate how many U.S. industries would relocate, it estimated that in 2010, they would have paid from $5 billion to $9.3 billion in federal corporate taxes.[21] In addition, as Bootstrap advocates have long argued, and as emphasized in the *Economist* report, only Puerto Rico itself can resolve its crisis; it can revive its economy only by becoming more "competitive." With so many of the operating costs to do business in Puerto Rico significantly higher than on the mainland, the economy would grow again only if it could offer incentives not available in the states. This is precisely the crux of the question of whether statehood is economically viable.

Statehood proponents point to the U.S. urban enterprise zone program, whereby manufacturing and other firms established in zones of perpetually high unemployment and poverty, like Puerto Rico, get a series of temporary federal incentives, including federal tax credits. Puerto Rico's pro-statehood resident commissioner, Jenniffer González Colón, introduced a bill on March 5, 2019, the Economic Development Act for Distressed Zones, based on the enterprise zone concept. A year later, responding to the coronavirus pandemic and the concern it raised regarding U.S. dependence on Chinese drug and pharmaceutical production, now seen as a serious danger to American national security, she presented another bill to attract the big pharmaceutical industries that had left after the loss of Section 936. The bill would provide the "distressed zones" tax credits in her earlier bill.

The Manufacturers' Association president, Carlos Rodriguez, engaged in a new drive to restore the Section 936 tax incentive, pointed out that it simply would not work: "We don't think these incentives are sufficient to bring new manufacturing to Puerto Rico."[22]

On April 22, 2020, Teresita Fuentes, a CPA who had served as secretary of the treasury under the pro-statehood governor Ricardo Rosselló, agreed. She wrote in the *Weekly Journal* that a manufacturer would have to pay a 21 percent federal tax rate in order to claim a tax credit. "The likely outcome," she stated, "is an increased effective tax rate and the loss of foreign tax credit benefits. Further, any tax exemption granted by Puerto Rico would cancel out." She pointed out, "For years I have advised global companies and have sat at the table as they make multi-million-dollar decisions to establish and move global operations based on cash flows, tax rates and business incentives." When asked who would recommend the González Colón distressed zone bill as an incentive to establish an operation in Puerto Rico, she replied, "Certainly a legal theorist . . . [but not] a qualified tax professional working in good faith."[23]

In the United States, the enterprise zone model has been controversial. Fuentes wrote that studies by the Congressional Research Service, the research branch of Congress, and other government entities "have failed to link these zones with improvement in community outcomes and have questioned the measurable positive impact of these types of programs."[24] That was the point made by the PRMA and the economists: to be a substitute for Section 936, it had to be an incentive available only to Puerto Rico.

The statehood movement got a big boost in 1958 and 1959, when the first noncontiguous states, Alaska and Hawaii, respectively, entered the Union. Although the U.S. Constitution does not set requirements for statehood, the House and Senate Interior Affairs Committee, in its report approving Alaska's entry into the Union, spelled out the three historical requirements: "that the inhabitants be imbued with and sympathetic towards the principles of democracy as exemplified in the American form of government, that a majority of the electorate desire statehood, and that a proposed new state has sufficient population and resources to support state government and to provide its share of the cost of the Federal Government."[25] Alaska and Hawaii both had strong economies and high per capita incomes achieved under full federal taxation. Proving that Puerto Rico is economically prepared—an economy that has always depended on full federal tax exemption—would raise unprecedented issues in Congress. Above all, as posed by the Status Commission and other studies, how will the island economy catch up to the rest of the nation?

In a *Newsweek* interview on October 1, 2018, Governor Rosselló reiterated what has always been the response: You can't put a price tag on the political rights of statehood—on the right of American citizens in Puerto Rico to have voting representation in Congress and to participate in presidential elections.

The Statehood Debate

Beyond economics, there are other important and complicated issues in the statehood debate. In the second half of the twentieth century, the new generation of statehood advocates carried the accusation that rights were being denied to a new level. That Puerto Ricans were being denied their political rights because they are "nonwhite" made this part of the national battle for civil rights. Puerto Ricans, like blacks and other minorities, they insisted, are the victims of American ethnic and racial discrimination. Puerto Rico has been denied statehood because it is Puerto Rican.

Race had always been an undercurrent in Puerto Rico's relationship to the United States. A good part of the early "anti-imperialist" battle against annexing Puerto Rico was racial. Those in favor argued that, unlike Cubans and Dominicans, most Puerto Ricans are white—76 percent, according to the subsequent U.S. Census. Just 12.4 percent are black. Even if this was true, the anti-imperialist leader Carl Schurz, who had led the U.S.

Senate fight against annexing Hawaii or any offshore island, argued, it is simply wrong to believe that a people of another ethnic heritage could be assimilated as Americans. There is no instance, he declared, of democracy working in "tropical climates."[26]

Since the massive migration of Puerto Ricans to the mainland after World War II, Puerto Ricans have been subjected to discrimination. While not as brutal as that against African Americans, it is similar to that of previous mass migrations. At the beginning, many Puerto Rican migrants believed that it was essentially ethnic, that once their children spoke English without an accent the discrimination would fade away. Most Americans knew little or nothing about Puerto Rico, often confusing it with Costa Rica. What they knew was what they saw on Broadway and in the Hollywood movie *West Side Story*, where Puerto Ricans spoke with a heavy accent, their faces were darkened to brown, and they were members of New York knife-wielding gangs. It was a major task of the early Bootstrap program to change the stereotype.

Now most Puerto Rican leaders on the mainland, no longer insisting that Puerto Ricans are "white," describe themselves, regardless of their race, as part of the "nonwhite" minority. Some politicians, academics, and others compare the bringing of slaves from Africa to the diaspora of Puerto Ricans driven to abandon their homeland by the oppression and exploitation of American colonialism.

Governor Pedro Rosselló, in his 2007 book, *El triumvirato del terror* (The Triumvirate of Terror), claimed that the discrimination against Puerto Ricans is manifested in a "conspiracy" in the United States to block statehood. He accused the U.S. Justice Department of bringing cases of corruption against members of his administration and party in order to "criminalize the statehood movement."[27]

During Rosselló's administration, the local U.S. District Attorney carried out investigations of widespread corruption that resulted in the conviction of over forty members of his administration and NPP leaders. When a U.S. attorney publicly linked corruption to the New Progressive Party, Rosselló wrote letters to the U.S. Attorney General protesting what he saw as proof of the anti-statehood "conspiracy."

The second part of the "triumvirate," Rosselló wrote, is the "Creole elite." This was surprising since the elite included prominent statehood advocates in the private sector, including the Ferré family, who were founders of the NPP and owned the island's principal daily newspaper, *El Nuevo Día*. Since its founding in 1970, the newspaper had been a bulwark of support of the NPP and of opposition to the Popular Democratic Party. But when it began to campaign vigorously against the corruption in the Rosselló administration, describing it as the "most corrupt period in island history," it ignited a war between Rosselló and the Ferré family. The Creole elite also included Jaime Fonalledas Enterprises, owner of big shopping centers and other real estate on the island. Fonalledas and his wife, Zoraida Fonalledas, were also prominent statehood advocates. Also named was the "Carrión conglomeration," headed by Richard Carrión, president of the island's largest bank, the Banco Popular de Puerto Rico, who had always avoided being identified politically or ideologically.[28]

According to Rosselló, it is easy to understand why the Puerto Rican wealthy, the Creole elite, even those who professed support for statehood, are part of the anti-statehood conspiracy: they benefit greatly from keeping Puerto Rico a colony. As Romero Barceló had argued in 1973, if Puerto Rico was a state Puerto Ricans would have to pay federal taxes.

Even more surprising was the harshness of Rosselló's attack on the Creole elite. He also used Romero's slavery analogy, accusing the "conspirators" of being like the American "house slaves" who, in exchange for privileges, happily sustained the slave plantations. He compared them to the Jewish "enablers" who cooperated with the Nazis in the concentration camps.[29]

The third part of the anti-statehood "triumvirate," not surprisingly, is the Popular Democratic Party.

There is in Rosselló's book an undertone of independentista anti-Americanism, manifesting a peculiarity of the island's status politics: the convergence of statehood and independence ideology. The book is dedicated "to all the Puerto Ricans that have suffered the onslaught of the persecution due to their belief and ideals," making common cause with independence leaders. For Rosselló, the enemies of independence — United States, the Puerto Rican economic elite, and the Popular Democratic Party — are the enemies of statehood.

"Why now the statehood persecution?," he asked. "Simple. Statehood is the current threat to the colonial regime."[30]

On May 9, 2019, after President Trump made anti-statehood state-ments, Puerto Rico Senate president Rivera Shatz wrote, "The problem is not Trump . . . it's the colony." Also using the language of anti-American independentistas, he accused the United States of the "crime . . . of 121 years" of colonialism.[31] On the opposite ends of Puerto Rico's status poli-tics spectrum, the statehood proponents and the independentistas have always had a common bond: both are engaged in a battle against the same enemy and its enablers, "American colonialism."

Cultural Death

Culture has always been at the heart of the political status conflict. The independence argument is based essentially on culture: American colo-nialism has consisted of a policy to exterminate Puerto Rican culture, to erase the Puerto Rican national identity, with its early policy of Americani-zation, of forcing Puerto Rico to abandon Spanish for English, and the "forced" migration of hundreds of thousands of Puerto Ricans to the mainland. This is an argument shared by many island academics, students, artists, writers, and journalists, as well as commonwealth supporters and independence advocates.

This, not the economy, they say, is the real danger of statehood: state-hood means inescapable assimilation, an existential threat to a nation with its own history, its own centuries-old cultural heritage. The argu-ment is made that many statehooders are really not motivated by true pro-American sentiments or loyalty but because they are ashamed of being Puerto Rican. Statehooders, they say, want to renounce their Puerto Rican identity to become "American."

In the political status conflict, independentistas saw exaltation of Ameri-can culture as anti-Puerto Rican and statehooders saw exaltation of Puerto Rican culture as anti-American. In 1955, statehood leaders had vigorously opposed Muñoz's creation of the Institute of Puerto Rican Culture.

One of the big changes Ferré and the new statehood leaders made in 1967, when they broke away from the Statehood Republican Party to form the New Progressive Party, was to change the statehood proponents' attitude toward culture. Ferré insisted that statehooders were as Puerto Rican, as pro–Puerto Rican, as the independentistas. He coined the phrase,

"estadidad jíbara," or native statehood. Puerto Rico would become a Hispanic state, retaining its Spanish language and cultural identity.

To make the point, as governor, Ferré strongly supported the Institute
of Puerto Rican Culture, which years earlier he had opposed. He named
its founder, Ricardo Alegría, a vocal anti-statehood proponent of independence, to continue heading the institute. Romero Barceló picked up
the "jíbaro statehood" argument, ridiculing the fear that statehood would
strip the Puerto Rican of his native, "jíbaro" culture, that he would no
longer eat "rice and beans." In his 1973 pamphlet, *Statehood Is for the
Poor*, he declared "neither our language nor our culture [is] negotiable."[32]
In the following years, he insisted that if he was forced to give them up, he
would no longer support statehood.

The observable reality on the island has been that after a century under
the United States, Puerto Rican culture has not only survived, but flour-
ished. Puerto Ricans, of course, have changed; they have become "Americanized" in their lifestyle and consumerism. But almost all Puerto Ricans,
including those living on the U.S. mainland and second- and third-gen-
eration individuals, who identify themselves as Puerto Ricans and speak
Spanish with difficulty if at all, are proud of their identity. The anthropolo-
gist and historian Ricardo Alegría, while sharing the fear of assimilation,
has also pointed out that the attempt to Americanize Puerto Ricans created among many a sort of mental block against English. This is one reason so few Puerto Ricans outside the tourist areas are bilingual, with many
hardly able to speak English at all.[33]

But, as in economics, the idea of "jíbaro statehood," of a Spanish-
speaking Hispanic state, raises difficult questions that have to do as much
with *American culture*. Statehood advocates point out that English is *not*
the official language of the United States. While there is an English-language test required for naturalization as a U.S. citizen, there is nothing in
the Constitution that requires Congress to impose it as a condition of
being admitted to the Union.

Statehood advocates also point out that English and Spanish are both
"official" languages on the island. When the pro-commonwealth governor
Rafael Hernández Colón eliminated English as an official language in 1992,
the first act of the new pro-statehood governor in 1993 was to restore it.

Statehood leaders accuse advocacy groups such as the English First Foundation, which lobbies to make English the official language, of being anti–Puerto Rican, "reactionary and racist." English First answers that it favors a bilingual Puerto Rico but that English should be "first." Through the years, many other members of Congress, some of them pro-statehood, have expressed the same idea.

Several U.S. political leaders, and others, have pointed out that while English is not the "official language," it is essential to the survival of the United States as a nation. A member of the 1964 Status Commission, Senator Henry M. Jackson, chair of the Senate Interior Committee, with jurisdiction over Puerto Rico, wrote in the Commission report that precisely because the United States is a nation of immigrants, English is the "common language [that] has brought us together. . . . [S]urely at a time when we are trying to eliminate ghettos of all kinds, we should not establish within our federal-state system a 'language ghetto.' A condition precedent to statehood must be the recognition and acceptance of English as the official language."[34]

A number of American historians, both conservative and liberal, some of whom strongly support liberal immigration policies, have written that while cultural diversity is central to American civilization, so is cultural assimilation. They have expressed concern that not assimilating ethnically different groups that consider themselves distinct cultural nations could lead to conflicts such as those in Canada with Quebec and Spain with the Basque Country and Cataluña. Among them is the liberal historian Arthur Schlesinger Jr., who warned in his 1992 book, *The Disuniting of America*, that it is the will to assimilate into American culture, not racial or ethnic identity, that defines an American: "A cult of ethnicity has arisen both among non-Anglo whites and among nonwhite minorities to denounce the idea of a melting pot, to challenge the concept of 'one people,' and to promote, protect and perpetuate separate ethnic and racial communities." This, he writes, is "the explosive issue of our times."[35] And it is the issue raised by the concept of estadidad jíbara, based on the negation of "the melting pot."

Sports and Beauty Queens

Closely related to the cultural issue in the statehood debate is the fate of the Puerto Rico Olympics Committee and participation in other international sporting events and in international beauty contests. No fewer than five Puerto Ricans have been crowned Miss Universe.

Since 1948, the International Olympics Committee (IOC) has recognized the island's National Olympics Committee. Since then, Puerto Rico has sent its own athletes to compete under the Puerto Rican flag. The large number of Puerto Rican Big League baseball stars and professional boxing and tennis champions is a source of considerable pride on the island.

If partisan politics and the status conflict tear Puerto Ricans apart, nothing brings them together like a tragedy such as Hurricane María or a Puerto Rican winning in a sports event or a beauty contest. In 2004, the island erupted in celebration when the Puerto Rico basketball team beat the United States 92 to 73. It erupted in celebration again in 2018 when the Puerto Rican Alex Cora, manager of the Boston Red Sox, led the team to the World Series championship.

Statehood opponents insist that once a state, the island would lose its Olympics standing. Statehood leaders express confidence that the island would retain it. What qualifies a country to have a National Olympic Committee is not clear: the International Olympic Committee Charter refers to "countries," defining them as independent states recognized internationally. But the IOC has recognized three U.S. territories: the U.S. Virgin Islands in 1967, Guam in 1986, and American Samoa in 1987. Whether it would recognize Puerto Rico if it becomes an integral part of the United States is obviously a different question.

The "Blood Tax": Vieques and National Defense

Aside from the political case of being disenfranchised U.S. citizens, the most credible and effective argument used by statehood advocates in Puerto Rico, and powerfully in Washington, is that Puerto Ricans pay much more than a federal tax; they pay a "blood tax." If Americans have been confused about the island's status battle, particularly about how Puerto Ricans identify themselves, one thing has always been clear: the long history of Puerto Rican participation and casualties in American wars.

A total of 65,034 Puerto Ricans participated in World War II, the Puerto Rican 65th Infantry Regiment earning 114 medals. In the Korean War, 756 Puerto Ricans were killed, and the 65th Infantry Regiment earned 3,644 medals, four of them Medals of Honor. In the Vietnam War, 455 islanders were killed and 3,775 wounded. On June 10, 2014, President Barack Obama awarded the Congressional Gold Medal to the 65th Infantry Regiment.

It is precisely the "blood tax," statehood proponents insist, that dramatizes the inequity in the island's colonial status. Puerto Ricans who paid the ultimate price were denied the right to vote for or against the president or to have a voice in the Congress that sent them to war.

The issue of Puerto Rican loyalty came up again in 1993 when Governor Pedro Rosselló, with the support of all the island parties, as well as business and religious leaders, led a crusade to get the U.S. Navy out of Vieques, the island municipality off Puerto Rico's east coast. Like sporting events and beauty contests, the war against the navy united the Puerto Ricans on the island and the mainland, generating up to then the biggest public protests in island history.

But for the United States, particularly for the navy, this was a matter of vital importance to national defense. Again there was deep misunderstanding and miscommunication. For Puerto Ricans, it was a patriotic issue: stop bombing our beloved island of Vieques. The United States saw the Vieques "hysteria" as Puerto Rican partisan politics pure and simple. For Puerto Rico, it was absurd, an insult to Puerto Rican intelligence, to assert that American national security hinged on the 52-square-mile island of Vieques.

The battle over Vieques, in fact, touched on a fundamental element in the Puerto Rico–U.S. relationship. Puerto Rico's strategic value to the navy had impelled the United States to take the island in the first place in 1898. In the 1940s, believing that World War II would extend into the Caribbean, Puerto Rico became a virtual U.S. armed camp dotted with army, navy, and air force bases. Their mission was to protect the Panama Canal, as well as the vital sea lanes used to transport petroleum and other critical materials in the Atlantic.

In his memoirs, Rexford Tugwell wrote that the reason he wanted to become governor of Puerto Rico was his belief that should Britain fall to the Nazis, the island would become a vital battleground. Citing President Roosevelt's "interests in the [Caribbean] area as part of our national defense," Tugwell was anxious to help his nation and his president in "war work."[36]

In 1952, when explaining and defending in Congress the creation of the commonwealth, Muñoz emphasized how important "common defense" was to the Puerto Rico–U.S. relationship and to Puerto Ricans. It was, he said, one of the four "pillars" of commonwealth status; the others were common citizenship, common market, and common currency.

But in November 1961, President Kennedy, after his tumultuous reception during his visit to Puerto Rico, brought up what was for Muñoz a particularly sensitive issue. The navy had training operations on the two island municipalities off Puerto Rico's east coast, Vieques and the 11.6-square-mile island of Culebra. Now Kennedy told Muñoz that the navy wanted to take over the islands totally.

Muñoz was anxious to get Kennedy's support for a new effort in Congress to improve Puerto Rico's commonwealth status, and he knew well how important these military matters were to the president and all Americans. But a few days later, he diplomatically wrote to the president that what he wanted was not possible. There were, of course, political problems. One of them, as Kennedy had warned, was that it would be necessary to exhume thousands of bodies buried in the cemeteries. The other was constitutional: as municipalities, they could not be eliminated without legislative approval; even for Muñoz, it was politically impossible. Kennedy dropped the request. But this was the beginning of what would escalate by the mid-1990s into the most serious and emotional conflict between Puerto Rico and the United States.

In preparation for World War II, the Roosevelt administration had converted the military air base in Ceiba, on the island's east coast, into what became the largest naval installation in the world, then called "the Pearl Harbor of the Atlantic." The plan was to house the British Navy should the United Kingdom fall to the Germans. By the 1960s, the Roosevelt Roads complex at Ceiba had grown to include Viequez and Culebra as well as bases at nearby St. Thomas and St. Croix. The navy acquired two-thirds of Vieques from sugar farmers by purchase and expropriation. The island's eastern tip was used for live target practice and Marine amphibious training. Most of the navy's land was used as a buffer zone for the 23,000 civilians in the town of Santa Isabel.

Since 1898, American visitors have felt that contrary to what the Puerto Ricans professed, they were actually for independence. Tugwell, in the 1940s, had feared that political unrest and the resurgence of na-

tionalist anti-American violence would disrupt American military operations in Puerto Rico. Following the war, the navy had the same concern,
fearing that political agitation on Vieques and Culebra would imperil
their operations and eventually their presence. There were occasional anti-
navy protests, mostly by anti-American, pro-independence groups but
also by Vieques and Culebra fishermen. Throughout, the navy vehemently insisted that the operations and the massive naval, air, and Marine
training operations were irreplaceable elements of national defense. And
it was convinced, and for a time convinced President Kennedy, that the
best way to ensure their security and permanence was simply to depopu-
late the islands entirely.

The first political battle took place in the 1970s. Governor Hernández
Colón decided to lobby in Washington to end naval operations in Culebra, arguing that since they would be transferred to nearby, depopulated
islands and the navy would retain Vieques, it would not, after all, affect
national defense. The navy put up strong resistance, fearing that if it lost
Culebra, it would eventually lose Vieques. Even after Defense Secretary
Elliot Richardson informed Hernández Colón in May 1973 that the navy
would leave in 1975, the navy kept battling. It was not until November
that resistance in Congress was overcome and the funds for the transfer
were approved.[37]

The navy's fear that it would also lose Vieques began to become reality
on April 19, 1999. A civilian guard, David Sanes, a forty-five-year-old
Vieques native, was killed by two training navy fighter bombs that ex-
ploded five hundred yards from a bomb-proof shelter. The navy declared
that it was an accident, that Sanes should have been inside the shelter like
the other guards. But his death ignited the political explosion that the
navy had long feared. Governor Rosselló led the charge, and his demand
that the navy leave the island got instant and virtually unanimous support
in all Puerto Rico. It attracted the U.S. media and a growing number of
U.S. political, environmental, civil rights, and entertainment personali-
ties, who joined the protest on the island and the mainland. Independence Party president Ruben Berríos carried out a civil disobedience protest, camping out illegally on navy land.

The navy insisted that the reports and images of a small defenseless island being bombed incessantly, mercilessly, were simply bogus. It declared
that this was the first civilian fatality and that, in any case, the navy had

stopped using live ammunition and was instead using nonexplosive duds on a small tip of Vieques, miles away from the civilian population. The accusation that it was destroying the spectacularly beautiful Vieques environment, the navy declared, was also absurd. In fact, the navy insisted, it was protecting the two-thirds of the island under its control from the land speculators that the navy alleged were also behind the protests. To counter the news photos of the bomb-pitted target area, the navy flew visitors over the large buffer zone to demonstrate its pristine natural state.

The island government and protesters quoted scientific studies that alleged that the bombing caused an abnormally high cancer rate in Vieques. These reports, the navy insisted, were also bogus. The reports, in fact, were subsequently disproven by U.S. and Puerto Rican Health Department studies.

But the navy defense, carried out mostly in Congress and the White House, had no support in Puerto Rico, and in March 2003, it lost the battle. The United States decided to end all bombing on Vieques. A year later, the navy closed the Roosevelt Roads base.

The Vieques battle had an economic consequence. Ceiba became one of the island's most economically depressed areas. There were several tourist hotels built on Vieques, but soon the residents were accusing the central government of neglect, especially in providing health and transportation facilities. The navy left a huge infrastructure complex, an airport, housing, and other facilities at the Roosevelt Roads base. Subsequent island government administrations came up with several plans to use the abandoned facilities for industrial and tourist development. A decade later, these plans were mostly unrealized.

Winning the Vieques battle also had consequences for the island's status politics. Again, there seemed to be a contradiction. On the one side, there was the "blood tax." Puerto Rico's participation in American wars proved its commitment to what Muñoz had often described as one of the pillars of the Puerto Rico–U.S. relationship: American national defense. But on the other side, the question was whether the explosion of anti-navy sentiment, of intransigence, refusing to even consider the navy's arguments as to national defense, revealed something about the true loyalty of Puerto Ricans. In the late 1930s, the fervent New Dealers who had tried so hard to help Puerto Rico emerge from extreme poverty, in Washington and on the island, questioned whether Puerto Ricans were truly loyal to the United States. They were dismayed that so many did not seem outraged by the assassination of the American police chief in San Juan. Even the loyalty of Muñoz, the one island politico trusted in Washington, was questioned. One of his few remaining supporters in Washington, the journalist Ruby Black, pleaded in emotional letters that he make clear that he did not agree with the nationalist anti-American violence.[38]

One thing was clear. The Vieques war was still another element in the century of misunderstanding between Puerto Ricans and Americans. Since the beginning, when taking and keeping Puerto Rico was a big factor in the grand design for a great American navy, in defense of the Panama Canal, throughout World War II it had been indisputable that the island was of great strategic value to national defense. No more. Although not in any juridical or political sense and certainly not visibly, the Vieques battle shifted the relationship between Puerto Rico and the United States.

Through the years, many visitors, witnessing how deeply and emotionally they identified themselves as *Puerto Ricans*, wondered if Puerto Ricans value their American citizenship purely for the economic and other benefits. If Schlesinger is right that it is the *willingness,* indeed the *aspiration*, to be assimilated into American culture, not racial or ethnic identity, that defines an American, it is obvious that Puerto Ricans, as much as they have changed in the past century, have not assimilated into becoming "American."

Will Puerto Rico Become a State?

The sense of inevitability of statehood for Puerto Rico stems in large part from the response of the U.S. government, especially after Puerto Ricans became U.S. citizens in 1917. The response has been that it can happen if Puerto Ricans clearly want it to happen and if Puerto Rico's economy continues to grow. This was the conclusion of the 1967 United States–Puerto Rico Commission on the Status of Puerto Rico report, which has been reiterated by every president, including Donald Trump, and many members of Congress. And it has been the conclusion of numerous reports, many from the U.S. government and the General Accountability Office.

As to whether statehood is or can be economically viable, the answer has been, at present, no. The Puerto Rican economy is based on the special relationship that exists with the United States. But it has also been argued that, in the final analysis, it is a "political" question that will depend on the political will in Puerto Rico and the United States to take the measures necessary to the economic transition to statehood.

In 2020, the New Progressive Party decided to hold another status vote, the sixth, this one a vote of yes or no on statehood, and to again ask the U.S. Justice Department for the $2.5 million to pay for the plebiscite. On July 29, 2020, U.S. Deputy Attorney General Jeffrey A. Rosen replied in a five-page letter to the Puerto Rico Election Commission, again rejecting the request, reiterating the accusation that the Puerto Rico government is "misleading" and "confusing" voters. The department again disputed that the 2012 plebiscite was conclusive in supporting statehood and rejecting commonwealth status. It held the same position as it did on the 2017 plebiscite.

The letter stated that comparing the plebiscite to referendums in Alaska and Hawaii is wrong. There the vote took place to ratify congressional approval of statehood: "To the extent that the plebiscite materials' statement about finality and their reference to Alaska and Hawaii imply that this plebiscite is the last time that Puerto Rico would conceivably vote on statehood, they do not perceive an accurate depiction on how the statehood process would be likely to unfold and are therefore likely to result in voter confusion."[39]

This letter was even harsher than that of April 13, 2017, but the drive for statehood was undeterred. On May 16, in a ceremony at La Fortaleza, surrounded by a large number of NPP leaders, including former governor Carlos Romero Barceló, Governor Wanda Vázquez Garced, who had replaced Rosselló in 2019, signed a bill calling for still another status vote, a statehood yes-or-no referendum concurrent with the November 3, 2020 elections.

The New Progressive Party's Pedro Pierluisi was elected governor. Jenniffer González Colón was reelected resident commissioner. It was the eighth time in the past fourteen elections that Puerto Rico elected a pro-statehood governor, the tenth time it elected a pro-statehood resident commissioner. Statehood won the referendum: 52 percent in favor, 48 percent against.

The drive for statehood will continue. For many Americans, the question that has nagged since 1898 remains: What do Puerto Ricans really want? Is the statehood movement a manifestation of loyalty to the United States, of identity with American culture and values? Or is it the promise of hundreds of millions more in federal funds?

Curiously, while historically territories have become states by proving that they have a strong economy that can take on all the attendant obligations, in Puerto Rico the statehood campaign, especially in Washington, is based on Puerto Rican poverty.

The two Justice Department letters denying the federal funds for the plebiscites make a serious allegation: the government of Puerto Rico, under the New Progressive Party, has been "misleading" and "confusing" the voters in its campaign to get them to support statehood. Are Puerto Ricans aware of the consequences of making the island a state? But at bottom, the question of whether Puerto Rico will become a state rests, as it always has, on whether statehood is economically feasible.

In February 14, 1962, Puerto Rico's top government leaders, led by Muñoz, met secretly with representatives of President Kennedy and top State and Justice Department officials at the Hay Adams Hotel in Washington. Kennedy had committed himself to help make major improvements in the commonwealth status. But as they got into the discussions, Kennedy's representatives, led by Richard Goodwin, his Latin America adviser, seemed to share the sense of the inevitability of statehood.

They kept asking Muñoz: Tell us again, why is statehood impossible? Muñoz would go through the economic reasons. But unsatisfied, they persisted. What if all those problems were resolved, would you still be opposed? Yes, Muñoz answered.

It has always been difficult for Americans to accept that statehood is not economically feasible. The 1967, the Status Commission, like many studies since that emphasized statehood is contingent on Puerto Rico's continued economic growth, assumed that the economy will grow. But today, this optimism, so strongly felt by Governor Calderón and others as they struggled to reverse the island's decline, has been, as the diplomats say, "overtaken by events": the loss of Section 936, the demise of Operation Bootstrap, the economic and fiscal crisis.

If the essential assumption has been that Puerto Rico's continued rapid economic growth will make statehood economically viable, the answer to the question "Will Puerto Rico become a state?" is evident, as, in fact, it has been since 1898.

CHAPTER NINE

The Future of Puerto Rico

In the aftermath of the bitter Vieques battle and as Puerto Rico sank into the economic and fiscal crisis, the U.S. government was forced to step in to prevent the collapse of the island economy. After 122 years, in a cold calculation of costs and benefits, Americans can say, "Let's face it. We didn't know what we were doing in the Spanish-American War. We didn't know what we were getting into when we took and kept Puerto Rico. Luis Muñoz Marín was right when he wrote in 1946, 'The United States possesses Puerto Rico by mistake.'[1] We tried to make it work, but it hasn't. Isn't it time that we finally admit it? Isn't the solution Puerto Rico's independence?

"In 2016 the governor of Puerto Rico and the president of the opposition party went to Congress with a desperate plea to help the island pull out of the economic spiral it got itself into through no fault of ours. We responded, keeping the government afloat by suspending payment of their $70 billion debt, creating the PROMESA Fiscal Board to get the government to make the hard decisions it was politically unwilling or unable to make, to be fiscally responsible, to balance its budget, to get out of bankruptcy, to at least begin to pay its debt and restore its credit.

"Even though we created the Fiscal Board at their urgent request, all we get from the political leadership is that the Fiscal Board is the number one enemy of the Puerto Rican people. All we have gotten from Puerto Rico is endless wailing that we are abusing them, that we are denying them their rights, that they are a colony. After Hurricane Maria, we committed to $82 billion in disaster relief. Since we created PROMESA they have not paid a cent in principle or interest.

"Although Puerto Ricans have always been exempt from federal income taxes, they contribute to the U.S. Treasury in other ways. But since 1898, Puerto Rico has received from the United States, especially after President Johnson's War on Poverty, greatly increased welfare, anti-poverty federal spending, and billions more. According to the island's Planning Board, in 2019 Puerto Rico received $30.04 billion in federal funds while contributing $4.5 billion.

"As the *Wall Street Journal* correctly points out, 'Political corruption in Puerto Rico is as thick as the humidity.'[2] And all we hear from the government and the politicians is that the United States must send them billions more and reward them by making Puerto Rico a state.

"Puerto Rico has always been a big drain on our Treasury, on the states. Will someone please explain to us why it wouldn't be a much bigger, permanent drain as a state? The only solution is independence."

Why Not Independence?

Is it conceivable that in the future Puerto Rico will reach the same conclusion, that the only way out is independence? If one concludes that the commonwealth formula has failed and if one accepts that the economic reality makes statehood impossible, isn't independence the only solution?

The principle of self-determination gives the right to independence regardless of the economic consequences. Puerto Ricans are, of course, free to assume the responsibility. Since Puerto Rico can always exercise this right, as long as it does not become a state in the Union independence will always be an option. But is it a realistic option? Is it realistic to expect that it will happen?

The Puerto Rico Independence Party (PIP) gets equal treatment and equal public funding under electoral law. Its independence message is emotionally powerful: all Latin American people opted for independence, and Puerto Rico is a Latin American nation, so if you are proud of being Puerto Rican you have a patriotic duty to favor independence.

PIP candidates are usually attractive and articulate. In the 2020 election, Juan Dalmau Ramírez, generally considered the most impressive of all the candidates for governor, got 13.7 percent of the vote. This was a big increase from the 2016 election, when the PIP candidate got 2.13 percent of the vote. Some analyists interpreted this as significant growth in independence sentiment, especially when the 14.2 percent that another pro-independence candidate received is factored in.

But political status played a small role in the 2020 campaign. Dalmau and the others focused on the economic and pandemic crises. One thing was clear: the Puerto Rican electorate manifested its unhappiness with the two major parties, as the PNP vote decreased by 9 percent and the PDP by 7 percent.

Although independentistas insist even more than statehooders that a price cannot be placed on "patriotism," they discount the idea that independence would ruin the island economy. The problem, the independence advocates insist, is colonialism. A sovereign Puerto Rico could negotiate favorable terms with the United States. After a century of colonialism the United States has the moral obligation to ensure that the island's economy will not sink and should agree to terms such as retaining free trade with the mainland. Some argue that Puerto Ricans should retain U.S. citizenship and its benefits.

But this takes Puerto Rico into the ideological political status world where everything is hypothetically possible. What would be the point of the United States agreeing to independence and then giving the republic all the benefits without any of the obligations of a commonwealth or a state?

The Rejection of Independence

For as long as Puerto Rico has had politics and parties, the one constant has been the rejection of independence. When the wars of independence began in Latin America, Puerto Ricans remained loyal to Spain. When Puerto

Rican party politics began in the mid-nineteenth century, what divided the parties was how to achieve self-government *within* the Spanish regime.

In the next century, under the Americans and after the disappointment of the civil government established under the Foraker Act, several parties began to include independence as an option. It was the shock of the 1936 Tydings bill that changed what was perceived as political rhetoric into a reality, provoking the famous saying, "It is one thing to call the devil, another to see him coming." With President Roosevelt supporting the bill, it provoked what was now the palpable fear of independence.

The Muñoz era began in 1940 when he convinced the jíbaros that a vote for him was not a vote for independence. But the growth in the statehood movement was largely due to the campaign message that Muñoz and the Popular Democratic Party, in supporting autonomy, were in fact leaving the door open to bring independence in through the kitchen. The only way to close that door was, of course, statehood.

For Muñoz and party leaders, it seemed evident that the island's economic growth under Operation Bootstrap and the massive migration were not separating but increasingly integrating the island into the United States. The real danger, some leaders believed, was that they were taking the island toward assimilation and statehood.

This "irrational" fear of independence, Muñoz and others believed, must be the result of a "defect" in many Puerto Ricans: it is one thing to rationally reach the conclusion that independence will not work, as he himself had, but another to *fear* it. In Muñoz's view, this was tantamount to a demeaning fear of one's own freedom.

But there was a rational basis for that fear. In the 1930s, the Harvard-educated Pedro Albizu Campos, resenting that he was the victim of racial discrimination when assigned to a black regiment during World War I, became radically anti-American. A charismatic, powerful orator, he drew large crowds and media attention. But the Nationalist Party got only 5,257 votes in the 1932 election, a little over 1 percent. He immediately renounced the electoral system, calling for a campaign of violence similar to that of Sinn Fein and the Irish Republican Army.

Two Nationalists assassinated the American police chief in San Juan in 1936; others attempted to assassinate island leaders and federal judges. In 1937, a violent confrontation in Ponce left eighteen Nationalists and two policemen dead. In 1950, Nationalists attempted to assassinate Governor Muñoz during an islandwide uprising that caused twenty-eight deaths, among them sixteen Nationalists. Two days later, on November 1, 1950, two Nationalists attempted to assassinate President Harry Truman in Washington. On March 1, 1954, in Congress, Nationalists shot and wounded five members of the House; all survived.

At the beginning, Albizu Campos and his party saw themselves as part of the nationalist movement in Europe: they were admirers of Mussolini fascism and adopted the black shirts of Franco in Spain. By the 1960s, the radical independence advocates turned to the Frantz Fanon anticolonialist national liberation movement and to the Cuban Revolution. Imprisoned and twice pardoned by Governor Muñoz, Albizu Campos, diagnosed as paranoid, spent the last nine years of his life in a hospital and died on April 21, 1965.

In the late 1960s, the independence movement split. Rubén Berríos, a young Yale-educated lawyer, became the Independence Party's leader. While anti-American and revering Albizu as a patriotic martyr, he favored electoral participation, aligning his party with Social Democratic parties in Latin America and Europe.

Dissidents formed the Puerto Rico Socialist Party, which described itself as Marxist-Leninist and aligned itself with the Cuban Revolution. The Castro government recognized it as Puerto Rico's legitimate representative with a "consular office" in Havana. It also had UN recognition. Dedicated to the class struggle, the PSP gained significant influence in labor unions. It originally refused to participate in elections, but it did in 1976 and 1980, failing to reach a single percentage point.

In the 1960s, a clandestine group began to carry out terrorist attacks on the island and the mainland. According to the U.S. government it was trained by Cuba and was a part of the Cuban Revolution. Having carried out over one hundred bombings and other terrorist attacks, the Armed Forces of National Liberation, or FALN, later known as the Macheteros, was considered the most dangerous terrorist group in the United States. In 1979, its convicted leader, William Morales, escaped from a hospital prison and was given sanctuary in Cuba.

In the early twentieth century, island leaders like Luis Muñoz Rivera insisted that their ideal was independence but that the island was simply too small and too poor to survive economically. Then, in midcentury, the fear was that an independent Puerto Rico could suffer the fate of so many Latin American republics under the yoke of dictatorships, especially one as brutal as that of Generalissimo Rafael Trujillo in the neighboring Dominican Republic. Now the fear was that the island would become another Cuba. For many Puerto Ricans, there was nothing irrational in associating independence with the history of violence on the island and of dictatorship in Latin America.

Puerto Ricans, however, had another reason for opposing independence. They saw on TV the horrendous images of bodies washing up on the beaches, of Haitians, Dominicans, men, women, and children, attempting to get into the United States. In late 2018, they saw the images of thousands of Central Americans trekking toward the U.S. border. Throughout the Trump administration they saw the call for a wall to keep them out. As American citizens, however, Puerto Ricans know that to escape the island's economic crisis, to rejoin family on the mainland, to seek a good job, they have only to buy a plane ticket.

In the 1950s, the hundreds of thousands of Puerto Ricans, most from the poorest rural areas, who migrated to the mainland diffused the population explosion, which was vital to the island's economic growth. After 2005, the migration consisted mostly of young professionals seeking to escape from the economic recession and then the devastation of Hurricane María. The island lost much of its productive population.

But Puerto Ricans on the mainland and the island see themselves as one family, in large part because it is so easy and inexpensive for Puerto Ricans to come and go between the island and mainland and because of their particularly strong bond with their ethnic identity. Those on the mainland outnumber those on the island by over a million. For Puerto Ricans, independence is more than a political or economic issue; it means separating the greater Puerto Rican family.

Despite its small electoral support, independence is an integral part of the island's status politics. It is supported by vocal intellectuals, academics, students, journalists, and important cultural and professional organizations. Puerto Rican student organizations at U.S. universities, seeing mainland Puerto Ricans as another minority group that is the victim of discrimination, also generally favor independence.

When the Independence Party fails to get enough votes to retain its legal status, the governments of either of the two major parties quickly restore it. Puerto Ricans, regardless of how they vote, *expect* the Independence Party to be on the ballot and the independence option in plebiscites. The island constitution guarantees minority representation in the legislature regardless of the votes: the Independence Party is represented in the House.

There is still another argument made by statehood as well as independence advocates. Since Puerto Rico is a colony under the constitutional territorial clause, Congress can unilaterally do whatever it wants with Puerto Rico, including making it independent. This is what inspired the nationalist violence and has been the hope of some independentistas. Independence will not be achieved at the ballot box, but conditions on the island and in the United States will convince the U.S. government to decree it.

But will Puerto Rico, in some future, turn toward independence? In Puerto Rico's political status world, all options are equal; but in the island reality, they are not. There is the reality of U.S. citizenship. In 1967, the U.S. Supreme Court ruled that Congress cannot involuntarily strip American citizenship from a citizen.

This points at an essential and personal difference between the prospect of statehood or independence. Puerto Ricans can easily be persuaded that if the island becomes a state, they have nothing to lose: indeed, if the statehood advocates are right, they have much to gain in federal funds and programs. But independence, as emotionally appealing as the calls to patriotism and nationalism are, means voluntarily giving up American citizenship and everything that goes with it. From abstract status ideology, it becomes real and personal. This is, of all factors, the fundamental basis of Puerto Rico's rejection or fear of independence. If statehood is economically unreal, then independence is politically unreal.

Commonwealth Status

In his memoirs, which were published posthumously in 1982, Muñoz pinpoints the exact moment in his 1940 campaign that became the genesis of commonwealth status. He was campaigning on the rural road between Río Grande and Palmer, talking to a small group of jíbaros, urging them not to sell their votes to the traditional parties, which repaid them by breaking their promises. The traditional parties made glowing promises of social and economic justice but sold out to the corporations that literally bought the elections, paying the jíbaros $2 for their vote.

"Trust me and my party to carry out a program of reforms that will improve your lives," Muñoz told them. But why should the jíbaros trust this man who was seen as having wasted his father Muñoz Rivera's legacy, a bohemian called by his friends El Vate, the Poet, and a political failure. But Muñoz sensed at this gathering that his message was resonating. Then he noticed the face of one jíbaro — the look of "doubt, fear, anguish." The man tried to express his feelings but could not. He said, "But, and if . . . ," and ran a finger across his neck. The others, who understood what he meant, nodded in agreement. Muñoz also understood: we agree with everything you are saying, but what if you bring about independence? Muñoz wrote that he never forgot the name of that "personally virile but politically terrified" worker: Nicanor Guerra.[3]

Muñoz made what he called in his memoirs "the great decision."[4] A few days later, campaigning before several hundred people at the Plaza de Armas in San Juan, a man cried out, asking what the Popular Democratic Party would do to demand independence if it won the elections. "I had no doubt about the answer . . . ," Muñoz wrote. "Political status is not at issue in the elections of 1940. A vote for the Popular Party will not be counted for or against any political status. They will be counted only in favor of the party's economic and social program."

The man who asked the question turned away, deeply disheartened. But, Muñoz continued, "it was at that moment that the Popular Party assured its victory in 1940 and assured what it was able to do in the next 30 years for that man and for all Puerto Rico."[5] This was the beginning of the "democratic revolution" that followed. He repeated the pledge in 1944, when his and Tugwell's reform was well under way. Muñoz went on to win overwhelmingly, reelected by landslides in 1948, 1952, and 1960. The economy took off. In 1948, Puerto Rico elected its governor for the first time. In 1952, it inaugurated its new status as a commonwealth.

The idea of a commonwealth was the result of a radical transformation within Muñoz. He had always put economic reform before political status.

He fervently favored independence, convinced that the capitalist United States would never permit radical reforms. The transformation began, as he told the economist Jude Wanniski in 1977, when he became convinced that under the Roosevelt New Deal the United States was no longer the enemy but now the ally of his program of reforms.[6]

But as he launched his new Popular Democratic Party in 1940, he faced a dilemma: while he and 90 percent of the leadership favored independence, 90 percent of Puerto Ricans rejected it. Everyone, of course, knew that he was an independentista, and it was obvious that if he campaigned for independence, he would lose.

But it was more than a political calculation. Muñoz had already begun to doubt, or as he put it, to "agonize," over whether independence *was* the solution to Puerto Rico's horrid economic conditions. And if not independence, as he was convinced that statehood was simply unrealistic, then what? The answer, Muñoz concluded, was to create an autonomous status. But this required a revolution of a different kind: a new political culture where status was not each party's ideology, its ideal, regardless of economic realities, but the practical solution to what had bedeviled Puerto Rico as the insoluble dilemma, ending the futile, sterile war between two unreal status options.

When the commonwealth was inaugurated on July 25, 1952, Muñoz believed that Puerto Rico was finally on its way to ending the status war. But when he retired in 1964, it became increasingly evident that he had failed.

Something didn't add up. In the late 1940s, he had beaten back a pro-independence rebellion within the leadership of his party, and by the 1950s, the independence vote began to decline. But the statehood surge began precisely after the creation of the commonwealth and the economy was growing as never before. It should have been the reverse. It should have been evident to everyone that the commonwealth was precisely the tool that worked, but it was not.

In 1954, just two years after the commonwealth was created, one of the founders of commonwealth status was concerned. University of Puerto Rico chancellor Jaime Benítez sent Muñoz an unusual letter. Throughout their lives close friends, Benítez rebuked Muñoz. In his annual legislative message, Muñoz had reiterated that the commonwealth was a work in process. But he went further, saying it was essential to its survival that it be significantly improved. This, Benítez said, was a grave mistake. Muñoz's insistence that survival depended on its "growth," he wrote, had the opposite effect: it weakened the commonwealth and undermined confidence, creating doubts and instability. "I find it unjustifiably risky to play a type of roulette where one risks losing a great deal more than what one wins if no one hits the right number."[7]

Benítez was using an argument Tugwell liked to use with Muñoz: if you want a plant to grow faster, don't pull it out by its roots to see what is wrong.

Muñoz ignored the advice.

In 1959, with the entry of Alaska and Hawaii into the Union having ignited the resurging statehood movement, Muñoz decided to return to Congress to correct the "defects" in the commonwealth but also with proposals for sweeping changes, giving the island full control over all matters not directly vital to the U.S. relationship. The creation of the commonwealth in 1952 had been relatively easy for Congress to understand: it consisted of amending the Jones Act, the existing organic act that established the Puerto Rico–U.S. relationship. Now Muñoz was asking for what seemed a different status that was very complicated and for some members of Congress constitutionally questionable.

Congress was confused. With the growing publicity in the United States and around the world about Puerto Rico's economic miracle, with the commonwealth working so well, why fix what was not damaged? The initiative failed. It was Muñoz's first defeat in Congress since becoming governor in 1948. Something had indeed changed.

Muñoz decided to try a different approach in 1962. "We are merely realistic," he liked to say.[8] The approach should be, he believed, to bring the status issue down from abstract, ideological politics to hard economic reality. The Status Commission created in 1964 by President Johnson and Muñoz had exactly this mission: to carry out a comprehensive, objective study of each status alternative, conducted by the best professionals in Puerto Rico and the United States.

The Status Commission was composed of island and U.S. political leaders and members of Congress. The study would be done by a large staff of economists, academics, and scholars. Numerous federal agencies submitted studies and reports; public hearings were held on the island

and in the United States. There was testimony from over a hundred witnesses, in addition to ten comprehensive background studies.

Muñoz expected that the professional and technical studies would finally confirm what to him was the evident reality, that statehood was not economically viable. The U.S. Bureau of the Budget reported that statehood would result in a net cost of $188 million. But the Status Commission's report, although prepared by the commonwealth-friendly staff director, Ben Stephansky, former U.S. ambassador to Bolivia, far from leading to the end of the status conflict, enflamed it by concluding that all status options were viable.

This was not, of course, what Muñoz wanted and expected. But it was not surprising. The commission, balanced with Puerto Rican political leaders with different status ideologies and members of Congress of both parties, was structured to be rigorously status neutral. It could not even imply that one option was superior or inferior to the others. It was considered essential for its credibility that its report and conclusions get the approval of its pro-statehood members, Luis A. Ferré and Miguel Angel García Méndez, as it did.

The Muñoz plan called for the first status plebiscite to be held in 1967. This was another change in his thinking. He had always opposed holding a status plebiscite. The 1951 referendum was limited to a yes or no vote on the creation of the commonwealth; there were no options. The original idea was that the commission's studies and report would "educate" the voters on the economic and other realities of the status conflict. Now Muñoz hoped for an overwhelming commonwealth victory over statehood. He campaigned on the slogan that he thought by now should be obvious to all Puerto Ricans: commonwealth was "the reality of the progress that we live."

But again he was disappointed. The commonwealth victory was comparable to the PDP landslides, getting 60 percent of the vote to statehood's 39 percent. But it was not the crushing, definitive victory that he wanted. Although the Statehood Republican Party boycotted the plebiscite, the Ferré-led United Statehooders exceeded the SRP vote three years before. The statehooders celebrated what they saw as a great victory. Days after, Ferré bolted from the Statehood Republican Party and converted his plebiscite movement into the New Progressive Party.

The following year, to everyone's shock, what the Muñoz generation, which had seen nothing but the political invincibility of Muñoz and the Popular Democratic Party, could not imagine happened. Ferré won the election; the statehood movement was in power and would go on to become the majority party.

Will the Commonwealth Survive?

By the beginning of the new millennium, it was obvious that support for commonwealth status was declining, if indeed even the leadership of the Popular Democratic Party still supported it. Muñoz retired in 1964. In 1980, he died at the age of eighty-two. Operation Bootstrap was killed by the elimination of Section 936. The statehood party was the majority party. High-level PDP leaders engaged in soul searching as to the purpose, the essence, of the commonwealth but could find no answer. This was a question no traditional party had ever had to ask itself. Statehood and independence are ideals that transcend any leader, any party, and are not questioned. And while the PDP leader who succeeded Muñoz, Rafael Hernández Colón, vigorously defended commonwealth status until his death on May 2, 2019, some PDP leaders joined the essential attack by statehood and independence advocates: commonwealth status must be discarded as "colonial."

No longer could commonwealth advocates use Munoz's 1967 plebiscite campaign slogan. Now the reality that Puerto Ricans lived was the economic and fiscal crisis. Nor could the Muñoz slogan be used in Washington. Members of Congress and administration officials who often were hard pressed to explain exactly what it is, or even if it fits into the U.S. Constitution, had defended commonwealth status if that was what the Puerto Ricans want and if it *works*. But as Puerto Rico kept electing the statehood party, sending resident commissioners to Congress demanding statehood in thirty-four of the past fifty-one years, inevitably the support declined.

The Juridical War

The war against Puerto Rico's commonwealth status was always waged on two fronts. One front was the political parties whose opponents were clearly winning as commonwealth support declined. The other was the juridical front where politicians, lawyers, constitutional experts, and academics, in the United States as well as in Puerto Rico, battled over the legitimacy of commonwealth status. Could it exist within the American constitutional system? Or was *commonwealth* a word used by Muñoz and his followers to mislead Puerto Ricans?

Since Muñoz first went to Congress in 1950 to begin the process of creating the commonwealth, this was in fact an issue. In the juridical world, it was always seen as an "experiment," as Chief Justice Earl Warren described it soon after it was created, "perhaps the most notable American political experiment in our time."[9] U.S. constitutional experts and politicians were intrigued by the commonwealth status and the compact theory. The Harvard professor Carl J. Friedrich wrote in 1959, "Puerto Rico's unique achievement is a novel combination of freedom and justice. It is that because it does not fit the familiar patterns of colonial dependence or sovereign independence. . . . [E]xisting categories do not suffice for comprehending what has happened."[10]

Until that time, it was generally accepted that there were two ways to be part of the United States, as a state or as a territory, incorporated or unincorporated. Commonwealth was a third way. Puerto Rico would be united with the United States through a bilateral compact agreed to by both that could be changed or repealed only by mutual consent.

The argument against commonwealth status was that Congress never intended to enter into a "compact," only to allow Puerto Rico to adopt its own constitution.[11] Muñoz and his lawyers argued from the beginning of the congressional process that the purpose was not to replace the 1917 Jones Act with another "organic act" but to change the foundation of Puerto Rico's relation to the United States. That law, Law 600, not only authorized Puerto Rico to enact its constitution, but also represented a "compact."

The juridical battle began. Legal scholars and academics in Puerto Rico and the United States wrote that the congressional record showed that this was not the "congressional intent." Even if it had been, it was not constitutional, since one Congress cannot bind another; it cannot enter into a "bilateral compact." Political opponents insisted that all this was a Muñoz fantasy, that commonwealth was a myth.

Commonwealth advocates countered that Law 600 referred to itself "in the nature of a compact" and was in fact a compact because it required the approval of Puerto Rico to go into effect. The approval of the constitution, including changes made by both Puerto Rico and Congress, required mutual consent. Law 447, in which Congress gave its final approval, also called itself a "compact."

This was, at the beginning, U.S. policy, as explicitly declared when the United States told the United Nations that Puerto Rico was no longer a "non-self-governing territory," no longer a "colony." On November 27, 1953, the UN approved Resolution 748 declaring that "the people of Puerto Rico, by expressing their will in a free and democratic way, have created a new constitutional status."[12]

And up to the present, this is the argument of commonwealth supporters. As José A. Hernández Mayoral and Roberto Pratts argued in a October 29, 2020, case before the U.S. Supreme Court, numerous Court decisions have established the juridical legitimacy of the commonwealth: "With the creation of the commonwealth, Puerto Rico boasts a relationship with the United States that has no parallel in our history. . . . Public Law 600 allowed Puerto Rico to obtain state-like sovereignty through a popularly adopted constitution, while preserving its fiscal autonomy indispensable to maintain its government."[13]

But if the Justice Department letters regarding the plebiscites were a big blow to the statehood movement, the PDP and commonwealth supporters received an even worse blow from the U.S. government in the early 1990s, when the U.S. Justice Department began to reverse its policy of backing the constitutionality of the commonwealth. In 2005, President George W. Bush's Task Force on Puerto Rico's Status contradicted the essential constitutional underpinning of the commonwealth.

The bilateral compact, the Justice Department declared, does not exist. The law creating the commonwealth was effectively another "organic act." "To the extent," the report states, "a convenant to which the United States is a party stands on no stronger footing than an Act of Congress, it is for purposes of federal constitutional false, subject to unilateral alteration or revocable by subsequent Acts of Congress."[14] Just as Congress is free to amend or repeal any law, Congress is free to unilaterally amend or repeal Puerto Rico's status.

For the Justice Department, the answer to the Question at the heart of the "constitutional experiment" was clear: "The terms of the Constitution do not contemplate an option other than severing independence, statehood or territorial status."[15] That confirmed what the legal as well as the political commonwealth opponents had alleged from the beginning: "commonwealth" was the name Muñoz and the PDP gave the same colonial status Puerto Rico always had. Since then, the U.S. government and the media have referred to the island not as the commonwealth of Puerto Rico but as "the territory of Puerto Rico." In Puerto Rico, not only for the opponents, but for a growing number of its traditional supporters, it was now a "colonial commonwealth."

If there were still any doubts, the commonwealth opponents declared, they were dispelled when Congress in 2016 created the PROMESA Fiscal Board, asserting its sovereignty over Puerto Rico under the constitutional territorial clause. It empowered the Fiscal Board to overrule the island's elected government and for many was the definitive proof that the island was indeed a U.S. colony.

Commonwealth status, it seemed, had effectively ceased to exist.

Raymond Carr's Conclusion

In 1983, the Twentieth Century Fund decided to attempt to answer the question, is there a solution to Puerto Rico's political status issue? A liberal think tank founded in 1919, the Fund had long been involved in Puerto Rican issues. Governor Luis Muñoz Marín had been one of its trustees. Three of the Status Commission's staff members were trustees.

Due to the Fund's relationship with Muñoz, it was important that the study not be seen as favoring commonwealth or any other status. Searching for an obviously status-neutral author, the Fund decided to ask the noted British historian, Raymond Carr, a respected scholar and author on Spanish history and Oxford professor. In 1987, he was named warden of St. Antony's College at Oxford.

Carr underlined that if he were to undertake the study, he would be free to criticize commonwealth status and Muñoz himself, and he did.

Published in 1984, the study's title, *Puerto Rico: A Colonial Experiment*, made clear his starting point on the island's status.[16]

Reminiscent of Dr. Henry K. Carroll's 1899 mission and firsthand report as President William McKinley's special envoy to Puerto Rico, Carr lived for months on the island, researched much of the literature and important documents related to the status issue, and spoke extensively to the leaders of all the parties and political groups and many others. He found, as others had, that the history of the Puerto Rico–U.S. relationship is the history of misunderstanding of two distinct peoples, "two societies bound together since 1898 [that] do not fully understand each other." Carr focused a good part of his study on the relationship between status and economics, describing the benefits of commonwealth status and the drawbacks of statehood. He did not foresee violence in Puerto Rico like that at the time in Northern Ireland and threatened in Quebec.

The Fund's director, M. J. Rousset, in the book's introduction, anticipating Carr's conclusion, wrote that the status issue "is likely to continue for the rest of this century, and beyond."[17] Carr effectively confesses that he failed in his search for a solution. He had been trying to find something that did not in fact exist. "There are, a historian must conclude, problems whose intractability may appear to render them insoluble," he wrote.[18] But there is a solution.

The Solution

Toward the end of his life, Muñoz wrote in his memoirs, "I repeat it because it is the historical key that historically repeats itself. Status politics have always impeded the realization of the ideals of life and civilization."[19] It was the "great decision" of putting aside the status battle in the 1940s that made possible Operation Bootstrap and the "economic miracle."

Many in Puerto Rico, including commonwealth supporters, insist that it is absurd to believe that the island can return to Operation Bootstrap, to a strategy that belongs to another age, to a radically different Puerto Rico, a different United States, a different world.

But Puerto Rico's basic economic reality has not changed. As in 1940, Puerto Rico's fundamental illness is the lack of jobs. The island is near the bottom of all world economies, with a 37 percent labor participation rate. The essential strategy to create jobs has not changed. The answer is not more federal funds; it must be attracting private investment. As numerous studies have shown — the 1964 Status Report, the 1975 Tobin Report, the many PROMESA Fiscal Board reports — and as the island's private sector endlessly insists, there is no mystery; the island's viability depends today, as it has always depended, on making the island economically competitive again and on a single-minded Puerto Rico government determined to promote that advantage.

If returning to the golden era of Fomento is not possible, what made Operation Bootstrap work has not changed. Making Puerto Rico competitive again depends on the survival of the fundamental structure of Puerto Rico's economic relationship to the United States. But will this structure, commonwealth status, survive?

The answer to Carr's question — is there a solution to the status conflict? — is no if this refers to the ideological status battle. It is embedded in Puerto Rican culture. But beneath the ideological battle, there is a reality. The rise of Puerto Rico was possible because of its commonwealth status. This essential reality will not change. Statehood and independence will remain unrealistic options. So, in looking as far into the future as one can, Puerto Rico will remain in a commonwealth-autonomous relationship with the United States.

PART II

The Historical Context

CHAPTER TEN

A "Troubled" Relationship

"Relations between the United States and Puerto Rico have been troubled since Puerto Rico was acquired in the aftermath of the Spanish-American War," Twentieth Century Fund director M. J. Rousset wrote in the introduction to Raymond Carr's book, *Puerto Rico: A Colonial Experiment.*[1] For Americans asking how Puerto Rico fell into such a deep economic, fiscal, and political crisis, there is a deeper mystery: how did the United States itself fall into the troubled relationship in the first place?

"The subject of Puerto Rico," the naval historian Ivan Musicant wrote in *Empire by Default*, "hardly arose in American political and expansionist circles during the diplomatic activity that led up to the war." Instead, "prior to the war, all attention centered on Cuba, and the United States did not develop plans to annex Puerto Rico before the war, or indeed for some time thereafter."[2]

The Puerto Rico–U.S. relationship was born out of a sea of confusion, indecision, and conflict that in the following century would underscore the relationship. It was born out of a decision that has confounded historians as much as Puerto Ricans. Why the United States decided to take

177

Puerto Rico during the 1898 Spanish-American War is evident. Why, after the war, without a plan, a policy, a purpose, it decided to *keep* the island is not.

The purpose of the war was to liberate Cuba from Spain and end a long and brutal civil war that, dramatized by American sensationalist newspapers but also witnessed by members of Congress, had revolted the American public and ignited anti-Spanish war fever. The pacifist, irresolute President McKinley, who had tried hard to avoid war, finally relented.

McKinley and much of the United States insisted that the intention was not to create an overseas American colonial empire but humanitarian. In his war message to Congress, he pleaded, "In the name of humanity, in the name of civilization[,] . . . the [civil] war in Cuba must stop."[3] But as Musicant put it, it was a war by "default." Or as Stanley Karnow put it in his *America's Empire in the Philippines*, it was not that the United States *went* to war against Spain but that it "stumbled" into it.[4]

The United States made it clear that it had no intention to incorporate Cuba or the Philippines into the nation. Nor was there the intention to incorporate Puerto Rico, but while little thought was given to the island, a small number of military strategists and "imperialists," led by Theodore Roosevelt and Senator Henry Cabot Lodge, saw its great strategic value at the entrance to the Caribbean. They were concerned that the planners in Washington would overlook little Puerto Rico. When Roosevelt, who had resigned as assistant secretary of the navy to organize the Rough Riders to fight in Cuba, warned Lodge, "Do not make peace until we get Puerto Rico," Lodge replied, "Puerto Rico is not forgotten and we mean to have it."[5]

Through the centuries, the 3,515-square-mile island, one-twelfth the size of Cuba, had been poverty stricken and a drain on the Spanish imperial treasury. But it was coveted by Spain's European rivals for its location as the gateway to the New World. Almost from the 1493 discovery and colonization of the island, it was attacked, first by French privateers, then in the late 1500s and early 1600s repeatedly by large British and Dutch fleets. All failed. Spain built massive fortifications and several military roads but little else.

In spite of the lack of planning and sometimes chaos—Colonel Roosevelt had to fight to get on the ship to take the Rough Riders to Cuba, leaving behind their horses—the United States destroyed the Spanish navy and took Cuba and the Philippines with surprising ease. In Puerto Rico, the 8,000 Spanish regulars and especially the 7,000 to 9,000 local militiamen had little will to fight: the expected Spanish resistance rapidly crumbled. There were six engagements, in the end costing six American lives and leaving thirty-six Americans wounded. The operation had lasted only nineteen days. As Ambassador John Hay described it, it had been a "splendid little war."[6]

But what to do with Puerto Rico? The island's strategic value was particularly evident to Captain Alfred Mahan, the influential head of the Naval War College. His 1890 work, *The Influence of Sea Power upon History*, and succeeding books made him highly influential in Europe and in the emerging "imperialist" movement in the United States. A lesson of history, Mahan wrote, was that to be a great world power, a nation needs a great navy that needs coaling stations around the world.[7] For the influential Anti-Imperialism League, the Spanish-American War was conducted to mimic the British Empire, which had such coaling stations.[8]

Not only did Puerto Rico have in San Juan a magnificent harbor, but Mahan's design for making America a great global power required an "Isthmian Canal" linking the American Atlantic and Pacific coasts. The need was dramatized by the newly commissioned battleship *USS Oregon*, making its way from the Pacific coast to join the American fleet off Cuba. It had to travel 13,792 miles, which took sixty-six days.

Mahan foresaw that once the United States built the canal Puerto Rico would be vital for its defense. He wrote in his 1918 book, *Lessons of the War with Spain*, that the naval bases in Puerto Rico were as important for the protection of the Panama Canal as British bases in Malta were to protect Egypt and the Suez Canal: "It would be very difficult for a transatlantic state to maintain operations in the Western Caribbean with a United States fleet based upon Puerto Rico and the adjacent islands."[9] But once they took Puerto Rico and its San Juan harbor, the American soldiers crossed the island, along with members of the U.S. media, among them several of the most famous journalists, and found a level of poverty and backwardness that they had never seen before and an ethnically different, Spanish-speaking, racially mixed people. The question of what to do with Puerto Rico became what to do with one million Puerto Ricans.

The Puerto Rican Reaction

Governor General Manuel Macías y Casado ended 405 years of Spanish rule at noon on October 18, 1898. As the Spanish flag was lowered over La Fortaleza, one of the greatest colonial empires in history came to an end.

As a Spaniard, Macías had a deeply personal reason for being depressed. It was more than the end of the Spanish Empire; Spain was now a minor power, humiliated by what was considered in most of Europe a second-rate, "mongrel" nation of cowboys and moneylenders. Spaniards resented the government's mishandling of the war and its outrageous deception that Spain was winning.[10] From the glory days of the conquistadors, the transport ships were now bringing back thousands of defeated, emaciated, and sick Spanish soldiers. For years, Spaniards referred to the Spanish-American War as El Desastre, the Disaster.

Having to turn over Puerto Rico had been particularly painful. During the wars of independence in the nineteenth century in South and Central America, only little Puerto Rico had remained steadfastly loyal. While the Cubans were fighting for independence, Puerto Rican leaders traveled to Madrid seeking more self-government and at the same time integrating more into Spanish politics and government.

A week before the American invasion, on July 17, the island's political leader, Luis Muñoz Rivera, son of a Spanish officer who had fought in Venezuela and migrated to Puerto Rico, elected head of the new government under the Autonomy Charter, assured Governor General Macías, "We are Spaniards and wrapped in the Spanish flag we will die!"[11] But as Macías lowered the Spanish flag, he and the other Puerto Rican leaders did not.

In past centuries Puerto Ricans had demonstrated their loyalty fighting alongside Spanish troops against the British and Dutch. But now they welcomed the twenty-five thousand American troops crossing the island as liberators.

Three days after landing in Guánica, the Americans proclaimed that this was indeed their purpose. General Nelson Miles, in full military dress, entered Ponce and issued a proclamation: "We have not come to make war upon the people of a country that for centuries has been oppressed, but on the contrary to bring you the protection, not only to yourselves but to your property, to promote your prosperity, and to bestow upon you the blessing of the liberal institutions of our government."[12]

This was almost identical to the American proclamation halfway around the world to Filipinos. But Puerto Rican leaders saw it as a message from the president of the United States to them. Most of the political leaders, including Muñoz Rivera, who had been criticized by other politicians as being excessively Spanish, interpreted the proclamation as a commitment to incorporate Puerto Rico into the United States, leading eventually to statehood. Along with José Celso Barbosa, the black Puerto Rican physician who got his degree at the University of Michigan, Muñoz Rivera welcomed the perceived promise of incorporation. Barbosa created the local Republican Party, declaring that its goal was statehood.

For Barbosa and others, the Americans represented not only economic and political liberation, but freedom from the old Spanish racism. Until the previous century, to marry a Spaniard, a Puerto Rican had to take a blood test to prove there was no trace of Jewish or black blood. Long considered the leader of the autonomy movement, Muñoz Rivera, insisting that his personal choice was independence, now favored "territorial status" leading to statehood.

Muñoz Rivera and Barbosa had a textbook understanding of the American system of government. To them, statehood meant, not assimilation, but achieving their life goal of self-government. States, after all, were "sovereign"; "states rights" gave them autonomy. Muñoz Rivera went further, arguing that as a state, Puerto Rico would effectively achieve independence. For them and other leaders, statehood meant becoming a "republic within a republic."[13]

A century of mutual misunderstanding had begun. The island leaders and many others had misread General Miles's proclamation. In Washington there was no plan as to the island's future status, much less to eventually make it a state.

But why not, as with Cuba and the Philippines, commit to eventual independence? There were some political leaders in the United States, like the vocal anti-imperialist Carl Schurz and others, who loudly called for it. It was evident that the war had made the United States a world empire, but McKinley insisted that the war had been fought on humanitarian grounds. He was influenced by the reports of American military officers on the island: "the cultural shock of encountering a poverty-stricken population, two-thirds of whom were illiterate with living standards inconceivable outside the Negro South."[14]According to Carr, General George W. Davis, the military governor, "was deeply distressed by Puerto Rican poverty and did what he could to relieve it."[15]

In 1899, President McKinley named a civilian, the Reverend Henry K. Carroll, as his commissioner for Puerto Rico. For several months, Carroll visited the entire island, remote rural areas as well as towns. He listened not only to the political leaders but also to hundreds of workers, businessmen, professionals, and academics on every economic, social, and political topic. Ultimately, Carroll issued an eight-hundred-page report describing in great detail the overwhelming backwardness that he witnessed. But despite this grim scenario, he was optimistic that Puerto Ricans were in fact better prepared for self-government than most Latin Americans.

McKinley and Congress received contradictory recommendations. The military officers, most of whom were not professional soldiers, like Carroll, sympathized with the Puerto Ricans. But they disliked and distrusted the political leadership and insisted that the island was not ready for self-government.

As Congress was engaged in the unprecedented and difficult task of setting up a civil government, it was influenced by General Davis, who strongly believed that Americans, having removed the Spanish government, now had a moral obligation not to abandon the uneducated Puerto Rican masses to the mercy of the political elite bred in Latin traditions incompatible with democratic practices.[16] He was referring to leaders such as Muñoz Rivera who seemed steeped in the evils of Spanish politics. What Puerto Rico needed, he argued, in addition to immediate economic and social relief, was a long period of American democratic "tutelage."

Carroll urged the opposite: what Puerto Ricans needed was not tutelage but the opportunity to govern themselves "by having . . . responsibilities laid upon them, by learning from their blunders."[17] Reporting that Puerto Ricans *could* become Americans, Carroll endorsed American citizenship.

As Anders Stephanson put it, "Once the future of the territories had been settled, no single theme so dominated the debate as that of 'duty.' It sparked one of McKinley's very few pithy formulations. 'Duty determines destiny.'"[18] Carroll's report reinforced his attitude as a pious Methodist and patriotic American: having taken the island, it was the Americans' humanitarian duty to help it overcome centuries of Spanish political and economic backwardness. In 1899, the humanitarian responsibility became even greater as the island was devastated by Hurricane San Ciriaco. Wasn't it a dereliction of duty for Americans to turn their backs on a destitute people that had greeted them as liberators?

On December 10, 1898, Spain and the United States signed the Treaty of Paris, officially ending the war. The treaty ceded Puerto Rico to the United States as compensation and decreed that Congress would determine its status. But McKinley made his decision: the United States would keep Puerto Rico. In secret instructions to civilian commissioners he sent to the island, he wrote that the island would "become the territory of Puerto Rico."[19]

But what did this mean? The US. Constitution declares, "The Congress shall have Power to dispose of and make all needful Rules and Regulations respecting the Territory and all other Property belong to the United States."[20] As the United States expanded westward to the Pacific, "territory" was the status of lands owned by the United States, populated increasingly by Americans and immigrants, to be governed by Congress until it met the demographic, political, and economic conditions to enter the Union as a state.

But while there was never a question as to the future status of the "territories," when the United States decided to keep Puerto Rico, it had no idea as to its future status, no intention to make it a state. What did McKinley have in mind? Some historians believe that just as he stumbled into the Spanish-American War and decided to take the Philippines without being able to locate it on a map, he stumbled into this fateful decision, setting off the century of the troubled relationship.

Now in Puerto Rico and the Philippines "the U.S. found itself exercising severing authority over several million inhabitants of alien races, unaccustomed to Anglo-Saxon law or institutions, many of them yet incapable of full self government."[21] The United States had no experience in the organization and administration of offshore colonies; indeed, it refused to accept the fact that it was now a colonial power. What, after all, was the gain for the United States? As it did in Cuba, it could have had in Puerto Rico the naval base Captain Mahan coveted without taking over the entire island and its population. The question Puerto Ricans asked was, what *is* our political status?

"Mr. Nobody from Nowhere"

Congress approved the 1900 Foraker Act to establish civil government. It bitterly disappointed the island leadership. The law failed to give the island the self-government that the political elite expected, but even more important to them, it left the island without a political status. At the congressional hearing, the influential businessman José Hanna, who had lobbied for the American invasion, lamented, "We are Mr. Nobody from Nowhere. We have no political status, no civil rights."[22]

In Washington, the Foraker Act was seen as unprecedentedly generous. Although it created a colonial, U.S.-appointed government, it was pointed out that the island was given more self-government, an elected lower house of an insular legislature, than had existed in past territories. Above all, the act was seen as economically generous, granting federal tax exemption and free trade. U.S. excise taxes on several Puerto Rican goods were rebated to the island, providing a major source of revenue when the island became a big rum producer.

But nothing was further from the minds of the island's political leadership than "economic generosity." Their goal was full self-government, a totally elected legislature. Carroll had warned McKinley and Congress, "[The Puerto Ricans] may be poor but they are proud and sensitive, and could be bitterly disappointed if they found that they had been delivered from an oppressive yoke to be put under a tutelage which proclaimed their inferiority."[23]

Carroll was right: the island leadership insisted that the Foraker Act was an insulting manifestation that Americans did indeed consider the Puerto Rican leadership inferior, incapable of self-government. The great expectations of the American invasion had resulted in the island possessing far less self-government than it had under the Spanish Autonomy Pact. Instead of delivering General Miles's promised "blessings of the liberal institutions of our government," the Americans delivered colonialism.[24]

Muñoz Rivera's dominant Federal Party denounced the act as "unworthy of the Americans that impose it, and the Puerto Ricans who have to endure it." And although Barbosa's Republican Party accepted the bill as necessary American "tutelage" to prepare Puerto Ricans for statehood, it was also disappointed. The act decreed that Puerto Ricans were "citizens of Puerto Rico," but what was Puerto Rico? As José Hanna had feared, effectively without citizenship, Puerto Ricans had become Mr. Nobody from Nowhere.

Three years later, the Supreme Court, in the famous Insular Cases, resolved the constitutional issue by creating a new status: Puerto Rico was an "unincorporated territory." Unlike an "incorporated territory," the island was not headed toward eventual statehood. The decision as to what "fundamental rights" of the Constitution applied would be made by Congress. The Constitution, according to the Court, "did not follow the flag."[25]

For island leaders, the decision confused the status issue even more. A dissenting opinion by Chief Justice Melville Fuller agreed with them: the island was left "like a disembodied shade."[26] As an unincorporated territory, Puerto Rico belonged to but was not a part of the United States. It was *annexed* but not *incorporated.* The United States found itself in uncharted constitutional waters, raising questions "among the most difficult the Supreme Court has ever faced, calling as they did for the application of constitutional principles entirely unforeseen by the framers of the Constitution."[27]

But while Puerto Rico's political leadership decried the lack of self-government provided in the Foraker Act and what seemed to them the obscurity of the Insular Cases, the Court's decisions left intact the two elements that were indispensable to the economy and what in the following century evolved into the essential structure of the U.S.-Puerto Rico relationship: federal tax exemption and free trade.

The United States took and kept the island in large part for its geographic location. Now it had created a political status for the island. But there remained a question: what to do with the million people on the island.

What to Do with the Puerto Ricans

At the beginning the answer seemed evident: urgently attack the deplorable, inhumane conditions in which Puerto Ricans were living, made even worse by 1899's Hurricane San Ciriaco. The initial military governments began building roads, hospitals, and schools and eradicating the endemic diseases that made so many Puerto Ricans seem so passive. At the same time, the United States launched the "tutelage" policy to prepare Puerto Ricans for self-government, teaching them how democratic institutions, clean elections, and effective government functioned. There were setbacks. Under the military governors, attempts to hold municipal elections degenerated into verbal and physical violence and had to be suspended and attempted again.

"Tutelage" was in fact "Americanization." It was decreed that all instruction in the public schools would be in English. Scores of young, idealistic American men and women teachers came to the island, a kind of early Peace Corps, many to live in remote, isolated rural areas and teach barefoot children. Decades later, it became evident that the English-only education policy not only did not work, but seriously damaged the entire educational program. The children did not learn English or much else.

From the beginning, there was support for making Puerto Ricans American citizens. The Carroll Report recommended it. Senator Joseph Foraker strongly supported it and included it in his original bill. But he and others began to wonder if citizenship would subject the island to full federal taxation. Faced with the doubt, citizenship was removed from the bill.

In 1906, President Roosevelt sent a message to Congress calling for full American citizenship. Members of Congress regularly introduced citizenship legislation. But it was not until the 1916 Jones Act replaced the Foraker Act that citizenship was granted. Although the act also extended self-government with a fully elected legislature with substantial powers over the still-appointed American governor, the bill sparked another bitter political fight on the island.

Congress assumed that it was granting what Puerto Ricans wanted. But Muñoz Rivera, the island's resident commissioner in Congress, was conflicted. His dominant Union Party divided into two factions, one favoring and the other opposing citizenship. He himself seemed divided emotionally. In a long speech delivered on the House floor, Muñoz Rivera, who had forced himself to learn English, again made clear his personal preference for self-rule leading to independence. But he added that he would accept citizenship if Congress offered statehood. Members of

Congress, always confused about island politics, were again baffled: was Muñoz Rivera for or against citizenship?

A month after returning to Puerto Rico, on November 15, 1916, Muñoz Rivera died. President Wilson signed the Jones Act on March 2, 1917. Given the option of rejecting citizenship, 287 Puerto Ricans did. Pro-independence leaders have always dismissed this, alleging it was a false option, since rejecting it meant falling back into the Mr. Nobody from Nowhere limbo. But there was no question that nearly all Puerto Ricans saw citizenship as a boon.

The Jones Act gave Puerto Rico an elected legislature with power over the budget and appointment of several cabinet members. It also retained the vital federal tax exemption and free trade. But this was not the full self-rule the leaders wanted. And now the leaders argued over what exactly were the consequences of American citizenship. Had Congress, in fact if not intentionally, as some of the Union Party leaders and independence advocates insisted, sealed the island's future status by closing the door to eventual independence? On the other side, the statehood advocates believed that in granting citizenship Congress effectively converted the island into an "incorporated territory," guaranteeing eventual statehood.

Once again the question ended up in the U.S. Supreme Court. It held that Puerto Rico remained an unincorporated territory, and that in approving the Jones Act Congress did not intend to put Puerto Rico on the road to statehood. If Congress had intended to make this irreversible decision, with all its political and economic implications, it would have done so *explicitly*, not by inference.[28] Citizenship, the Court ruled, did not convert the island into an incorporated territory.

And again the difficulty and complexity of fitting Puerto Rico into the U.S. constitutional system became apparent. Few American leaders had wrestled with the consequences of the Spanish-American War as much as William Taft. President McKinley named him the first civil governor of the Philippines in 1901. After serving as the twenty-seventh president of the United States, in 1921, President Harding appointed him Chief Justice of the Supreme Court. Referring to the 1922 opinion on Puerto Rico's political status, he wrote, "Few questions have been the subject of such discussion and dispute in our country as the status of the territories acquired from Spain in 1899."[29]

The Root of the Political Status Conflict

The granting of American citizenship, while it did not change the island's status, did change the nature of the Puerto Rico status conflict. Disappointed by the Supreme Court ruling, statehood advocates insisted that as American citizens, Puerto Ricans were being denied the rights enjoyed by fellow citizens on the mainland. Puerto Ricans, they said, were second-class citizens. Some went further, insisting that while citizenship did not incorporate the island, Puerto Ricans now had a *right* to statehood.

The United States saw it differently. The conflicting perception of rights went back to 1898, when Secretary of War Elihu Root wrote that as "citizens of Puerto Rico," the islanders had the right to demand not to be deprived of life, liberty, or property without due process, but they did not have the right to determine their form of government or their status. Now the United States responded that American citizenship did not change this: Puerto Ricans were not being denied rights, for there is no such thing as a right to statehood. Statehood is a concession—a power exercised exclusively by Congress and the president.

There was another change in Puerto Rico's status politics. From the beginning of the relationship to this day, for many island leaders and others there has never been a mystery about why the Americans took and kept Puerto Rico or about its political status. One word explains it all: colonialism.

But by midcentury several leaders began to question if this was true. What was in it for Americans? On February 10, 1946, Senate president Luis Muñoz Marín wrote a long article in *El Mundo*, insisting that colonialism simply made no sense for the Americans. He compared it to European colonialism: the 110 million inhabitants of Britain, France, and Belgium controlling 700 million inhabitants in their colonial empires. There was a reason: they believed that their high standard of living depended on their empires.

But why would 140 million Americans, among the most prosperous people in the world, want to control 2 million Puerto Ricans, among the poorest? Clearly the American standard of living does not depend on keeping Puerto Rico a colony. Of course, Muñoz went on, American compa-

nies make profits on the island, but in the past decade Puerto Rico has received substantially more in U.S. funds than have left the island in private
profits. And the United States does not need to "own" the island to have
naval bases on it: it has bases all over the Caribbean, Cuba, the Dominican
Republic, Trinidad, Panama, and other Central American countries.

"The case of Puerto Rico, as I have said, is peculiar," Muñoz wrote.
"It does not mold itself to the general design of colonial cases. The United
States does not possess Puerto Rico by the need to better its standard
of living. The United States possess Puerto Rico by mistake. Mistake
of the Spanish-American War, corrected in Cuba, to be corrected in
Puerto Rico."[30]

Puerto Rico was, of course, a colony in that it did not have full self-
government, under its own constitution, until 1952, when Muñoz and
Congress created the autonomous commonwealth. But this question —
is the history of the Puerto Rico relationship to the United States a history of colonialism? — is at the core of what became a century of miscommunication and misunderstanding. That in turn is at the core of Puerto
Rico's status politics.

CHAPTER ELEVEN

A Century of Miscommunication
and Misunderstanding

A key to the question of what went wrong in the U.S.–Puerto Rico relationship is that they are "two societies, *bound together* since 1898, [that] do not fully understand each other."[1] It has been a century of miscommunication and misunderstanding. Americans have misunderstood the Puerto Ricans, their politics, their reactions. The Puerto Ricans have misunderstood the Americans even when their intention was to benefit them. Americans and Puerto Ricans speak different languages. But even speaking the same language, they have misunderstood each other as to the meaning of words and concepts vital to the U.S.–Puerto Rico relationship.

In 1906, President Theodore Roosevelt, visiting the island on his return from the Panama Canal, declared, "We are giving them [Puerto Ricans] good government and the island is prospering."[2] Puerto Rican leaders saw it differently: without self-government and American citizenship, Puerto Ricans saw themselves still as "Mr. Nobody from Nowhere."

In 1909, President William Taft described Puerto Rico as "the favorite daughter of the United States." The Puerto Rican–controlled House of Delegates, in a spat with the American governor over judicial appointments, refused to approve the government budget. Taft sent a message to Congress describing in detail all the things the Americans had done for Puerto Rico. "To him," the historian Morales Carrión writes, the problem was that the Americans "had been too generous . . . [and] the ungrateful colonials must be called to order."[3]

Americans had reasons to believe their rule was a success. Dr. Bailey K. Ashford, who came to the island during the Spanish-American War as a young lieutenant and stayed, discovered that ringworm was causing the anemia afflicting thousands of Puerto Ricans. It explained why Puerto Ricans looked, as Roosevelt had described them in 1906, so "pathetic and childlike."[4] Ashford's discovery cured 300,000 islanders — one-third of the population. The island's death rate plunged to twenty-two per thousand. After serving in World War I, he returned to the island and founded what became the School of Tropical Medicine. Ashford became the father of public health on the island.

From the start the economy improved. Free trade with the United States increased: exports by 400 percent from 1901 to 1910, rose from $17.5 million to $68.5 million. There was an influx of private capital for tobacco but mostly for sugar production. Most dramatic was the American education drive that had begun under the military government. By 1901, the number of students had increased to 42,070 in 874 common schools; by 1910, there were 114,367 students in 1,912 schools.

In Washington it seemed evident that the vast majority of Puerto Ricans were grateful. There was a statehood party. Santiago Iglesias, the Spanish-born militant recognized as the father of the Puerto Rico labor movement, freed from El Morro prison by the Americans in 1898, was vocally pro-American.

In 1919, President Wilson received glowing reports from the appointed governors. Governor Arthur Yager, who was named by Wilson in 1912 and would become the longest-serving American governor, reported in 1919 that the progress on the island could "not be equaled by any people anywhere in the world in the same length of time." He was most proud of the fact that of the 5,943 government workers, only 208 were

American—many of them young teachers who migrated to the island. And he predicted an even better future: "The next two decades will see even more wonderful progress and development."[5]

What, then, was the truth? Was it an example of American enlightenment or an example of misrule and economic exploitation, a dismal "broken pledge"—the title of an influential 1931 book by Bailey W. Duffie and Justine W. Duffie denouncing what it described as American exploitation?[6]

For young Luis Muñoz Marín, writing in U.S. newspapers and magazines and in his father's newspaper, *La Democracia*, the statistics of progress may have been accurate, but they did not describe the reality of the extreme poverty, of the exploitation of big sugar corporations paying the plantation workers 55 cents a day, in some cases 35 cents, and on the coffee farms, 30 cents. What to the Americans seemed desperately needed economic development, for the critics was capitalist exploitation. In an article in the *American Mercury*, Muñoz denounced "the development of large scale absentee-owned sugar estates, the rapid curtailment in the planting of coffee . . . and the concentration of cigar manufacturing in the hands of American trust" that have combined "to make Puerto Rico a land of beggars and millionaires, of flattering statistics and distressing realities."[7]

Successes such as Dr. Ashford's breakthrough discovery, the dramatic reduction in diseases and improvements in sanitation, triggered what economists came to see as Puerto Rico's most fundamental ill: a population explosion, growing almost 30 percent in a decade, from 1.1 million in 1910 to 1.3 million in 1920. By 1940, it would reach 2 million. In fact, both sides were right: the statistics of progress and improvement were correct, but unable to keep up with the runaway population growth, Puerto Rico was not progressing but moving backward.

Some Puerto Ricans, including the young Muñoz and later Moscoso, began to promote birth control, provoking the outrage of the Catholic Church. In 1946, as Operation Bootstrap was beginning, Muñoz dramatically proclaimed that unless the island arrested its runaway population growth—projected to reach 4 million by 2000—his economic and social reforms would fail.[8] Only rapid economic growth, he argued, could defuse the population bomb and avoid a catastrophe.

But even the recognition of population growth as the root cause of Puerto Rico's ills provoked political controversy. This argument, critics said, shifted the blame for Puerto Rico's dismal condition from the Americans, from "colonialism," to the Puerto Ricans themselves.

Are Puerto Ricans "Ungrateful"?

In 1928, it seemed that the unflappable President Calvin Coolidge had snapped. A year after his May 21, 1927, solo flight across the Atlantic, Charles Lindbergh flew into Puerto Rico and was honored at a joint session of the island legislature. He was asked by the House and Senate leaders to take a message to President Coolidge, who had recently attended the sixth Inter-American Conference in Havana.

The message was written in a typical island rhetorical style and respectfully repeated a plea often made by island leaders, that the United States finally end the island's unacceptable colonial status: "Grant us the freedom that you enjoy, for which you struggled, which you worship, which we deserve and you have promised."[9] Signed by the pro-independence and pro-statehood legislative leaders, "freedom" meant either one.

Coolidge could have, as had past presidents, ignored the message as typical Puerto Rican political posturing. But because it was delivered by a national hero and received media attention, he reacted with indignation. No, he shot back in a long letter, Puerto Rico is enjoying the most liberal status in its history. The United States gives the island more internal self-government than that of any state, in fact, more powers of government than Puerto Ricans are prepared for. Listing all the things the Americans had done and accomplished in the three decades, Coolidge pointedly declared that it was not true that Puerto Rico is "a mere subjected colony." He ended with advice to island leaders: come back down to earth and make petitions "that may be granted without a denial of such hope."[10]

In the United States, the word *colony*, ubiquitous in island politics, was unacceptable. "What distinguishes American colonialism," wrote Raymond Carr, "is that Congress refused to admit it possessed a colony."[11] Now the word "waved a red flag" that infuriated the famously "silent" president.[12] As with President Taft twelve years earlier, Coolidge seemed personally offended by what seemed Puerto Rican ingratitude.

The Two Hurricanes

In 1928, there were what Morales Carrion called "two hurricanes" that settled the issue of whether Puerto Rico was an American success or a shameful failure. The first was San Felipe, which struck the island on September 13, 1928, leaving three hundred dead and half a million homeless and wiping out the coffee industry. The hurricane, of course, could not be blamed on the Americans, but like all big hurricanes in Puerto Rico, it also had the effect of temporarily peeling away the political rhetoric and the official reports, exposing the cold reality of how Puerto Ricans lived.

The other "hurricane" was President Herbert Hoover's appointment of Theodore Roosevelt Jr. as governor. The forty-two-year-old eldest son of his famous father had followed in his footsteps, serving also as assistant secretary of the navy. After Puerto Rico, he went on to become governor of the Philippines and to distinguished service in World War II, rising to brigadier general and earning a posthumous Medal of Honor.

After Hurricane San Felipe, Roosevelt wrote an article in the *New York Herald Tribune* titled "Children of Famine," in which he wrote, "Riding through the hills, I have stopped at farm after farm where lean, underfed women and sickly men repeated again and again the same story—little food and no opportunity to get more."[13] In spite of the vast improvement in public health resulting from Dr. Ashford's work, he wrote, "we were and are a prey to diseases of many kinds. Our death rate from this disease was 4½ times the death rate in the continental United States. Our death rate from malaria was 2½ times the rate. . . . Some 35,000 people in our island are now suffering from tuberculosis, some 20,000 from malaria, and some 60,000 from hookworm. This condition is all the more deplorable because the climate here is exceptionally healthy."[14]

After the hurricane, followed in 1929 by the Great Depression, Roosevelt's description of the suffering in Puerto Rico was not surprising. But contrary to what his father had described in 1906, Roosevelt was convinced that he was witnessing American failure. Before arriving in Puerto Rico, he was influenced by Muñoz, meeting and befriending him. He also came to a conclusion different from his father's regarding the Spanish-American War. He agreed with the journalist Walter Lippmann that the "mistakes" of the United States had left it unprepared to become a world power.[15]

In his 1937 book, *Colonial Policies of the United States*, while recognizing American efforts in Puerto Rico, the road building, health, and educational programs, Roosevelt saw that the attempt to Americanize the Puerto Rican people had failed: "The hopeless drive to remodel Puerto Ricans so that they should become similar in language, habits and thoughts to continental Americans" was a mistake. Puerto Ricans were not learning English and were not assimilating. Unlike other Americans who assumed that the island would eventually become a state, he believed that it was economically unrealistic: the island would not be able to bear the weight of federal taxation.[16]

The only possible solution, he wrote, was for the island to seek some form of "dominion" status: somewhere between independence and statehood. This was an idea that had floated around for years but had mostly been dismissed by island leaders, including a younger Muñoz. Two decades later, however, it was the precursor of the Muñoz-led Puerto Rico creation of autonomous commonwealth status.

Roosevelt had arrived in Puerto Rico to tackle his job with his father's "great zeal and gusto." Learning Spanish, he became personally involved in the suffering of the Puerto Rican poor. But when he left the island in 1929, Morales Carrión wrote, "he had grown tired and sick of the politicians and of the people themselves."[17] He felt defeated, as a decade later did others who had also tried to help Puerto Rico: his distant relative, Franklin Delano Roosevelt and the New Dealers.

The New Deal

The old idea in Washington that Puerto Ricans were ungrateful for American generosity and goodwill resurfaced powerfully when a giant effort was made to extend the New Deal to Puerto Rico. The effort became, instead, another example of the disfunction of the U.S.–Puerto Rico relationship.

Muñoz was to play a central role in the drama. Although a leader of the independence movement and an early admirer of pro-violence Nationalist leader Albizu Campos, Muñoz was nonviolent, not anti-American, and, as he wrote to a friend in 1922, nonideological.[18] A Marxist in his youth, he believed that American failure was the failure of capitalism and the result of the opposition of the conservative Republicans in Washington as in Puerto Rico to socialist reforms. Himself Americanized, having been brought up and educated both in the United States and on the island, he saw himself as part of the American progressive movement, an admirer of the imprisoned Socialist labor leader Eugene Debs.

The election of Franklin Delano Roosevelt in 1932 sparked a wave of optimism in Puerto Rico, as it did in the United States. Sparked in part by Eleanor Roosevelt's and Rexford Tugwell's visit to Puerto Rico in 1934, when they were moved by witnessing Puerto Rico's poverty and backwardness, the Roosevelt administration decided to extend the New Deal programs to Puerto Rico.

Muñoz, the vociferous critic of American colonialism, changed. As he confessed to the economist Jude Wanniski, the Roosevelt New Deal forced him "to revise my theory of empire." The United States, he now believed, was not the great obstacle to the deep economic and social reforms Puerto Rico needed but the hope that made them possible. He became the de facto political representative of the New Deal on the island and, although only a minority senator, Puerto Rico's de facto representative in Washington. Fluent in English and American liberalism and trusted by the progressives in Washington as his father, Muñoz Rivera, never was, he established a relationship with Eleanor and then Roosevelt himself.

As the United States set up the Puerto Rico Economic Relief Administration to spend hundreds of millions of dollars on infrastructure and social programs, Washington feared that the island's tribal politics would sabotage it. As always, island politics were confusing, contradictory. Here was the independentista Muñoz dedicating himself to implementing the American programs on the island while the statehood Republican Coalition Party, in control of the legislature, was against them.

In the logic of Puerto Rico politics, however, there was nothing confusing. Muñoz had become so identified with the New Deal, the Republican Coalition was convinced that it had to obstruct the New Deal economic and social relief programs in order to defeat him and the Liberal Party in the 1936 elections. Partisan politics, as it would again and again, trumped economic policy.

As the New Deal became mired in politics, an outbreak of anti-American violence occurred. Muñoz refused to condemn the two Nationalists who on February 23, 1936, assassinated the American police chief in San Juan, Francis E. Riggs, when the United States did not condemn the police killing of the Nationalists after capturing them. The New Dealers in Washington and on the island turned against Muñoz.

Had the Americans misunderstood Muñoz? Had they, in fact, misunderstood the Puerto Ricans? Americans were assured, especially by the statehood leaders, of how loyal Puerto Ricans were, how much they treasured their American citizenship, and how vehemently they rejected independence.

Senator Millard Tydings, author of the Philippines independence bill and a personal friend of the slain police chief, introduced a bill in Congress to give Puerto Rico independence if Puerto Rico asked for it. He made it clear the move had Roosevelt's blessing. The bill shocked the Puerto Ricans: Roosevelt, after all, had been seen since 1933 as Puerto Rico's great friend. Muñoz had dedicated himself to dramatizing how much Roosevelt personally cared, as did Eleanor, about the island.

Now the Tydings bill was seen in Puerto Rico as an American betrayal. Again Washington was confounded. Instead of embracing what he had fought for all his life, Muñoz bitterly denounced the bill. He argued that it would not give Puerto Ricans real freedom but economic conditions so onerous, especially in removing free trade, that it enslaved them in starvation. It was, he decried, revenge. The Americans, and the president himself, were retaliating not only against the killing of the American police chief but also against Puerto Ricans' so-called ingratitude.

In the labyrinth of island politics, Muñoz saw the bill as a Machiavellian plot concocted by the head of the New Deal on the island, Ernest Gruening, the liberal newspaper and magazine editor who had supported Muñoz for years but who now was personally hurt by Muñoz's refusal to condemn the Nationalists. The real purpose of the bill, Muñoz believed, was Gruening's determination to punish him and the Liberal Party in the coming elections, igniting in voters the fear of independence that would defeat them.

To add to the confusion, statehood leaders came out *in favor* of the independence bill. Hurt by the American slap in the face, they proclaimed, as they did in the past and would again in the future, that if the Americans rejected them—and rejected statehood—they would favor independence. But in their political calculations, "Gruening's revenge" would propel the party back into power. Gruening, the liberal New Dealer, was now the ally of the anti–New Deal island Republicans.

What was intended to correct three decades of American failure, to finally make good on the "broken pledge," in the view of the New Dealers in Washington, had degenerated into a "deranged saraband"[19]—the slow Spanish dance in triple time.

Muñoz unsuccessfully urged the Liberal Party to boycott the 1936 election in protest, confirming in the minds of even his Washington supporters that he was another Latin American politico. On Election Day, the "Gruening revenge" worked, and the Republican Coalition Party was reelected. Liberal Party leaders accused Muñoz of causing its defeat by promoting the boycott and expelled him from the party.

Senator Tydings visited the island shortly thereafter. He wrote to Roosevelt that he had bad news: "I am sorry to report that there is no real independence sentiment here. . . . [I]t certainly would be better for us, and, conversely, much worse for Puerto Rico."[20]

Rexford Tugwell wrote in his memoirs that in Washington, the old Teddy Roosevelt progressive, Interior Secretary Harold Ickes, who had supervised the New Deal on the island, simply gave up. Nothing could be accomplished in what he described as the "barrel of snakes" of island politics. According to Gruening, Roosevelt himself felt that Puerto Rico was a hopeless cause.[21] The New Deal in Puerto Rico effectively ended. The Liberal Party, after the defeat, disappeared. It seemed to everyone that Muñoz's political career also ended. The "troubled relationship" seemed to have hit rock bottom. In Washington, the view that Puerto Rico was hopeless seemed irrefutable. There was nothing the United States could do to help Puerto Rico.

The Meaning of Self-Determination

On August 14, 1941, President Roosevelt and Winston Churchill signed the Atlantic Charter: the United States and the United Kingdom committed themselves to "respect the right of all people to choose the form of government under which they will live; and they wish to see *sovereign* rights and self-government restored to those who have been forcibly deprived of it."[22] The Charter became the foundation of the United Nations and the 1946 UN Charter signed in San Francisco. Self-determination was the principle that drove the decolonization process after World War II.

For Puerto Rican leaders, this was a commitment to "decolonize" the island. The United States had often insisted that its policy on Puerto Rico was the Wilsonian principle of the right of self-determination. The standard and safe reply of any politician or other visitor to the island when asked about the political status has always been that it is a matter for the Puerto Ricans to decide.

But Tugwell reminded Muñoz and other leaders that the Atlantic Charter was not an act of Congress that applied directly to the island.[23] Still, having supported Puerto Rico electing its own governor since 1942, he also favored self determination, telling the island legislature on February 13, 1945, "It is already time, past the time that Puerto Ricans elect the form of government they want to live under."[24]

The 1936 Tydings bill, in fact, had reflected what was by then American policy: if Puerto Rico asked for independence, it would grant it. Seven years later, Tydings tried again, this time offering independence with much less economically onerous provisions. In the 1940s, Tugwell wrote in his memoirs that he warned Muñoz and other PDP leaders to be very careful about demanding independence for they would be surprised by how quickly they would get it. Later, in 1960, he wrote, "I often said when I was governor[,] . . . with President Roosevelt's concurrence[,] . . . if Puerto Ricans should choose to sever the old relationship, we continentals would see them go in peace with our best wishes."[25] After the creation of the commonwealth in 1952, President Dwight D. Eisenhower and subsequent presidents expressly committed the United States to Puerto Rico's independence.

But when Americans tell Puerto Ricans that their status is their choice, as President Carter had, the statement is misleading. Puerto Rico's status is *not* their choice. "Self-determination" is the right to independence, not the right to statehood or commonwealth status. Becoming a part of the United States is a U.S. decision.

The confusion over the meaning of self-determination became evident in the early 1990s, when Governor Rafael Hernández Colón made another big effort in Congress to resolve the status issue by proposing improvements in the commonwealth. During the process, various senators expressed surprise that the term "self-determination" was being misused in Congress and in Puerto Rico. Oklahoma senator Don Nickles said, "I think when you are talking about Puerto Rico[,] . . . if you are talking about self-determination dealing with independence, I do not know of anybody here that would disagree if they wanted to choose that. But if you talk about statehood and/or if you are talking about commonwealth, you are talking about something of a mutual concern. You are talking about a marriage, and I think that is entirely different. . . . [O]r a change in the Commonwealth[,] . . . that is something that I think . . . has to be mutually beneficial, and something that we consider."[26]

The right of Puerto Ricans to "choose" statehood in the sense of petitioning for statehood is one thing. But through the years, U.S. politicians and others, usually seeking support in national politics, have carelessly misled Puerto Ricans into believing that the right to self-determination is the right to statehood, still another element in the century of misunderstanding.

National Politics

Democratic Party chairman Paul Butler, visiting the island in 1960, was surprised to learn that he had been misled into believing that there was a Democratic Party on the island. He ordered the head of the local Democratic Committee, José Benítez, to organize it. Muñoz was then surprised when Benítez, long associated with the PDP, announced he was organizing a new party, the Democratic Party of Puerto Rico, supporting statehood. Benítez believed that he had found an unbeatable combination. It was evident that most Puerto Ricans, when they thought about national politics, naturally considered themselves Democrats. Add to this the obvious growing support for statehood, and he would have a powerful political party.

He was wrong. After a lot of publicity that was amply covered by the English-language *San Juan Star*, just one political rally was held, at which a handful of people showed up. The party disappeared.

Complicating the U.S.–Puerto Rico relationship has been the confusion regarding national politics on the island. Although Puerto Rico does not vote for president of the United States, it does have statelike participation in the national party nominating conventions: 53 Democratic delegates and 23 Republican delegates.

In the United States, Muñoz was considered a liberal Democrat. Many believed that the Popular Democratic Party was affiliated with the national Democrats. PDP leaders, like the colorful mayor of San Juan, Felisa Rincón de Gautier, actively campaigned for Democrats among mainland Puerto Ricans. But Muñoz insisted that he belonged to no national party and that the PDP was never affiliated, wanting to be free to establish Washington relationships with both parties, with Richard Nixon as well as John F. Kennedy. But Muñoz held tight control over the island's Democratic National Committee.

The national committees of both parties on the island were composed mostly of wealthy American residents and Puerto Ricans who contributed to the mainland parties and could afford to attend the presidential nominating conventions. They had influence over federal appointments of judges, postmasters, and other federal officials. At the national conventions, they worked to get pro-commonwealth or pro-statehood language in the party platforms. In close nominating elections, their votes were as coveted as any others. But national politics on the island was to get much more confused.

Since Barbosa created the island's Republican Party in 1899, it had been affiliated with the national party. Statehood Republican Party leader Luis A. Ferré was known in the GOP as the Puerto Rican "Mr. Republican." Presidents Ronald Reagan, Gerald Ford, and George H. W. Bush supported statehood, ensuring they had the Puerto Rican votes at the national conventions. When GOP candidates such as Senator Howard Baker of Tennessee and Senator Bob Dole of Kansas campaigned in the primaries, they crisscrossed the island shouting "Estadidad ahora," "Statehood Now." Media reports later indicated that once the candidates left the island, the slogan was virtually forgotten.

The historical link broke when the new generation of statehood leaders emerged in the 1960s. They pointed out that the GOP and U.S. presidents had in fact done nothing for statehood. In spite of the endorsements, Republican national leaders, particularly in Congress, were naturally aware that statehood would virtually guarantee two Democratic senators and five or six Democratic representatives in Congress.

In 1967, when Ferré left the Statehood Republican Party, he remained a Republican and retained control of the local GOP committee, but his New Progressive Party was not affiliated with any national party. Now the new leaders associated themselves with a national party, depending on which one was in power, often switching from party to party.

After President Carter was elected in 1976, NPP San Juan mayor Carlos Romero Barceló, a Nixon supporter, switched to the Democratic Party and with White House support maneuvered control of the island's Democratic Committee. Now the national party situation in Puerto Rico became more confused, with the New Progressive Party controlling both national committees on the island.

This was considered a major step forward for the statehood movement. Edward Kennedy remained associated with the PDP. When he challenged President Carter in 1980 he received support from party leader Hernández Colón, who, unlike Muñoz, participated actively in national Democratic politics. But the historical link between the PDP and the national Democratic Party, especially under Presidents Kennedy and Johnson, was broken. NPP leaders believed they had overcome a handicap in the United States as well as in Puerto Rico. No longer identified exclusively with conservative Republicans, statehood advocates now worked for the support of the Democratic Party and of the American liberals who had always been naturally disposed to favor statehood. By the early 2000s, the traditional national political alignment had been reversed: GOP leaders opposed statehood, and Democrats supported it, linking Puerto Rico's statehood with Washington, DC, statehood.

In the 1990s, Governor Pedro Rosselló also switched from Republican to Democrat. His son, Governor Ricardo Rosselló, became a Democrat. His replacement in 2019, Wanda Vásquez, although also of the NPP, switched from Democrat to Republican. Some NPP resident commissioners sat with the Democrats in Congress; others, with the Republicans: Pedro Pierluisi (2012–16) was a Democrat and Jenniffer González Colón (2017–20), a Republican.

As Butler found in 1960, national politics in Puerto Rico seem to be a house of mirrors in which it is difficult to determine at any given time who is a Democrat and who is a Republican. The intense loyalties in Puerto Rico's political culture are to the local parties. The content and commentary in the island media is predominantly on local, not national, politics. There is little real interest in the ideological liberal versus conservative battles that separate national politics.

Although there is growing interest and media coverage of national issues and politics in Puerto Rico, in large part a result of the communications revolution and the Trump presidency, party identification of island leaders, as in the past, is often not a matter of loyalty or conviction but of political expediency related to their political status strategies in Washington.

Two Languages: The "Painful Correspondence"

William Dorvillier lived the reality of the two languages in Puerto Rico. Born in Massachusetts, he came to Puerto Rico for his honeymoon in the 1940s and stayed for the next half century. Unable to speak Spanish, he convinced Angel Ramos, publisher of the island's leading newpaper, *El Mundo*, to start an English-language paper, the *World Journal*, aimed at the many Americans on the military bases. When the war ended and the Americans left, Ramos decided to close the paper.

Dorvillier, who never learned Spanish, persisted and in 1959 convinced Mike Cowles, owner of *Look* magazine in the United States, to start an English-language daily. The *San Juan Star* was a journalistic success. The next year, it was the smallest and youngest newspaper to win a Pulitzer Prize. Dorvillier, a Catholic, was known for his hard-hitting editorials against the island's Catholic bishops when they decided to organize a political party to oppose the island's governing party.

But the *San Juan Star* hit the language barrier. The one English-language radio station went off the air. The *Star*'s circulation never reached the level it needed to achieve financial success. Although it was admired for its aggressive investigative reporting, it was never accepted by the island media as a Puerto Rican newspaper. After several ownership changes, the paper closed in 2008.

When Muñoz attempted to get Congress to make big changes in Puerto Rico's commonwealth status in 1963, Dorvillier foresaw the difficulty of the Puerto Ricans communicating with the Americans. "For the past ten years," he wrote, "a painful correspondence has been going between Puerto Rico and Congress in which neither side has understood a word the other was saying."[27]

José Trías Monge was Muñoz's Harvard- and Yale-educated legal con-
sultant. He spoke English, but when he sat with Kennedy officials in the
early 1960s to work out the details of the commonwealth improvement
plan, he found that the biggest, in the end insurmountable, obstacle was
that as much as they wanted to please the Puerto Ricans, they simply did
not understand what they were talking about.[28] As had Muñoz's 1959 attempt to improve the commonwealth's status, this one also failed.

Long before the Bush Task Force on Puerto Rico effectively changed the
island's name from the Commonwealth of Puerto Rico to the territory of
Puerto Rico, there has been confusion in the U.S. over the word *commonwealth*. On February 4, 1952, Puerto Rico's legislature approved a resolution declaring, "The body politic created by our Constitution shall be des-
ignated 'The Commonwealth of Puerto Rico.'"[29] The law of Puerto Rico
and the United States approving the constitution referred to "the Constitution of the Commonwealth of Puerto Rico."[30] But what is a commonwealth? Massachusetts, Virginia, and Pennsylvania call themselves common-
wealths. The British refer to their "commonwealth of nations."

In the island's status politics, the words *commonwealth*, *territory*, and
compact do not come down to a matter of semantics. When the island is
called "the Commonwealth of Puerto Rico," it is recognition that commonwealth exists as a status; when "territory of Puerto Rico" is used, it
means that Puerto Rico is still a U.S. colony. Another term that is prob-
lematic is "political status." In the United States, the "political status of
Puerto Rico" means the political, economic, and juridical relationship
between the United States and Puerto Rico as spelled out by law. The
question is, Does it work? In Puerto Rico the question is, are you a statehooder, commonwealther, or independentista? It is the relationship but
much more: it is an ideal. Through the years, especially in Washington,
Americans using these words are oblivious to the fact that they are minefields in Puerto Rican status politics.

The century of miscommunication and misunderstanding between
the United States and Puerto Rico reached a climax when President
Obama signed the law creating the Puerto Rico Oversight, Management,
and Economic Stability Act, or PROMESA. Obama believed it was an
answer to Puerto Rico's desperate SOS for relief of its $70 billion debt,
$130 billion if pension funds were included. The purpose of PROMESA

was to allow Puerto Rico to restructure its debt while helping the government make the spending adjustments to return to a balanced budget.

PROMESA, whose translation is "promise," was for Puerto Rico leaders just the opposite. It was the return to the dark days, as Hernández Colón put it, of "unrepentant colonialism." Puerto Rican leaders and Americans had never disagreed more over the meaning of a word.

The Spanish philosopher José Ortega y Gassett wrote that in Spanish culture, you will never understand its politics if you go by what is said. In the century of "painful communication," Americans and Puerto Ricans have not understood each other. This is the root of the mistakes and failures and the root of Puerto Rico's status politics.

The Pandemic, the "Curse," the "Fix"

On Sunday evening, March 15, 2020, Puerto Rico went into lockdown. Suddenly Puerto Rico was eerily still, eerily quiet. No people, no cars on the streets and roads; shopping centers were empty and theaters, restaurants, and bars closed.

Two days earlier, late on Friday, three coronavirus cases had been confirmed. Governor Wanda Vázquez Garced declared a national emergency—closing the tourist piers in Old San Juan, ordering the National Guard to screen travelers arriving at local international airports, closing the public schools and universities and urging the private schools to do the same, and canceling all cultural, entertainment, and sporting events. On Sunday morning, a fourth case was confirmed, and the governor issued an executive order decreeing a mandatory curfew and mandatory social distancing.[1]

Of course, the coronavirus had spread worldwide. But Puerto Ricans had reason to ask, was there no end to the string of the island's bad luck? The lockdown, of course, was still another devastating blow to Puerto Rico's battered economy.

The list of misfortunes was long: the now fourteen-year-long economic depression, which saw the economy decline by 15 percent; in 2015, the humiliation of the government of Puerto Rico telling the world that it had terribly mismanaged the economy, digging the island into a hole that it could not climb out of, that it was bankrupt; the humiliation of having to send a desperate SOS to Washington; the humiliation of Congress creating a federal oversight board—the PROMESA Fiscal Board—with powers that superseded those of the island's elected government.

Puerto Rico, not long ago celebrated throughout the world as the showcase of democracy, now, in the summer of 2019, was a showcase of political immaturity. Governor Ricardo Rosselló was caught in juvenile, repulsive private conversations, which added to a pattern of corruption. There were massive street demonstrations and walls painted with huge letters reading, "RICKY RENUNCIA." For the first time in history, an elected governor was forced to resign.

There were two hurricanes in September 2017. Puerto Rico was lucky with the first, category 5 Irma, but not the second, Maria, which was the most destructive Atlantic hurricane in recorded history. As Puerto Rico celebrated the Christmas season, on December 28, 2019, the island began to shake. There were eleven earthquakes of magnitude 5 or greater. Puerto Rico was under overlapping declarations of states of emergency: first because of the earthquakes and then because of the coronavirus.

But remarkably enough, in the gloom of this latest calamity, the coronavirus pandemic, there appeared a ray of light, a ray of hope. Could it finally give Puerto Rico what it desperately needed, an opportunity to revive its economy?

The Opportunity

In the United States, as the coronavirus crisis took hold, one of the alarm bells that went off in the White House, in Congress, and in the media was U.S. dependence on Chinese pharmaceutical products, including drugs vital to fight the virus. A March 11, 2020, *New York Times* story reported, "An article posted [. . .] by the state news agency Xinhua argued that the world should thank China, rather than blame it for spreading the virus, saying that if China banned the export of drugs 'the United States would sink into the hell of a novel coronavirus epidemic.'"[2]

On July 21, 2019, Rosemary Gibson, author of the book, *China Rx: Exposing the Risk of America's Dependence on China for Medicines*, wrote a column for the *Seattle Times* titled "U.S. Dependence on China for Medicine Is a Major Problem." She wrote, "Over the past 30 years much of the U.S. drug manufacturing industry has relocated offshore. . . . China now dominates global drug production."[3]

Her book received a great deal of attention in Washington and the health industry. On October 30, 2019, she testified at the House Energy and Commerce Subcommittee hearings that U.S. dependence on Chinese drug manufacturing "poses devastating public health consequences." She called on Congress to get the pharmaceutical industry to return to the United States as a matter of national security: "A robust and resilient industrial base of manufacturing generic medicines and their essential ingredients should be a national health security, public health and national security priority."[4]

The *New York Times* quoted Gibson in a March 11, 2020, story: "If China shut the door on exports of core components to make our medicines, within months our pharmacy shelves would become bare and our health care system would cease to function. In the event of a natural disaster or global pandemic, then the United States will wait in line with every other country for essential medicines."[5] According to Food and Drug Administration data, the *Times* reported, "72 percent of manufacturing facilities making active pharmaceutical ingredients for American drugs were overseas, with 13 percent in China."[6]

That same day, Florida senator Marco Rubio, a 2016 GOP presidential candidate, and former House Speaker Newt Gingrich wrote an article for Fox News: "In the face of the pandemic, the absence of domestic capacity in critical medical sectors has critically endangered both the U.S. public health system and our economy." Rubio said that he sounded the alarm in his February 12, 2019, report, "Made in China and the Future of American Industry."[7] The day before, on March 10, at a closed-door White House meeting, the *Miami Herald* reported, "Rubio and President Donald Trump agreed that the U.S. needs to encourage more domestic drug manufacturing and lessen its dependence on China to produce medicines."[8]

Leading the drive at the White House was President Trump's senior trade adviser, Peter Navarro, who had written a long memo on January 29, 2020, warning that the coronavirus crisis in China threatened the United States with millions of Americans sick or dead and billions in economic costs. On February 12, he wrote another memo, echoing Rosemary Gibson: "This is a wake-up call for an issue that has been latent for many years but is critical to US economic and national security. If we have learned anything from the coronavirus and swine flu H1N1 epidemic of 2009 it is that we cannot necessarily depend on other countries, even close allies, to supply us with needed items, from face masks to vaccines. . . . The policy of the US government is Buy American. The question is why aren't we fully applying this principle to . . . pharmaceuticals such as antibiotics." He called for "'onshoring' the pharmaceutical supply chain."[9]

The media, both conservative and liberal, picked up the issue. On February 13, 2020, Breitbart News ran a frightening story that began, "The coronavirus outbreak has exposed the United States' dangerous dependence on China for pharmaceutical and medical supplies, including an estimated 97 percent of all antibodies and 80 percent of the active pharmaceutical ingredients needed to produce drugs in the U.S." In an April 17, 2020, article, the *New York Times* columnist Bret Stephens wrote, "Just as there are no atheists in foxholes, there should be no big-pharma haters in pandemics. . . . [O]ne lesson from this pandemic is how dependent we are for our survival on an innovative and robust pharmaceutical industry. Maybe we should do more as a country to cultivate it than tear it down."

In the Senate, Republican senator Tom Cotton of Arkansas and Congressman Mike Gallagher of Wisconsin introduced a bill on March 13, 2020, "to cut U.S. reliance on pharmaceutical products from China." "This is a national security imperative that to many Americans is a matter of life or death," they wrote. "It's past time for us to develop an aggressive plan to move critical pharmaceutical supply chains away from China."[10] On March 11, 2020, New Jersey Democratic senator Bob Menendez and Tennessee Republican senator Marsha Blackburn introduced the Secure America's Medicine Cabinet Act to give U.S. pharmaceutical production and innovation a powerful boost. Pointing out that on February 27, 2020, the "FDA announced the shortage of one drug used to treat patients with coronavirus," Blackburn said, "without intervention, the FDA expects the pharmaceutical industry will continue to rely on Chinese companies to make active pharmaceutical ingredients. . . . The status quo has made us vulnerable. The fix, however, is sitting right in front of us."[11]

The Fix: Puerto Rico

If allowing the nation to fall into dependence on China for vital drugs was, as Gibson described it, "a blunder of epic proportions," what exactly was the "blunder"?

A big part of the answer was found in a March 8, 2020, *New York Post* op-ed: the decision in Congress in 1996 to eliminate Section 936. And the fix was restoring the tax incentive to bring back to U.S. jurisdiction, to Puerto Rico, the pharmaceutical, biochemical, and medical device industries.[12]

Two days later, on March 10, Virginia senator Tim Kaine, Democratic Party vice presidential candidate in 2016, was quoted as saying, "Puerto Rico is very well prepared. . . . [I]t is a pillar of the pharmaceutical industry."[13]

The long March 16, 2020, *Forbes* article, "Puerto Rico Can Help the U.S. End Its Dependence on Chinese Pharmaceutical Ingredients," spelled out in detail why restoring the Section 936 incentive was the fix. It was what attracted the pharmaceutical industry to Puerto Rico in the first place; eliminating it was what drove it to China and elsewhere, creating the dependency crisis.

Others in the United States and Puerto Rico joined the drive. Two days after the *Forbes* article, on March 18, the federally created PROMESA Fiscal Board sent a letter to President Donald Trump, Senate majority leader Mitch McConnell, and House Speaker Nancy Pelosi. Puerto Rico, the board declared, is poised "to play a leading role in bolstering national security." The letter continued, "There is a well-developed ecosystem of highly skilled employees who have the technical skills needed to work in a highly regulated and safety-oriented operating environment. Puerto Rico is also fully within the customs territory of the United States and manufacturing is subject to FDA and other federal agency oversight."[14]

The following day, the Puerto Rico Manufacturer's Association, which had lobbied hard against the elimination of Section 936 in 1996, made the same appeal in a letter to the president and congressional leaders. The association emphasized the magnitude of the mistake of having repealed 936: Puerto Rico lost its dominance in the pharmaceutical industry and "the U.S. Treasury did not receive the additional tax revenue it expected." This proved, the letter continued, that the argument against Section 936 as "corporate welfare" was wrong: in fact, 936 gave no tax benefits that the industries have not achieved by simply relocating from Puerto Rico to China and India.[15]

The minority pro-commonwealth Popular Democratic Party came out behind the pro-936 campaign. On March 16, 2020, former governor Aníbal Acevedo Vilá sent a letter to Senator Charles Grassley. It was phasing out 936 in 1996, he reminded the senator, that ruined the island economy: "There is no other U.S. jurisdiction which has experienced such a prolonged and deep contraction in output. The underlying force that created the downturn was the Washington-driven decision to repeal 936."[16] Urging Congress to restore 936, Acevedo Vilá wrote:

> By turning on Puerto Rico's mighty manufacturing engine, we can solve two critical problems at once—we can provide a secure and reliable source of critical drugs and medical devices under the U.S. flag, and solve in great part Puerto Rico's social-economic crisis. By bringing back product lines to Puerto Rico from overseas jurisdictions you will put bread on our tables, put revenue and growth into our budget and economy, and bring security to the U.S. by having these critical products manufactured under U.S. laws and with U.S. customs and by U.S. citizens and U.S. companies.

On March 23, 2020, the PDP approved a resolution supporting Acevedo Vilá's appeal to Congress.

With all the support Puerto Rico was receiving in Washington as well as in Puerto Rico, questions remain. Will the push to restore a Section 936–type incentive reignite the old status battle? Will the New Progressive Party, historically opposed to 936 as "incompatible with statehood," again oppose the tax benefit?

Former pro-statehood treasury secretary and former Ernst & Young partner Teresita Fuentes wrote that she hoped that this time the NPP would not oppose. A tax expert with decades of experience advising big corporations on where to locate their operations, she saw 936 as the means to generate the economic growth that in the future would make statehood viable. She belonged to the Luis A. Ferré camp of "moderate" statehood advocates. Although she believed that reviving the original 936 was no longer possible, she joined the campaign to get Congress to approve a similar tax incentive.

On March 25, 2020, she went further, strongly criticizing her party for having killed 936. In a column in the *Weekly Journal* on Section 936, "A Credit Repeal That Led to a Horrible Deal," she wrote that repealing it was a terrible mistake: "Puerto Rico lost. Some extremely prominent and successful companies moved their operations to foreign jurisdictions such as Ireland and Singapore, and the result was plant closure and unemployment in Puerto Rico. . . . Clearly it was the wrong move. . . . [T]he fact of the matter is Puerto Rico's economy went on a downward spiral right after or closely before its repeal."[17]

She described the anti-936 corporate welfare arguments as "obnoxious, ridiculous and dangerous." She attacked the fundamental argument that 936 was an "obstacle to statehood": "To those who call it corporate welfare just look at the quality jobs it creates; to those that think that it's anti-statehood just look as how undoubtedly American it would be right now to insure that the products that THE AMERICAN PEOPLE need were manufactured in Puerto Rico."[18] She pleaded for Puerto Rico to take advantage of this new opportunity to play an important role in American national security.

On March 18, 2020, Puerto Rico's NPP resident commissioner, Jenniffer González Colón, joined the campaign, sending a letter to the U.S. House and Senate leadership of both parties strongly supporting the drive to bring the pharmaceutical industry back to Puerto Rico: "Consistent with the President's remarks and widespread support for domestic production of pharmaceutical and medical supply chain, Puerto Rico is well positioned to help the U.S. close the gap immediately, with the current availability of specialized manufacturing equipment and highly trained personnel. The public health emergency has shown us that securing the supply of pharmaceutical, biological and medical devices and supplies on American soil is in the interest of our national security and health security."[19]

On April 5, 2020, she presented a bill "to provide federal tax incentives for the manufacture of vital medical supplies now made in foreign jurisdictions, which pose a risk to U.S. supply chain as evidenced by the pandemic caused by Covid-19." It called for giving new industries federal tax credits under a program aimed at "distressed zones" of high unemployment and poverty. But although González Colón was considered to be in the party's moderate pro-statehood wing, now she made it clear that her bill ruled out any 936-type federal tax exemption: "Every new economic initiative . . . must be within the federal tax system."[20]

On April 22, 2020, former treasury secretary Teresita Fuentes wrote another column criticizing the González Colón bill as precisely what she had asked the political leadership not to do. The bill, she wrote, was a "political façade": it was a substitute for Section 936 and would not work. "Why would an operation that left Puerto Rico and went foreign come back to Puerto Rico to pay additional taxes on operations that currently don't pay these?" She was pointing to the same defect that dogged previous pro-statehood proposals: why would an investor come to the island if it had the same incentives in the United States? And again she pleaded, "Let's leave the political discussion behind regarding the section [936] of the U.S. Code for another day."[21]

In fact, the NPP leadership had reiterated its categorical opposition to reviving a 936-type incentive on March 28, 2020. The island's Senate approved a resolution, submitted by NPP leader and Senate president Thomas Rivera Schatz, that, while supporting the drive to bring the pharmaceutical industry back to Puerto Rico, reiterated the NPP's opposition to any federal law that depended on the continuation of commonwealth status. The resolution revived many of the party's arguments used in Congress to repeal Section 936: to support 936 is to perpetuate the political rights and federal funding "inequalities" under the commonwealth. The solution is the "equity" of statehood.

In May 2020, Puerto Rico was into the third month of the coronavirus lockdown, and Governor Vázquez and her administration were under siege in Puerto Rico and in Congress. There were reports of mishandling federal crisis funds and of massive corruption. On April 20, 2020, Finance Committee chair Charles Grassley sent a scalding letter to the governor stating that there were "troubling revelations regarding instability of leadership in Puerto Rico's health system as well as a clear lack of accountability." "It appears," he continued, "that procurement and contracting in Puerto Rico often passed through a filter of political connections before resources intended for the people of Puerto Rico actually reach them and achieve the intended use, depriving the people of Puerto Rico of the primacy they serve." Grassley asked the governor to provide information and respond to a series of questions.[22]

The governor let the senator know on April 27 of her displeasure at his letter in an eight-page reply that began by referring to the political status issue. Describing the "severe hardships" of the people of Puerto Rico, she wrote, "There is no doubt that all these situations exacerbate the struggles of the U.S. citizens in Puerto Rico due to the longstanding inequities that result from our territorial status."[23] She was referring to her party's drive for statehood.

After their elections on November 3, 2020, Pierluisi and González Colón, as the previous governors, vowed to attack the economic and fiscal crisis. The opportunity to do so, "the fix," was there: the unexpected opening to revive the economy that arose from the coronavirus pandemic. But armed with the new statehood win in the referendum, they made clear that they would carry forward the battle for statehood.

Will Puerto Rico squander this opportunity to revive economic growth?

The answer is in the story of the rise and fall of Puerto Rico. Of the many factors, whether it is a rise or fall has always depended on (whether Puerto Rico overcomes or succumbs to the scourge of island history) the obsession with political status.

NOTES

Prologue

1. Avik Roy, "Puerto Rico Can Help the U.S. End Its Dependence on Chinese Pharmaceutical Ingredients," *Forbes*, March 16, 2020.
2. Ibid.
3. Ibid.
4. Ibid.
5. Scott Gottlieb, Statement by FDA Commissioner Scott Gottlieb, MD, on medical device manufacturing recovery in Puerto Rico, U.S. Drug and Food Administration, October 20, 2017.
6. Ken Roberts, "Puerto Rico's Pharma Industry: How Long Can It Wait for an Operational and Reliable Electrical Grid?," *Forbes*, October 28, 2017.
7. CNBC, "Here's How an Obscure Tax Change Sank Puerto Rico's Economy," September 26, 2017.

Introduction

1. Raymond Carr, *Puerto Rico: A Colonial Experiment* (New York: New York University Press, 1984), 316.
2. A. W. Maldonado, *Luis Muñoz Marín, Puerto Rico's Democratic Revolution* (San Juan: University of Puerto Rico Editorial, 2006), 350.
3. Mary Williams Walsh, "Puerto Rico's Bankruptcy Plan Almost Done, and It Could Start a Fight," *New York Times*, July 14, 2019, www.nytimes.com /2019/07/14/business/puerto-rico-bankruptcy-promesa.html.
4. Earl Warren, cited in Hearings before the Committee on Energy and Natural Resources 102nd Cong., 1st sess., S. 244, To Provide a Referendum on the Political Status of Puerto Rico, January 30 and February 7, 1991, at 164.

5. Brief for the United States as Amicus Curiae Supporting Respondents at 31, Sánchez Valle, 136 S. Ct. 1863 (2016) (No. 15-108).

6. Rafael Hernández Colón, Letter to Representatives Rob Bishop and Raul Grijalva, Fundación Rafael Hernández Colón, Ponce, May 24, 2016.

7. Angel Rodriguez, "Puerto Rico Politicians Weigh in on House Committee Approval of PROMESA," *Caribbean Business*, May 26, 2016. http://caribbean business.com/puerto-rico-politicians-weigh-in-on-house-committees-approval -of-promesa/.

8. Rubén Berríos, "Qué hacer ante la Junta," *El Nuevo Día*, July 1, 2016.

9. Danica Cotto, "Puerto Rico Files Bill to Obtain Statehood by 2025," AP News, January 4, 2017, www.apnews.com/75ec8c38f7924c449e16d15e614ac504.

10. P.R. Act No. 7-2017 (February 3, 2017).

11. Turnout for previous plebiscites was 78.2% in 2012, 71.6% in 1998, 73.5% in 1993, and 65.9% in 1967.

12. Cindy Burgos Alvarado, "Puerto Rico Governor Designates Four Members for Equality Commission," *Caribbean Business*, July 3, 2017, http:// caribbeanbusiness.com/puerto-rico-governor-designates-four-members-for -equality-commission/.

13. The U.S. Attorney's Office District of Puerto Rico Press Release, "Former Secretary of Puerto Rico Department of Education Julia Keleher Indicted with Another Individual for Bribery, Conspiracy, and Wire Fraud," July 10, 2019.

14. A. W. Maldonado, *Teodoro Moscoso and Puerto Rico's Operation Bootstrap* (Gainesville: University of Florida Press, 1997), xi.

15. Thomas Rivera Schatz, "El problema no es Trump, es la colonia," *El Vocero*, May 9, 2019.

16. Charles Rangel, *The Latin Americans: Their Love-Hate Relationship with the United States* (New York: Harcourt Brace Jovanovich, 1987), 5–8.

17. Ibid., 50.

18. Ibid.

19. Michael Corkery and Mary Williams Walsh, "Puerto Rico Governor Says Island Debts Are 'Not Payable,'" *New York Times*, June 29, 2015.

20. Editorial Board, "Puerto Rico's Political Meltdown," *Wall Street Journal*, July 25, 2019, www.wsj.com/articles/puerto-ricos-political-meltdown -11564010349.

Chapter One.   Operation Bootstrap

1. Rexford Guy Tugwell, "Puerto Rico: A Study in Democratic Development," *Annals of the American Academy of Political and Social Sciences* 285 (January 1953): 145.

2. Earl Parker Hanson, *Transformation: The Story of Modern Puerto Rico* (New York: Simon and Schuster, 1955), ix.

3. Kenneth E. Boulding, "The Fomentarian Revolution," Center for the Study of Democratic Institutions, June 1961.

4. Charles T. Goodsell, *Administration of a Revolution* (Cambridge, MA: Harvard University Press, 1965), viii.

5. Rafael Bernabe and César J. Ayala, *Puerto Rico in the American Century: A History since 1898* (Chapel Hill: University of North Carolina Press, 2009), 258.

6. Jude Wanniski, "A Conversation with Muñoz Marín," *Wall Street Journal*, August 24, 1977.

7. Ibid.

8. Boulding, "The Fomentarian Revolution."

9. Rexford Guy Tugwell, *The Stricken Land* (New York: Doubleday, 1947), 13–14.

10. Ernest Gruening, *Many Battles* (New York: Liveright, 1973), 181; original emphasis.

11. Ruby Black, *Eleanor Roosevelt: A Biography* (New York: Dell, Sloan and Pearce, 1940), 297.

12. A. W. Maldonado, *Luis Muñoz Marín, Puerto Rico's Democratic Revolution* (San Juan: University of Puerto Rico Press, 2006), 150.

13. Bailey W. Diffie and Justine W. Diffie, *Puerto Rico: A Broken Pledge* (New York: Vanguard Press, 1931).

14. Tugwell, "Puerto Rico: A Study in Democratic Development," 145.

15. Tugwell, *The Stricken Land*, 256.

16. A. W. Maldonado, *Teodoro Moscoso and Puerto Rico's Operation Bootstrap* (Gainesville: University of Florida Press, 1997), 57.

17. Bernabé and Ayala, *Puerto Rico in the American Century*, 269.

18. Maldonado, *Teodoro Moscoso and Puerto Rico's Operation Bootstrap*, 60.

19. Ibid., 260.

20. Arturo Morales Carrión, *Puerto Rico: A Political and Cultural History* (New York: Norton, 1983), 165.

21. Bernabé and Ayala, *Puerto Rico in the American Century*, 259–60.

22. Ibid., 275.

23. *Status of Puerto Rico, Report of the United States–Puerto Rico Commission on the Status of Puerto Rico*, vol. 3, 171. San Juan: Luis Muñoz Foundation.

24. *Status of Puerto Rico, Report of the United States–Puerto Rico Commission on the Status of Puerto Rico*, vol. 3, 170.

25. Carlos Romero Barceló, *La estadidad es para los pobres* (San Juan: n.p., 1973), 41.

26. Maldonado, *Teodoro Moscoso and Puerto Rico's Operation Bootstrap*, 229.

Chapter Two. *Operation Bootstrap and the Statehood Surge*

1. Arturo Morales Carrión, *Puerto Rico: A Political and Cultural History* (New York: Norton, 1983), 141.
2. A. W. Maldonado, *Luis Muñoz Marín, Puerto Rico's Democratic Revolution* (San Juan: University of Puerto Rico Press, 2006), 397.
3. Guillermo A. Baralt, *Desde el mirador de prospero: La vida de Luis A. Ferré, 1904–1999* (San Juan: Fundación El Nuevo Día, 1966), vol. 2, 55.
4. Ibid., 204.
5. Ibid., 55–56.
6. Ibid., 49.
7. Rexford Guy Tugwell, "What's Next for Puerto Rico?," *Annals of the Academy of Political and Social Science* 28 (January 1953): 146.
8. Ibid., 58.
9. Ibid., 65.
10. Ibid., 65.
11. A. W. Maldonado, *Teodoro Moscoso and Puerto Rico's Operation Bootstrap* (Gainesville: University of Florida Press, 1997), 190.
12. Ibid., 198.
13. Salvador Casellas, "Cómo salir de una recesión en tres años: Mis cuatro años en Hacienda" (unpublished MS, 2018).
14. Pablo J. Hernández Rivera, *Salvador Casellas: Testimonios y legado* (San Juan: n.p., 2018), 144.
15. Rafael Hernández Colón, *Contra viento y marea* (San Juan: Fundación Biblioteca Rafael Hernández Colón, 2014), 235.
16. Carlos Romero Barceló, *La estadidad es para los pobres* [Statehood Is for the Poor], 2nd ed. (San Juan: n.p., 1974), 3.
17. Ibid., 77.
18. Ibid., 2.

Chapter Three. *The Demise of Section 936*

1. Financial Oversight and Management Board for Puerto Rico, "New Fiscal Plan for Puerto Rico, Restoring Growth and Prosperity," October 23, 2018, 7, www.oversightboard.pr.gov.
2. Ignacio Rivera, interview by A. W. Maldonado, August 26, 2018.
3. CNBC, "Here's How an Obscure Tax Change Sank Puerto Rico's Economy," September 26, 2017.

4. José A. Hernández Mayoral, "Contribuciones federales: Razón insolayable para votar no," *El Nuevo Día*, October 23, 2020, 45.

5. U.S. General Accounting Office, *Tax Policy, Puerto Rico and the Section 936 Tax Credit*, June 1993.

6. U.S. Treasury Department, "The Operation and Effect of the Possessions Corporations System of Taxation," fourth report, February 1982.

7. Hubert Barton, interview by A. W. Maldonado, 1964; original emphasis.

8. Ronald Reagan, "Remarks to the Permanent Council of the Organization of American States on the Caribbean Basin Initiative," Ronald Reagan Presidential Library and Museum, February 24, 1982.

9. A. W. Maldonado, *Teodoro Moscoso and Puerto Rico's Operation Bootstrap* (Gainesville: University of Florida Press, 1997), 227.

10. Ibid., 228.

11. Hector Cardona, former general manager, Wyeth plant in Puerto Rico, interview by A. W. Maldonado, February 14, 2018.

12. Guillermo A. Baralt, *Contra viento y marea hacia el futuro* (San Juan: Asociación de Industriales de Puerto Rico, 2014), 223.

13. Félix Córdova Iturregui, *La eliminación de la Sección 936: La historia que se intenta suprimir* [The Elimination of Section 936: The History That Is Being Suppressed] (San Juan: Publicaciones Gaviota, 2020), 164.

14. A. W. Maldonado, "Who Is Responsible for the Death of 936," *San Juan Star*, July 11, 1996.

15. Peter Holmes, memo to Alex Maldonado, "Pharma vs. Non-Pharma Data in Puerto Rico," August 19, 2018. A. W. Maldonado files.

16. Córdova Iturregui, *La eliminación de la Sección 936*, 153.

17. Zadia M. Feliciano and Andrew Green, "U.S. Multinationals in Puerto Rico and the Repeal of 936 Tax Exemption for U.S. Corporations," Working Paper 23681, National Bureau of Economic Research, Cambridge, MA, August 2017, www.nber.org/papers/w23681.

18. Ibid.

19. Ibid.

20. Hector Cardona interview.

21. Hector Cardona interview.

22. Hector Cardona interview.

23. A.W. Maldonado, "The 'Big Lie' in the Repeal of Section 936," *San Juan Star*, October 1, 2006.

24. A. W. Maldonado, "How the Statehood Movement Blocked Section 956," *San Juan Star*, November 2, 2003.

25. Ibid.

26. Alejandro García Padilla, "Proposed Federal Tax Policy Promoting Economic and Healthcare Parity in Puerto Rico, Congressional Task Force Briefing Book," August 4, 2016, 6, 11.

27. Córdova Iturregui, *La eliminación de la Sección 936*, 237.

28. Ibid., 153.

Chapter Four. *The Turning Point*

1. Eliezer Curet Cuevas, *El desgobierno de Rosselló y Cifuentes* (San Juan: Management Aid Center, 1996), 365.

2. Ibid., 4.

3. Pedro Rosselló, *A mi manera* (San Juan: Sistema Universitario Ana J. Méndez, 2012), 73.

4. Curet Cuevas, *El desgobierno de Rosselló y Cifuentes*.

5. Ibid., 265.

6. Eliezer Curet Cuevas, *Economía política de Puerto Rico: 1950–2000* (San Juan: Ediciones M.A.C., 2003), 284.

7. A. W. Maldonado, interview with José Izquierdo Encarnación, secretary of transportation and public works, 2001–2, secretary of state, 2002–5, June 28, 2019.

8. Curet Cuevas, *El desgobierno de Rosselló y Cifuentes*, 284.

9. José Izquierdo Encarnación interview.

10. Juan Agosto Alicea, *Crisis: Al borde de la quiebra* (San Juan: Panamericana Formas e Impresos, 2011), 182–84.

11. Ibid., 168.

12. Curet Cuevas, *Economía política de Puerto Rico*, 178.

13. Letter from Juan Agosto Alicea to Governor Sila María Calderón, January 7, 2002. A. W. Maldonado files.

14. Agosto Alicea, *Crisis: Al borde de la quiebra*, 166.

15. Letter from Juan Agosto Alicea to Governor Sila María Calderón.

16. Curet Cuevas, *El desgobierno de Rosselló y Cifuentes*, 387.

Chapter Five. *The Breakdown of the Public Corporations*

1. Rexford Guy Tugwell, *The Stricken Land* (New York: Doubleday, 1947), 8.

2. Ibid., 81.

3. Ibid., 151.

4. Reece B. Bothwell González, *Puerto Rico: Cien años de lucha política* (San Juan: Editorial Universitaria de la Universidad de Puerto Rico, 1979), vol. 3, 329.

5. Luis Muñoz Marín, *La historia del Partido Popular Democrático* (San Juan: Editorial Batey, 2003), 33.

6. Luis Muñoz Marín, *Memorias, 1940–1952* (San Juan: Universidad Interamericana de Puerto Rico, 1992), xi.

7. Charles T. Goodsell, *Administration of a Revolution* (Cambridge, MA: Harvard University Press, 1965), 1.

8. Ibid., 171.

9. General Accounting Office, "Puerto Rico: Factors Contributing to the Debt Crisis and Potential Federal Action to Address Them," GAO-18-387, May 9, 2018, 25.

10. Juan Agosto Alicea, *Crisis: Al borde de la quiebra* (San Juan: Panamericana Formas e Impresos, 2011), 195.

11. Ibid., 227–28.

12. Ibid., 232.

13. Ibid., 231.

14. Ibid., 232.

15. Ibid., 272.

Chapter Six. The Demise of the Government Development Bank

1. James Tobin, *Informe al gobernador del Comité para el Estudio de la Finanza de Puerto Rico* (San Juan: Editorial de la Universidad de Puerto Rico, 1976), 1.

2. Ibid.

3. Pablo J. Hernández Rivera, *Salvador Casellas, testimonios y legado* (San Juan: n.p., 2018), 148.

4. Mary Williams Walsh, "Puerto Rico's Finance Plan Could Start a Fight," *New York Times*, July 15, 2019, B4.

5. Government of Puerto Rico, "New Fiscal Plan for Puerto Rico," submitted to the PROMESA Fiscal Board, January 24, 2018, 42. Financial Oversight and Management Board of Puerto Rico, San Juan.

6. Rexford Guy Tugwell, *The Stricken Land* (New York: Doubleday, 1947), 516.

7. Teodoro Moscoso, Oral Memoirs, tape recording, Luis Muñoz Marín Foundation, San Juan, 100.

8. Tugwell, *The Stricken Land*, 256.

9. Government of Puerto Rico, "New Fiscal Plan for Puerto Rico," 511.

10. Tugwell, *The Stricken Land*, 529–30.

11. Charles T. Goodsell, *Administration of a Revolution* (Cambridge, MA: Harvard University Press, 1965), 175.

12. Ibid.

13. Rafael Hernández Colón, *Contra viento y marea* (San Juan: Fundación Biblioteca Rafael Hernández Colón, 2014), 85.

14. Ibid., 86.

15. Juan Agosto Alicea, interview by A. W. Maldonado, January 31, 2019.

16. U.S. Government Accountability Office (GAO), "Puerto Rico: Factors Contributing to the Debt Crisis and Potential Action to Address Them," May 2018, 22, www.gao.gov.

17. Ibid.

18. Eliezer Curet Cuevas, *Economía política de Puerto Rico: 1950–2000* (San Juan: Ediciones M.A.C., 2003), 368.

19. Ibid.

20. Juan Agosto Alicea, *Crisis: Al borde de la quiebra* (San Juan: Panamericana Formas e Impresos, 2011), 166.

21. Ibid., 178.

22. Ibid.

23. Ibid., 177.

24. Ibid., 184.

25. Juan Agosto Alicea, Personal letter to Governor Calderón, January 7, 2002.

26. Agosto Alicea, *Crisis, al borde de la quiebra*, 189.

27. A. W. Maldonado, "Puerto Rico Should Hang Its Head in Shame," *San Juan Star*, March 5, 2006.

28. Ibid.

29. Guillermo A. Baralt, *Contra viento y marea hacia el futuro* (San Juan: Asociación de Industriales de Puerto Rico, 2014), 271.

30. Rodrigo Masses, former president of the Puerto Rico Manufacturers' Association, interview by A. W. Maldonado, February 14, 2018.

31. Baralt, *Contra viento y marea hacia el futuro*, 282.

32. Hernández Colón, *Contra viento y marea*, 282.

33. Carlos Romero Barceló, "El hombre que no se quiere ir," *El Nuevo Día*, June 9, 2019, 10.

34. U.S. GAO, "Puerto Rico: Factors Contributing to the Debt Crisis," 8.

35. Romero Barceló, "El hombre que no se quiere ir."

36. U.S. GAO, "Puerto Rico: Factors Contributing to the Debt Crisis," 27.

37. "Puerto Rico Will Default on $422 Million Government Development Bank Debt," Bloomberg News, May 2, 2016.

38. Government of Puerto Rico, "Government Development Bank for Puerto Rico Fiscal Plan," submitted to PROMESA Fiscal Board, April 28, 2017, 6. Financial Oversight And Management Board for Puerto Rico, San Juan.

39. Ibid., 7.

Chapter Seven. "That Is Nuts": Puerto Rico's Labor Policy

1. "After the Hurricane," *The Economist*, April 14–20, 2018, 18; original emphasis.

2. Financial Oversight and Management Board for Puerto Rico, "New Fiscal Plan for Puerto Rico: Restoring Growth and Prosperity," October 23, 2018, 140.

3. U.S. Government Accountability Office (GAO), "Puerto Rico: Factors Contributing to the Debt Crisis and Potential Action to Address Them," May 2018, 22, www.gao.gov.

4. Luis Muñoz Marín, Speech at ILGWU Foundation, Atlantic City, NJ, May 18, 1956, Luis Muñoz Marín Foundation, San Juan.

5. Héctor Luis Acevedo, *La generación del 40 y la convención constituyente* (San Juan: Universidad Interamericana de Puerto Rico, 2009), 379–82.

6. A. W. Maldonado, "Just Say No to Unionization," *San Juan Star*, February 26, 1995, 40.

7. A. W. Maldonado, "The Day the Island Government Was Ruined," *San Juan Star*, May 9, 2004, 40.

8. Steven Greenhut, *Plunder! How Public Employee Unions Are Raiding Treasuries, Controlling Our Lives, and Bankrupting the Nation* (Santa Cruz, CA: Forum Press, 2008), 1.

9. James Tobin, *Informe al gobernador del Comité para el Estudio de las Finanzas de Puerto Rico* (San Juan: Editorial Universitaria de Puerto Rico, 1976), 6.

10. PROMESA Fiscal Board, Letter to Governor Rosselló regarding proposed fiscal plan, February 5, 2018, 3.

11. Financial Oversight and Management Board for Puerto Rico, "New Fiscal Plan for Puerto Rico: Restoring Growth and Prosperity," 7.

12. Michael Corkery and Mary Williams Welsh, "PR Governor Says Island's Debts Are 'Not Payable,'" *New York Times*, June 29, 2015.

13. Financial Oversight and Management Board for Puerto Rico, "New Fiscal Plan for Puerto Rico: Restoring Growth and Prosperity," 51.

Chapter Eight. Will Puerto Rico Become a State?

1. Report of the United States–Puerto Rico Commission on the Status of Puerto Rico, Luis Muñoz Marín Foundation, San Juan, August 1966, 14.

2. Rafael Hernández Colón, *Estado libre asociado: Narturaleza y desarrollo* (Ponce: Editorial Calle Sol, 2014), 303.

3. Acting U.S. Deputy Attorney General Dana J. Boente, Letter to Governor Ricardo Rosselló, Office of the Deputy Attorney General, U.S. Department of Justice, Washington, DC, April 13, 2017.

4. Report of the United States–Puerto Rico Commission on the Status of Puerto Rico, 14.

5. New Fiscal Plan for Puerto Rico, Commonwealth of Puerto Rico, submitted to the Financial Oversight and Management Board for Puerto Rico, January 24, 2018, 7–9, www.oversightboard.pr.gov.

6. Fiscal Oversight and Management Board for Puerto Rico, Letter to Governor Ricardo Rosselló Nevares, February 5, 2018, 8, www.oversightboard.pr.gov (comments@oversightboard.pr.gov).

7. José A. Delgado, "Carlos Trujillo: 'El status es un asunto político domestico,'" *El Nuevo Día*, October 6, 2018.

8. John Wagner, "Trump an 'Absolute No' on Puerto Rico Statehood Because of San Juan's 'Horror Show' of a Mayor," *Washington Post*, September 24, 2018.

9. "José A. Aponte Will Not Permit Statehood," *El Nuevo Día*, June 15, 2019.

10. José A. Aponte, "Leader of the U.S. Senate Declares That Republicans Will Block Any Proposal for Puerto Rico Statehood," *El Nuevo Día*, September 23, 2020.

11. Ibid., 10.

12. Julio Ricardo Varela, "White Liberals Must Stop Pushing Puerto Rico Statehood for Their Own Purposes: Let Us Decide," *NBC: Think: Opinion, Analysis, Essays*, November 11, 2020.

13. "After the Hurricane," *The Economist*, April 14–20, 2018, 18–20.

14. Report of the United States–Puerto Rico Commission on the Status of Puerto Rico, 24.

15. Ibid, 14.

16. Ibid.

17. U.S. Government Accountability Office (GAO), "Puerto Rico's Political Future: A Divisive Issue With Many Dimensions," GGD-81-48, March 2, 1981.

18. Moody's Investment Service, Issue comment, November 4, 2020.

19. Eduardo Sanabria, CPA, Memorandum to Héctor Luis Acevedo, Alvarado Tax & Business Advisors, Guayabo, Puerto Rico, November 14, 2020.

20. Leysa Caro González, Ricardo Cortés Chico, and Javier Colón Dávila, "Incertidumbre y confusión en la recta final," *El Nuevo Día*, August 2, 2019.

21. U.S. GAO, "Puerto Rico: Information on How Statehood Would Potentially Affect Selected Federal Programs and Revenue Sources," GAO-14-31, March 4, 2014, 27.

22. José A. Delgado, "Dudas con el proyecto," *El Nuevo Día*, April 3, 2020, 23.

23. Teresita Fuentes, "Economic Distress or Political Chess?," *Weekly Journal*, April 22, 2020, 10.

24. Ibid.

25. José A. Hernández Mayoral and Roberto Prats Palerm, Amicus Curiae Brief before the Supreme Court of the United States, United States of America v. José Luis Vaello Maduro, October 29, 2020, 9.

26. Robert L. Beisner, *Twelve against Empire: The Anti-Imperialists, 1898–1900* (New York: McGraw-Hill, 1968), 22, 23.

27. Pedro Rosselló, *El triunvirato del terror* (San Juan: Harland Group, 2007), 21.

28. A. W. Maldonado, *La prensa y la política en Puerto Rico* (San Juan: Ediciones Puertos, 2015), 267.

29. Rosselló, *El triunvirato del terror.*

30. Ibid., 65.

31. Thomas Rivera Schatz, "El problema no es Trump, es la colonia," *El Vocero*, May 5, 2019.

32. Romero Barceló, *La estadidad es para los pobres* (San Juan: n.p., 1974), 84.

33. Ricardo Alegría, interview by A. W. Maldonado, December 1976.

34. Report of the United States–Puerto Rico Commission on the Status of Puerto Rico, 21.

35. Arthur M. Schlesinger Jr., *The Disuniting of America: Reflections on a Multicultural Society* (New York: Norton, 1998), 10.

36. Rex Guy Tugwell, *The Stricken Land* (New York, Doubleday, 1947), 95.

37. Rafael Hernández Colón, *Contra viento y marea* (San Juan: Fundación Biblioteca Rafael Hernández Colón, 2014), 34–35, 79–84.

38. Reece B. Bothwell González, *Puerto Rico: Cien años de lucha política* (San Juan: Editorial Universitaria de la Universidad de Puerto Rico, 1979), 605.

39. Jeffrey A. Rosen, Deputy Attorney General, Letter to Juan Ernesto Dávila Rivera, Chairman, Puerto Rico State Election Commission, San Juan, Office of the Deputy Attorney General, Washington, DC, July 29, 2020.

Chapter Nine. The Future of Puerto Rico

1. Luis Muñoz Marín, *Memorias* (San Juan: Fundación Luis Muñoz Marín, 2003), 354.

2. Editorial Board, "Puerto Rico's Political Meltdown," *Wall Street Journal*, July 25, 2019, www.wsj.com/articles/puerto-ricos-political-meltdown-11564010349.

3. Luis Muñoz Marín, *Memorias, 1940–1952* (San Juan: Universidad Inter-americana de Puerto Rico, 1982), 186.

4. Ibid.

5. Ibid., 188.

6. Jude Wanniski, "A Conversation with Muñoz Marín," *Wall Street Journal*, August 24, 1977.

7. Reece B. Bothwell González, *Puerto Rico: Cien años de lucha política* (San Juan: Editorial Universitaria de la Universidad de Puerto Rico, 1979), vol. 4, 190.

8. Earl Parker Hanson, *Transformation: The Story of Modern Puerto Rico* (New York: Simon and Schuster, 1955), vii.

9. Rafael Hernández Colón, *Estado libre asociado: Naturaleza y desarrollo* (San Juan: Editorial El Sol, 2014), 127.

10. Carl J. Friedrich, *Puerto Rico: Middle Road to Freedom* (New York: Rinehart & Company, 1959), 2.

11. David Helfeld, "Congressional Intent and Attitude toward Public Law 600 and the Constitution of Puerto Rico," *Revista Jurídica de la Universidad de Puerto Rico* 21 (1952): 254, 261.

12. *Documents on the Constitutional Relationship of Puerto Rico and the United States* (Washington, DC: Puerto Rico Federal Affairs Administration, 1988), 614.

13. José Hernández Mayoral and Roberto Prats Palerm, Amicus Curiae Brief before the Supreme Court of the United States, October 29, 2020, 12.

14. Report by the President's Task Force on Puerto Rico's Status, Executive Offices of the President, Washington, DC, December 2005, 7.

15. Ibid., 5.

16. Raymond Carr, *Puerto Rico: A Colonial Experiment* (New York: New York University Press, 1984).

17. Ibid., viii.

18. Ibid., 411.

19. Muñoz Marín, *Memorias, 1940–1952*, 188.

Chapter Ten. A "Troubled" Relationship

1. Raymond Carr, *Puerto Rico: A Colonial Experiment* (New York: New York University Press, 1984), vii.

2. Ivan Musicant, *Empire by Default* (New York: Henry Holt and Company, 1998), 517.

3. William McKinley, Declaration of War to the Congress of the United States, April 11, 1898.

4. Stanley Karnow, *America's Empire in the Philippines* (New York: Random House, 1989), 91.

5. Musicant, *Empire by Default*, 520.

6. Frank Freidel, *The Splendid Little War* (New York: Dell, 1958), 209.

7. Alfred T. Mahan, *Lessons of the War with Spain* (Boston: Little, Brown, 1918), 29.

8. Robert L. Beiser, *Twelve against Empire: The Anti-Imperialists, 1898–1900* (Chicago: University of Chicago Press, 1985), xxii.

9. Arturo Morales Carrión, *Puerto Rico: A Political and Cultural History* (New York: Norton, 1983), 135.

10. Juan Pan-Montejo, *Más que perder en Cuba: Espuma, 1898, y la crisis de fin de siglo* (Madrid: Alianza Editorial, 1998), 151.

11. Musicant, *Empire by Default*, 521.

12. Morales Carrión, *Puerto Rico: A Political and Cultural History*, 132.

13. Carr, *Puerto Rico: A Colonial Experiment*, 42.

14. Ibid., 34.

15. Ibid., 415.

16. Morales Carrión, *Puerto Rico: A Political and Cultural History*, 153

17. Ibid., 155.

18. Andres Stephanson, *Manifest Destiny* (New York: Farrar, Straus and Giroux, 1995), 87.

19. Morales Carrión, *Puerto Rico: A Political and Cultural History*, 135.

20. U.S. Const. art. IV, § 3, cl. 2.

21. Robert E. Cushman and Robert F. Cushman, *Cases in Constitutional Law* (New York: Meridith Publishing Company, 1963), 215.

22. U.S. Congress, House Committee on Insular Affairs, Committee Report and Acts Relating Thereto, 1st and 2nd sess., 1900–1901, 116.

23. Morales Carrión, *Puerto Rico: A Political and Cultural History*, 155.

24. Carr, *Puerto Rico: A Colonial Experiment*, 37.

25. Cushman and Cushman, *Cases in Constitutional Law*, 216.

26. U.S. Supreme Court, Gonzalez v. Williams, 192 U.S. 1 (1904).

27. Morales Carrión, *Puerto Rico: A Political History*, 15.

28. Balzac v. People of Puerto Rico, 258 U.S. 298 (1922), 215.

29. Cushman and Cushman, *Cases in Constitutional Law*, 219.

30. Luis Muñoz Marín, *Memorias, 1940–1952* (San Juan: Universidad Interamericana de Puerto Rico, 1982), 354.

Chapter Eleven. A Century of Miscommunication and Misunderstanding

1. Raymond Carr, *Puerto Rico: A Colonial Experiment* (New York: New York University Press, 1984), 13; emphasis added.

2. Arturo Morales Carrión, *Puerto Rico: A Political and Cultural History* (New York: Norton, 1983), 163.

3. Carr, *Puerto Rico: A Colonial Experiment*, 166.

4. Morales Carrión, *Puerto Rico: A Political and Cultural History*, 163.

5. Carr, *Puerto Rico: A Colonial Experiment*, 204.

6. Bailey W. Diffie and Justine W. Diffie, *Porto Rico: A Broken Pledge* (New York: Vanguard Press, 1931).

7. Luis Muñoz Marin, "The Sad Case of Puerto Rico," *American Mercury* (1929), 138.

8. Luis Muñoz Marín, *Memorias* (San Juan: Fundación Luis Muñoz Marín, 2003), 323.

9. Morales Carrión, *Puerto Rico: A Political and Cultural History*, 210.

10. Ibid.

11. Carr, *Puerto Rico: A Colonial Experiment*, 44.

12. Morales Carrión, *Puerto Rico: A Political and Cultural History*, 210.

13. Earl Parker Hanson, *Transformation: The Story of Modern Puerto Rico* (New York: Simon and Schuster, 1955), 63.

14. Ibid.

15. Clinton Rossiter and James Lare, *The Essential Lippmann* (New York: Random House, 1963), 488.

16. Theodore Roosevelt Jr., *Colonial Policies of the United States* (New York: Arno Press and the New York Times, 1970), 117–18.

17. Morales Carrión, *Puerto Rico: A Political and Cultural History*, 220.

18. Carmelo Rosario Natal, *La juventud de Luis Muñoz Marín* (Rio Piedras: Editorial Edil, 1989), 140.

19. A. W. Maldonado, *Luis Muñoz Marín: Puerto Rico's Democratic Revolution* (San Juan: University of Puerto Rico Press, 2006), 131.

20. Thomas Mathews, *Puerto Rican Politics and the New Deal* (Gainesville, University of Florida Press, 1960), 107.

21. Earnest Gruening, *Many Battles* (New York: Liveright, 1973), 181.

22. Yale Law School, The Avalon Project, Documents in Law, History and Diplomacy.

23. Rexford Guy Tugwell, *The Stricken Land* (New York: Doubleday, 1947), 595.

24. Reece B. Bothwell González, *Puerto Rico: Cien años de lucha política* (San Juan: Editorial Universitaria de la Universidad de Puerto Rico, 1979), 434.

25. Thomas Matthews, *Puerto Rican Politics and the New Deal* (Gainesville: University of Florida Press, 1960), x.

26. Rafael Hernández Colón, *Estado libre asociado: Naturaleza y desarrollo* (San Juan: Editorial El Sol, 2014), 275.

27. William J. Dorvillier, Editorial, *San Juan Star*.

28. José Trías Monge, *Historia constitucional de Puerto Rico* (San Juan: University of Puerto Rico Press, 1983), vol. 4, 182.

29. *Documents on the Constitutional Relationship of Puerto Rico and the United States* (Washington, DC: Puerto Rico Federal Affairs Administration, 1988), 191.

30. Ibid., 220.

Epilogue. *The Pandemic, the "Curse," the "Fix"*

1. "Puerto Rico Governor Declared State of Emergency to Fight Covid-19 Spread," *Caribbean Business*, March 13, 2020.

2. Ana Swanson, "Coronavirus Spurs U.S. Efforts to End China's Chokehold on Drugs," *New York Times*, March 11, 2020.

3. Rosemary Gibson, "U.S. Dependence on China for Medicine Is a Major Problem," *Seattle Times*, July 21, 2019.

4. Rosemary Gibson, Testimony before the House Committee on Energy and Commerce Subcommittee on Health: Safeguarding Pharmaceutical Supply Chains in a Global Economy, October 30, 2019, House Committee on Energy and Commerce, Committee Activity website.

5. Ana Swanson, "Coronavirus Spurs U.S. Efforts to End China's Chokehold on Drugs," *New York Times*, March 11, 2020.

6. Ibid.

7. Marco Rubio and Newt Gingrich, "Rubio, Gingrich: Coronavirus Lays Bare China's Power over Health, Economy," Fox News, March 11, 2020.

8. Alex Daugherty, "Rubio Wants More Domestic Drug-Making to Fight Coronavirus, Lessen Reliance on China," *Miami Herald*, March 11, 2020.

9. James Politi, "U.S. Trade Advisor Seeks to Replace Chinese Drug Supplies," *Financial Times*, February 12, 2020.

10. Tyler Olsen, "GOP Lawmakers Unveil Bill to Cut American Dependence on Chinese Drugs," Fox News, March 19, 2020.

11. Marsha Blackburn and Bob Menendez, "Press Release: Blackburn, Menendez Lead Bipartisan Bill to Increase U.S. Prescription Drug Manufacturing," March 11, 2020.

12. "'New York Post' Editorial Calls for Medicine Production in Puerto Rico," *El Nuevo Día*, March 8, 2020.

13. José A. Delgado, "Pharmaceutical Industry, Eyes on Puerto Rico," *El Nuevo Día*, March 10, 2020, 6.

14. José B. Carrion, Letter to President Donald J. Trump, March 18, 2020.

15. Carlos M. Rodriguez, Letter to President Donald J. Trump, March 19, 2020.

16. Anibal Acevedo Vilá, Letter to Senator Charles Grassley, March 16, 2020.

17. Teresita Fuentes, "A Credit Repeal That Led to a Horrible Deal," *Weekly Journal*, March 18, 2020.

18. Ibid.

19. Jenniffer González Colón, Letter to Sen. Mitch McConnell and Rep. Nancy Pelosi, Puerto Rico Priorities on COVID-19 Relief Package, March 18, 2020.

20. Jenniffer González Colón, "Press Release: Puerto Rico Resident Commissioner Leads Bipartisan Legislation That Would Secure the National Supply Chain," April 5, 2020.

21. Teresita Fuentes, "Economic Distress or Political Chess," *Weekly Journal*, April 22, 2020.

22. Charles (Chuck) Grassley, "Press Release: People Need Disisater Aid in Puerto Rico; It Can't Keep Going to Waste," Office of Senate Finance Committee Chairman, April 20, 2020.

23. Wanda Vázquez Garced, Letter to Senator Charles Grassley, Office of the Governor of Puerto Rico, La Fortaleza, San Juan, April 27, 2020.

This book would not have been possible without the research, editing, and support of Pablo José Hernádez Rivera.

INDEX

AAA. *See* Aqueduct and Sewerage Authority

AAFAF (Financial Advisory and Fiscal Agency Authority), 117

Abbot Laboratories, 68

Acevedo, Héctor Luis, 74

Acevedo Vilá, Aníbal, 96, 110–12, 113, 125, 212

Administration for the Financing of Health Services, 106

Administration of a Resolution (Goodsell), 87, 102

administrative revolution, Puerto Rico's need for, 87

AFICA (Puerto Rico Industrial, Tourism, Educational, Medical, and Environmental Financing Authority), 106

Agosto Alicea, Juan: on borrowing, debt, and financial crisis, 81–82; on GDB, 81–82, 102, 108, 109, 110, 112; on public corporations and their labor unions, 94–96

agriculture versus industrialization, 17, 19, 21, 23–24, 78

Alaskan statehood (1958), 143–44, 156, 167

Albizu Campos, Pedro, 161–62, 195

Alegría, Ricardo, 148

Alliance for Progress, 3, 46

American Mercury, 192

American Samoa, IOC separate recognition of, 150

Americanization/assimilation, 34–35, 40, 145, 147–49, 155, 161, 181, 186, 195

America's Empire in the Philippines (Karnow), 178

anemia, 191

anti-Americanism, 18, 146–47, 153, 155, 161–62, 195–97

Anti-Imperialism League, 179

Aponte, José, 111

Aqueduct and Sewerage Authority (AAA), 93–96, 105, 108, 125

Aqueduct Independent Union (UIA), 93, 94–96

Armed Forces of National Liberation (FALN or Macheteros), 162

Army Corps of Engineers, 136

Ashford, Bailey K., 191, 194

assassinations and assassination attempts, 155, 161–62

assimilation/Americanization, 34–35, 40, 145, 147–49, 155, 161, 181, 186, 195

Atlantic Charter, 198–99

Baker, Howard, 201
Baker, James, 58
Banco Popular de Puerto Rico, 146
Baralt, Guillermo, 42
Barceló, Antonio, 48
Barton, Hu, 57
Baucus, Max, 69
Baxter, 65
beauty contests, international, 150
Beaverbrook, Lord, 89
Bell, Charles Jasper, 101
Benítez, Jaime, 47, 55–56, 123–24, 125, 166–67, 200
Bernstein, Leonard, 2
Berríos, Ruben, 153, 162
Biden, Joe, 139
bilharzia, 19
Black, Ruby, 18, 155
Blackburn, Marsha, 210–11
"blood tax" (military service by Puerto Ricans), 150–51, 154
Bloomberg News, 116
Boente, Dana J., 135
borrowing, debt, and financial collapse, viii–ix, 3–4, 73–82, 207; Coliseum and other Olympics sites, construction of, 80–81, 82, 108; continued growth of debt, 114–15; Curet Cuevas's predictions regarding, 73–75; extent of spending and accumulated debt, 81–82; GDB, financing debt through, 77, 80, 81–82, 102, 106–7; health care

reforms, 75–77, 82, 108; loss of credit and announcement of bankruptcy, viii, 98, 99–100, 129; "perfect storm" of seven converging factors leading to, 129–30; public corporations' contribution to, 96; repeal of Section 936 and, 52–53, 70, 72; Super Aqueduct project, 82, 95; Urban Train (Tren Urbano), 77–80, 82, 96

Boulding, Kenneth E., 15–16
Bowles, Chester, 15
Breaux, John, 69
Breitbart News, 210
Bristol-Myers, 68
Bryan, Kevin, 70, 71
Buscaglia, Rafael, 102, 104, 107, 117
Bush, George H. W., 59, 201
Butler, Paul, 200, 202

Cabrera, Héctor, 68
Calderón, Sila, 69, 80–81, 93–94, 108–11, 112
capitalist exploitation of Puerto Rico by U.S., 16, 25–26, 84, 87, 89, 166, 192, 195–96
Caribbean Basin Initiative, 59
Caribe Hilton, 103
Carr, Raymond, 84, 172–73, 174, 177, 193
Carrión, Richard, and "Carrión conglomeration," 146
Carroll, Henry K., and Carroll Report, 173, 182–83, 184, 186
Carter, Jimmy, 199, 202
Casals, Marta, 1
Casals, Pablo, and Casals Festival, 1–2

Casellas, Salvador, 47, 56, 98
Castro, Fidel, 90, 162
Ceiba, military base at, 152, 154
Celso Barbosa, José, 32, 132, 181, 201
Century Foundation, 172
China Rx (Gibson), 209
China's pharmaceutical ingredients,
    U.S. dependence on, vii, 143,
    208–11
Christmas bonus, mandatory/
    guaranteed, 118, 119, 122–23,
    126, 127
Churchill, Winston, 198
Cifuentes, Álvaro, 62
citizenship, U.S., of Puerto Ricans, 18,
    19, 28, 35, 135, 137, 144, 150,
    155, 160, 163, 164, 186–88
Ciudadanos Pro Estado 51 (Citizens
    for State 51), 36, 39
Clinton, Bill, vii, ix, 28, 54, 61, 66,
    71, 73, 75, 76
Clinton, Hillary, 76
CNBC, ix, 54
COFINA (Puerto Rico Sales Tax
    Financing Corporation), 113, 115
Cold War, 26
Coliseum, 80–81, 82, 108
Colonial Policies of the United States
    (Theodore Roosevelt, Jr.), 195
colonialism: American colonial
    system, problematics of, 84–85,
    138, 146–47, 158–60, 194–95;
    Atlantic Charter and
    commitment to self-
    determination, 198–200;
    capitalist exploitation of Puerto
    Rico by U.S., 16, 25–26, 84, 87,
    89, 166, 192, 195–96;
    characterization of U.S.–Puerto

Rico relationship as, 188–89,
    193; economic problems of
    Puerto Rico attributed to, 9–11;
    European colonialism, 188;
    PROMESA viewed as return to,
    205; return of pharmaceuticals
    industry to Puerto Rico affected
    by status politics, 213–15; Spain
    and Spanish rule, 1, 9, 160–61,
    178–81, 183; territorial clause,
    claim of congressional power
    over Puerto Rico due to, 4–6,
    171–72, 183, 204; transition
    from colony to self-governing
    commonwealth, 15–16, 25;
    unincorporated territory,
    Supreme Court cases establishing
    Puerto Rico as, 185, 187; U.S.
    colonization of Puerto Rico
    (1898), 19, 30, 32, 55, 158,
    177–83
Colorado, Antonio, 59
Commerce Department, U.S., 141
Commonwealth Oil Refinery
    Company, 46
commonwealth status of Puerto Rico,
    2–5, 164–72; common defense
    and, 152; "dominion" status
    suggested by Theodore Roosevelt,
    Jr., presaging, 195; effective self-
    government and self-control
    under, 35–36; Fernos-Murray
    bill, 36, 37; "free association" or
    "sovereign commonwealth"
    status, 133, 135; historical
    development of, 164–69;
    juridical battle over, 169–72;
    juridical defect of restricted
    U.S. voting rights, 35–36;

commonwealth status of Puerto
Rico (*cont.*)
Operation Bootstrap and
economic growth, 28, 32;
plebiscites on, 6, 36–41, 133–36,
139, 156, 168; Puerto Rico
Federal Relations Act, 55;
repeal of Section 936 affecting,
72; self-determination, meaning
of U.S. commitment to, 199,
200; survival of, 169; territorial
clause interpretation affecting,
4–6, 171–72, 183, 204;
viewed as backdoor for
independence by statehood
supporters, 33, 161
competitiveness, economic, 24, 62,
84, 104, 120, 126, 127, 129,
130, 142, 174
Congressional Quarterly, 68–69
Congressional Research Service, 143
Constant Gardener, The (Le Carré), 65
Constitution of Puerto Rico: balanced
budget clause and debt limit in,
4, 104–7; commonwealth status
and, 4–5, 25, 32, 35, 55;
replacement of president by
secretary of state under, 8
Constitution, U.S., 5, 27, 37, 138,
143, 183
Constitutional Convention (1951),
89–90, 122, 123
construction/infrastructure/housing
industries, and Section 936, 56
consumerism, 34–35, 148
Controlled Foreign Corporation
status, 67, 68
Coolidge, Calvin, 193
Copaken, Richard, 58
Copeland, Aaron, 2

Cora, Alex, 150
Córdova Díaz, Jorge, 122
Córdova Iturregui, Félix, 71
coronavirus/COVID-19 pandemic,
vii, 8, 207–10, 214–15
Corrada del Río, Baltasar, 61
corruption, political, in Puerto Rico,
7, 11, 134, 145–46, 159, 208,
214–215
Cotton, Tom, 210
Cowles, Mike, 203
Creole elite, 145–46
Crisis: Al borde de la quiebra (Agosto),
82
Cuba, in Spanish-American War, 177,
178–79, 183, 189
Cuban Revolution, 3, 15, 58, 90, 162
Culebra (island), 152
culture of Puerto Rico and statehood
movement, 147–49
Cuomo, Andrew, 7, 136
Curet Cuevas, Eliezer, 73–77, 79, 82,
108
"curse" on Puerto Rico, 9, 11

Dalmau Ramírez, Juan, 160
Davis, George W., 55, 182
Debs, Eugene, 196
debt. *See* borrowing, debt, and
financial collapse
Deficit Reduction Act, 61
Democracia, La (newspaper), 192
Democratic Party, 39, 62, 63, 121,
139, 200–202
democratic socialism, 87, 118
Descartes, Sol Luis, 23, 29
diseases prevalent in historical Puerto
Rico, 19, 191, 194
Disuniting of America, The
(Schlesinger), 149

Dole, Bob, 201
Dorvillier, William, 203
Dubinsky, David, 2, 121–22

earthquakes (2019), 8, 9, 208
Ease of Doing Business Report
(World Bank, 2018), 92, 129
Economic Development Act for
Distressed Zones, 142–43
Economic Development
Administration (EDA), 124
economic rise and fall of Puerto Rico,
vi–ix, 1–11, 207–15; borrowing,
debt, and financial collapse,
viii–ix, 3–4, 73–82, 207 (*see also*
borrowing, debt, and financial
collapse); "Camelot" and
economic rise, 1–3; capitalist
exploitation, 16, 25–26, 84, 87,
89, 166, 192, 195–96;
competitiveness, need for Puerto
Rico to achieve, 24, 62, 84, 104,
120, 126, 127, 129, 130, 142,
174; coronavirus/COVID-19
pandemic and, vii, 8, 207–10,
214–15; "curse" on Puerto Rico,
9, 11; earthquakes (2019), 8, 9,
208; financial drain of Puerto
Rico on U.S., 158–59; living
conditions of ordinary Puerto
Ricans, 19, 25, 52–53, 181–82,
191–92; natural/unnatural
economic state in Puerto Rico,
43; "perfect storm" of seven
converging factors leading to,
129–30; political status of Puerto
Rico and, 9–11, 173–74 (*see also*
colonialism; commonwealth
status of Puerto Rico;
independence movement;

political status of Puerto
Rico; statehood movement);
population levels, 7, 19–20,
52–53, 163, 192; PROMESA,
institution of, 4–6, 208
(*see also* PROMESA); pulling
out of financial collapse,
130; Rosselló political crisis
and resignation, 7–8, 208;
Section 936, passage of, 3,
47–48, 56–58; Yom Kippur
Oil War of 1973 and, 29,
46–48, 54, 98–99. *See also*
Fomento; historical context of
U.S.–Puerto Rico relationship;
labor policy and employment;
Operation Bootstrap;
pharmaceutical and medical
products industry in Puerto
Rico; Section 936, repeal of;
tax exemption in Puerto Rico
economic viability of statehood,
139–44, 155–57, 195
Economist, The, 118, 125, 139–40, 142
EDA (Economic Development
Administration), 124
Eisenhower, Dwight D., 199
El Yunque rain forest, 53
electric power infrastructure: costs of
electric power in Puerto Rico, 92;
debt crisis, contribution to, 96;
Hurricane Maria and, viii, 92;
labor unions and, 91, 92; Operation Bootstrap and government
monopoly on, 17; PREPA, 88,
91, 92, 102, 105; private power
companies and, 89; as public
corporation, 88–89, 91, 92, 96;
Puerto Rico Water Resources
Authority, 17, 88, 89, 102

Electrical Industry and Irrigation
   Workers Union (UTIER), 91
electronics industries and repeal
   of Section 936, 53–54, 56,
   65, 67
eliminación de la Sección 936, La
   (Córdova Iturregui), 71
Embrel, 67
emigration: after Hurricane Maria, 7,
   118, 163; from countryside to San
   Juan, 77; culture of Puerto Rico
   and, 147; GAO 2018 report on,
   115; Latin American/Caribbean
   emigration efforts and Puerto
   Rican rejection of independence,
   163; population levels affected by,
   52–53, 163; racial discrimination
   and, 145; at time of Operation
   Bootstrap, 26, 161
Empire by Default (Musicant), 177
employment. *See* labor policy and
   employment
English First Foundation, 149
English versus Spanish language,
   147–49, 186, 203, 204
enterprise zone program, 62, 142–43
estadidad jíbara (native statehood),
   40, 148, 149
Estadistas Unidos (United
   Statehooders), 38–39

Fajardo area, 76
FALN (Armed Forces of National
   Liberation or Macheteros), 163
Fanon, Frantz, 162
fascism in Puerto Rico, 87, 162
federal minimum wage increases, 24,
   28, 45, 120–22
Federal Party, 184

Feliciano, Zadia, 66
FEMA, 136
Fernos-Murray bill, 36, 37
Ferré, Luis A.: culture of Puerto Rico
   and, 147–48; defeated by
   Sánchez Vilella, 34; elected as
   first pro-statehood governor,
   30–31, 40; on federal minimum
   wage increases, 45, 122; on
   Fomento, tax exemption, and
   Operation Bootstrap, 30–31, 35,
   41–45, 49, 50; food stamp
   program and, 99; Teresita
   Fuentes and, 213; GDB and,
   108; history of statehood
   movement in Puerto Rico and,
   32–33, 72; on labor policy,
   122–23; plebiscite of 1967 and
   birth of NPP, 38–41, 168–69;
   Romero Barceló compared, 48;
   Pedro Rosselló compared, 60;
   on Section 936, 58, 63; Status
   Commission report and, 168;
   U.S. national politics and, 201
Ferré family, 41, 146
finances. *See* economic rise and fall of
   Puerto Rico
Financial Advisory and Fiscal Agency
   Authority (AAFAF), 117
Fomento (Puerto Rico Industrial
   Development Company;
   PRIDCO): approval of Section
   936 and revival of, 99; beneficial
   effects of Section 936 on, 53, 57;
   commonwealth status made
   possible by, 72; creation of,
   21–22, 100–101; extension to
   Caribbean and Central America,
   59; Ferré and, 41–42; Fortuño

and, 113, 114; GDB and, 22, 100–102, 103; labor policy/ employment and, 91, 119–22, 124; links to U.S. via, 26; on making Puerto Rico competitive, 130; number of manufacturing plants attracted by, 24–25; Operation Bootstrap, introduction of, 16, 17, 20, 24–25; privatization of, 41; as public corporation, 88; repeal of Section 936 and, 28, 57, 59, 62, 67, 72; statehood movement and, 41–51, 72; tax exemption proposal of Moscoso and, 20–24
Fonalledas, Jaime and Zoraida, 146
Food and Drug Administration, U.S., viii, 209
food stamp program, 99
Foraker, Joseph, 186
Foraker Act (1900), 55, 161, 184–85, 186
Forbes, vii, viii, ix, 211
Ford, Gerald, 201
Ford, Henry, 2
Fortuño, Luis, 69, 72, 112–15, 128, 129, 133
Fox News, 209
Franco, Francisco, 1–2, 87, 162
free trade between Puerto Rico and U.S., 24, 185, 197
Friedrich, Carl J., 16, 170
Fuentes, Teresita, 143, 213, 214
Fuller, Melville, 185

Gallagher, Mike, 210
Gallisá, Carlos, 91
GAO. *See* General Accounting Office

García Mendez, Miguel Ángel, 33–34, 38, 168
García Padilla, Alejandro, viii, 3, 4, 11, 70, 116, 128, 129, 132
GDB. *See* Government Development Bank
GDP (gross domestic product), 66, 100, 103
GE (General Electric), 53–54, 65, 67
General Accounting Office (GAO), U.S.: 1981 Report of, 141; 2014 Report of, 142; 2018 Report of, 92, 107, 115–16, 123, 126, 129; on possibility of statehood, 141, 142, 155
General Electric (GE), 53–54, 65, 67
General Obligation bonds, 103, 105
Gibson, Rosemary, 209, 210
Gingrich, Newt, 209
GNP (gross national product), 25, 71, 114
González, José Ramón, 108
González Colón, Jenniffer, 6, 137, 139, 142–43, 156, 202, 213–14
Goodsell, Charles T., 87, 102
Gottleib, Scott, viii
Government Development Bank (GDB), 97–117; under Acevedo Vilá, 110–12; borrowing and debt, descent into, 77, 80, 81–82, 102, 106–7, 114–15; building for, 97–98, 117; under Calderón, 108–11; Coliseum construction bailed out by, 81, 108; credit rating (1987), 106; demise of, 96, 116–17, 130; Fomento and, 22, 100–102, 103; under Fortuño, 112–15; GAO Report of 2018 on, 92, 107, 115–16;

Government Development Bank (GDB) (*cont.*)
health care reform financing through, 77, 108; under Hernández Colón, 105–8; origins of and opposition to, 98, 100–102; political interference with, 107–9; private financing by, 103; as public corporation, 88; public corporations and, 84, 104–5; Puerto Rico's loss of credit (2014) and announcement of bankruptcy, 97–117; purpose and activities of, 102, 103–4; under Rosselló, 81, 82, 108, 109; "secret debt," refinancing of, 109; Section 936 funds, effects of loss of, 67; Section 936 funds deposited in, 56; trust in fiscal responsibility of, 104–6; Urban Train deficits funded by, 80; Yom Kippur oil crisis of 1973, austerity program and recovery, 98–99
Grant, Pedro, 91
Grassley, Charles, 69, 212, 214–15
Great Depression, 18, 19, 46, 70, 98, 194
Great Recession of 2008, 111–12, 163
Green, Andrew, 66
Greenhut, Steven, 125–26
gross domestic product (GDP), 66, 100, 103
gross national product (GNP), 25, 71, 114
Gruening, Ernest, 18, 197–98
Guam, IOC separate recognition of, 150
Guerra, Nicanor, 165

H1N1 epidemic/swine flu (2009), 210
Hanna, José, 184, 185
Harding, Warren G., 187
Hawaiian statehood (1959), 143–44, 145, 156, 167
Hay, John, 179
health and health care:
Administration for the Financing of Health Services, 106; coronavirus/COVID-19 pandemic, vii, 8, 207–10, 214–15; diseases prevalent in historical Puerto Rico, 19, 191, 194; reforms, borrowing and debt due to, 75–77, 82, 108
Hearst, Randolph, 2
Hernández, Zaida, 125
Hernández Colón, Rafael, 3, 4–5; Calderón and, 109; commonwealth status defended by, 169; English versus Spanish language and, 148; Fortuño compared, 115; GDB and, 105–8; government salary increases, decision to forgo, 47, 99, 110; labor unions and, 92, 93; oil crisis/embargo and, 81, 98–99, 106–7, 129; on political status of Puerto Rico, 134; on PROMESA, 205; repeal of Section 936 and, 54–56, 58–59, 70, 71; self-determination, on meaning of, 199–200; statehood movement and, 46, 47, 50; Urban Train under, 78; on Vieques, Culebra, and U.S. national defense, 153
Hernández Mayoral, José Alfredo, 1–3

Hernández Mayoral, Juan Eugenio, 71
Hiram Bithorn baseball stadium, 80
Hispanic Heritage Month, 139
*historia del Partido Popular
    Democrático, La* (Muñoz), 87
historical context of U.S.–Puerto
    Rico relationship, 177–205;
    American intentions following
    Spanish-American War, 181–83;
    Atlantic Charter and
    commitment to self-
    determination, 198–200;
    colonialism of U.S.–Puerto
    Rican relationship and, 188–89;
    European interest in Puerto
    Rico and conquest by Spain,
    178; Foraker Act (1900)
    establishing civil government,
    55, 161, 184–85, 186; Jones Act
    and U.S. citizenship for Puerto
    Ricans, 186–88; as
    miscommunication and
    misunderstanding, 151, 155,
    173, 181, 189, 190, 197, 200,
    203–5; New Deal, 17, 18, 19,
    83, 85, 120, 121, 154–55,
    195–98; Puerto Rican reaction
    to U.S. takeover, 180–81;
    Theodore Roosevelt, Jr.'s
    governorship, 194–95; Spanish-
    American War and colonization
    of Puerto Rico (1898), 19, 30,
    32, 55, 158, 177–83, 187, 189,
    191, 194; statehood movement
    and, 181, 188; success of
    American rule, different views
    regarding, 190–93; tutelage
    policy, 186; Tydings bill
    (1936), 161, 197–98, 199;

"ungratefulness" of Puerto Rico,
    claims of, 191, 193, 195, 197;
    unincorporated territory,
    Supreme Court cases
    establishing Puerto Rico as, 185,
    187; U.S. national politics in
    Puerto Rico and, 200–203
Hobsbawm, Eric, 16
Holmes, Peter, 69
hookworm, 194
Hoover, Herbert, 194
"hopelessness" of Puerto Rican
    situation prior to Operation
    Bootstrap, 18–20, 43, 104, 198
housing/infrastructure/construction
    industries, and Section 936, 56
Hurricane Irma (2017), 6, 52, 208
Hurricane Maria (2017), viii–ix, 6–7,
    52, 54, 92, 118, 136–37, 150,
    159, 163, 208
Hurricane San Ciriaco (1899), 9,
    183, 185
Hurricane San Felipe (1928), 194
hurricanes, threat of, 9

Ickes, Harold, 83, 198
Iglesias, Santiago, 191
ILGWU (International Ladies
    Garment Workers Union),
    121–22
immigration to U.S. *See* emigration
imperialism, U.S., 10, 26, 178, 179.
    See also colonialism
independence movement, 158–64;
    assassinations and assassination
    attempts, 155, 161–62; Atlantic
    Charter and commitment to self-
    determination, 198–200;
    commonwealth status viewed by

independence movement (*cont.*)
statehood supporters as
backdoor entry for, 33, 161;
convergence of statehood and
independence ideology, 146–47;
cultural arguments for, 147;
drop of pro-independence vote
to less than three percent, 37;
economic arguments against,
157, 162–63; "free association"
or "sovereign commonwealth"
status, 133, 135; historical
background, 161–63; increase
in pro-independence in 2020
elections, 160; Miles
proclamation at end of Spanish-
American War and, 181; Muñoz
giving up support for, 22, 35,
157, 161, 166; Nationalist
Party, 161–62; perceived fear of,
161, 165, 197; PIP (Puerto Rico
Independence Party), 23, 25–
26, 32, 38, 153, 159–60, 162,
164; racial discrimination and,
161, 163; rejected by Puerto
Ricans, 160–61, 163–64; self-
determinism arguments for,
159–60; Tydings bill (1936),
161, 197, 198, 199; U.S.
backing for, 158–59, 164;
Vieques, Culebra, and U.S.
national defense, 152–53
Industrial Development Company,
124
industrialization versus agriculture,
17, 19, 21, 23–24, 78
*Influence of Sea Power upon History,
The* (Mahan), 179
infrastructure/housing/construction
industries, and Section 936, 56

Institute of Puerto Rican Culture,
147, 148
Insular Cases, 5, 185
Inter-American Conference, 193
Inter-American Human Rights
Commission, 138
International Ladies Garment Workers
Union (ILGWU), 121–22
International Olympics Committee
(IOC), 150
Izquierdo Encarnación, José, 79

Jackson, Henry M., 149
Jaime Fonalledas Enterprises, 146
"*jíbaro* party" (party of rural workers),
PDP as, 34, 40
job loss and job creation. *See* labor
policy and employment
Joelson, Walter K., 53
John F. Kennedy Library and
Museum, Boston, 1
Johnson, Lyndon B., 46, 159, 167,
202
Jones Act, 167, 170, 286–187
junk status, Puerto Rican bonds
downgraded to, 98
juridical battle over commonwealth
status, 169–72
juridical defect of restricted U.S.
voting rights, 35–36
Justice Department, U.S., 135–36,
146, 156–57, 171–72

Kaine, Tim, 211
Karnow, Stanley, 178
Kennedy, Edward, 202
Kennedy, Jacqueline, 1
Kennedy, John F., 1–3, 37, 46, 55,
121, 152–53, 157, 201–2, 204
Korean War, 150–51

La Fortaleza, San Juan, 21, 30, 84, 85, 156, 180
La Guardia, Fiorello, 20
labor policy and employment: Christmas bonus, mandatory/ guaranteed, 118, 119, 122–23, 126, 127; Constitutional Convention (1951) on, 89–90; federal minimum wage increases, 24, 28, 45, 120–22; job creation, 20, 46, 52, 57, 62, 65, 105, 120–22, 128, 174; job loss due to Fortuño's spending cuts, 113; job loss due to repeal of Section 936, 67, 71; Operation Bootstrap and, 119–20; paradox of raising wages versus creating jobs, 120–22, 128; public corporation unions, 89–92, 93, 94–96, 124; public employees, full unionization of, 123–26; reforms, efforts to implement, 126–29; unemployment rates, ix, 7, 25, 26, 46, 47, 64, 118, 119, 173–74; worker protections in Puerto Rico compared to states, 118–19, 126, 128. *See also specific unions*
Latin Americans, Puerto Ricans as, 10
Latin Americans, The (Rangel), 10
Lausell Hernández, Luis, 91
Le Carré, John, 65
León, Vicente, 102
Lessons of the War with Spain (Mahan), 179
Liberal Party, 48, 196, 197, 198
LIFE magazine, 104
Lindbergh, Charles, 193
Lippmann, Walter, 2, 194
Lodge, Henry Cabot, 178

Longworth, Alice Roosevelt, 2
Look magazine, 203
Luchetti, Antonio, 88–89
Lugo, Hector René, 94–96

"Macarena, La," 74
Macheteros (Armed Forces of National Liberation; FALN), 163
Macías y Casado, Manuel, 180
Mahan, Alfred, 179, 183
malaria, 194
Maldonado, Jerry, 53
Maldonado, Raul, 7
Marxism/Marxism-Leninism, 21, 91, 162, 195
McConnell, Mitch, 139, 211
McKinley, William, 173, 178, 181–84, 187
McSally, Martha, 139
Mellon, Paul, 2
Mendez, Carlos "Johnny," 127
Mendoza, Inés, 1
Menendez, Bob, 210
Menotti, Gian Carlo, 2
Merck, 68
Miami Herald, 209
migration. *See* emigration
Miles, Nelson, 19, 180–81
Mills, Wilbur, 56
Minimum Wage Board, 121
minimum wage increases, federal, 24, 28, 45, 120–22
miscommunication and misunder- standing between Puerto Rico and U.S., 151, 155, 173, 181, 189, 190, 197, 200, 203–5
Moody's, 105, 141
Morales, William, 162
Morales Carrión, Arturo, 191, 194, 195

Morrow, Edward R., 2
Moscoso, Gloria, 45
Moscoso, Teodoro: Calderón
  compared, 109; Casals and, 2; on
  federal minimum wage increases,
  45; GDB, founding of, 100–
  101; GE plant and, 53; on labor
  policy and employment, 119–20;
  Law 154 imposing tax on tax
  exempt industries and, 114;
  plant executives and managers
  taking up role of, 67; positive
  publicity generated by, 104;
  public corporations and, 88, 89;
  replaced at Fomento by Ferré,
  44; return to Fomento under
  Muñoz, 45–46; Section 936,
  passage of, 47–48, 55–56;
  statehood movement and, 35,
  41–48, 50; tax exemption
  proposal of, 20–24, 27, 29, 103;
  Tugwell and, 17, 21–22, 24.
  See also Fomento
Movimiento Obrero Unido (United
  Workers Movement; MOU), 91
Mundo, El, 91, 102, 188, 203
Muñoz, Victoria, 60
Muñoz Marín, Luis: as anticapitalist,
  21, 22, 87, 166, 192, 195–96;
  assassination attempt on, 162;
  Antonio Barceló and, 48; on
  capitalist exploitation, 192;
  Casals and, 1–3; on colonialism
  of U.S.–Puerto Rican
  relationship, 188–89; on
  commonwealth status, 164–72;
  on consumerism in Puerto Rico,
  34–35; death of, 169; early
  Marxism of, 21, 101, 121, 195;
  fiscal policy on borrowing under,

76; GDB (Government Development Bank) and, 100–101,
  103–4; Hernández Colón
  compared, 105; independence,
  giving up support for, 22, 35,
  157, 161, 166; Institute of
  Puerto Rican Culture and, 147;
  introduction of Operation
  Bootstrap and, 16–20; on
  juridical defect, 35; labor policy
  and, 89, 90, 121–23; loyalty,
  American questions about, 155;
  on minimum wage, 45, 121;
  on national politics, 200, 201;
  New Deal and, 195–98; one-
  party system under, view of
  Puerto Rico as, 1–3; plebiscite of
  1967 and birth of NPP, 36–41,
  168–69; political career under
  Operation Bootstrap, 25–27;
  on political status of Puerto Rico,
  5, 16, 22; positive publicity
  generated by, 104; privatization
  of Fomento and, 41; public
  corporations under, 85–87, 89,
  90, 93; retirement from active
  political life, 33–34, 37; return of
  Moscoso to Fomento, arranging,
  45–46; Theodore Roosevelt, Jr.,
  and, 194; Sánchez Vilella and,
  34, 37–40, 46, 47; statehood
  movement and, 30, 31, 32, 43,
  140, 157; on status politics in
  Puerto Rico, 172, 183; tax
  exemption and, 20–24, 29, 44,
  55; Tugwell and, 18, 85–87, 167;
  Twentieth Century Fund/
  Century Foundation and, 172;
  on U.S. colonialism, 158; on
  Vieques, 152

Muñoz Rivera, Luis, 162, 165, 180–82, 184, 186–87, 196
Musicant, Ivan, 177
Mussolini, Benito, 100, 162

National Bureau of Economic Research, 66–67
National Guard, 92, 207
national politics in Puerto Rico, 200–203
national security and Puerto Rico, 150–55, 179
Nationalist Party, 161–62
naval stations, U.S., in Puerto Rico, 151–55
Navarro, Peter, 210
Negrón López, Luis, 39–40
New Deal, 17, 18, 19, 83, 85, 120, 121, 154–55, 195–98
New Progressive Party (NPP): anti-Bootstrap position of, 26–27; corruption investigation and "anti-statehood conspiracy," 145–46; culture of Puerto Rico and, 147–48; Curet Cuevas on, 73–75; election of Ricardo Rosselló and, 131–32; on federal minimum wage increases, 45, 122; financial crisis, requesting U.S. government intervention in, 4; GDB and, 111, 112–15; Hurricane Maria and, 137; on labor policy, 122, 125, 126, 128; *El Nuevo Día* and, 146; plebiscite of 1967 and birth of, 36–41, 133, 168–69; plebiscites instituted under, 6, 133–36, 139, 156, 157; political crisis under Ricardo Rosselló, 7–8; power-sharing with PDP, 111; Section 936, repeal of, 59–64, 66, 68; Section 936 replacement initiatives and, 69–71, 213–14; U.S. national politics in Puerto Rico and, 202. *See also specific governors*
New York Herald Tribune, 194
New York Post, 211
New York Times, 208–9, 210
Newsweek, 144
Nickles, Don, 200
Nixon, Richard, 201, 202
Northern Ireland, Puerto Rico compared to, 161, 173
NPP. *See* New Progressive Party
Nuevo Día, El, 74–75, 146

OAS (Organization of American States), 138
Obama, Barack, 4, 151, 204
Ogilvy, David, 104
oil crisis of 1973/oil embargo of 1973–1975, 29, 46–48, 54, 98–99, 106, 126, 127, 129
Olympics Committee of Puerto Rico, 80–81, 149–50
one-party system, view of Puerto Rico as, 30, 31
Operation Bootstrap, 15–29; agriculture versus industrialization, 17, 19, 21, 23–24; defined, 2, 24; economic miracle arising out of, 16–18, 24–27, 43; end of, with repeal of Section 936, ix, 3, 11, 29, 72, 129, 130; Ferré and, 30–31; free trade between Puerto Rico and U.S., 24; hopelessness of Puerto Rican situation prior to, 18–20, 43, 104, 198;

Operation Bootstrap (*cont.*)
  Independence Party, anti-
  Bootstrap campaign of, 25–26;
  labor costs affecting, 119–20;
  living conditions for ordinary
  Puerto Ricans under, 25;
  manufacturing decline under
  Ferré, 44; minimum wage
  increases, federal, Puerto Rico
  not subject to, 24, 27; political
  repercussions of, 15–16, 25–27;
  Section 936, passage of, 3,
  47–48, 56–58; statehood
  movement and, 26–29, 34–35,
  41–51; tax exemption plan
  proposed by Moscoso, 20–24,
  27, 29, 103; Yom Kippur oil
  crisis of 1973 and, 46–48
Operation Serenity, 34–35
Organic Acts, 27, 167, 171
Organization of American States
  (OAS), 138
Ormandy, Eugene, 2
Ortega y Gassett, José, 205

Pagan, Bolívar, 102
Panama Canal, 151, 155, 179, 190
Paris, Treaty of (1898), 183
PDP. *See* Popular Democratic Party
Peat Marwick, 81
Pedrín Zorrilla Mini-Coliseum, 80
Pelosi, Nancy, 211
per capita income, 10, 25, 43, 103
petrochemical industry, 42, 43, 46–47,
  56, 103
Pfizer, 68
pharmaceutical and medical products
  industry in Puerto Rico: as
  answer to U.S. dependence on

foreign pharmaceuticals, 211–15;
  beneficial effects of Section 936
  for, 56, 61, 65; China's
  pharmaceutical ingredients,
  U.S. dependence on, vii, 143,
  208–11; Controlled Foreign
  Corporation status, adopting,
  67, 68; coronavirus/COVID-19
  pandemic and, 207–10, 214–15;
  effects of repeal of Section 936,
  vii–viii, ix, 67–69; Hurricane
  Maria affecting, viii–ix; lobbying
  for retention of Section 936,
  61–62, 64; preparation for
  phase-out of Section 936, 64–65;
  statehood movement affecting
  return of, 213–15
Pharmaceutical Industry Association,
  61, 68, 111
Philippines: independence of, 22,
  197; in Spanish-American War
  (1898), 179, 181, 183
Pierluisi, Pedro, 4, 8, 69–70, 72, 132,
  134, 156, 202
PIP (Puerto Rico Independence
  Party), 23, 25–26, 32, 38, 153,
  159–60, 162, 164
Planning Board, 17, 78, 159
Playtex, 65
plebiscites on political status of Puerto
  Rico, 6, 36–41, 133–36, 139,
  156, 168
*Plunder! How Public Employee Unions
  Are Raiding Treasuries, Controlling
  our Lives, and Bankrupting the
  Nation* (Greenhut), 125–26
political status of Puerto Rico, 158–74;
  convergence of statehood and
  independence ideology, 146–47;

"dominion" status suggested by Theodore Roosevelt, Jr., 195; economic competitiveness, need for Puerto Rico to achieve, 24, 62, 84, 104, 120, 126, 127, 129, 130, 142, 174; economic problems and, 9–11, 173–74; financial collapse and, 3–6, 130; first gubernatorial elections (1948), 25; Foraker Act (1900) leaving island without political status, 184–85; miscommunication and misunderstanding between Puerto Rico and U.S. regarding, 151, 155, 173, 181, 189, 190, 197, 200, 203–5; Operation Bootstrap, political repercussions of, 15–16, 25–27; plebiscites on, 6, 36–41, 133–36, 139, 156, 168; PROMESA/ Fiscal Board and, 4–6, 9, 137, 172; repeal of Section 936 and, 71–72; return of pharmaceuticals industry to Puerto Rico affected by, 213–15; territorial clause, claim of congressional power over Puerto Rico due to, 4–6, 171–72, 183, 204; Twentieth Century Fund/Century Foundation and Raymond Carr on, 172–73; unincorporated territory, Supreme Court cases establishing Puerto Rico as, 185, 187; United States–Puerto Rico Commission on, 37–38, 48, 72, 132, 136, 140–41, 144, 149, 155, 157, 167–68. *See also* colonialism; commonwealth status of Puerto Rico; historical

context of U.S.–Puerto Rico relationship; independence movement; statehood movement; *specific parties*
Ponce Museum of Art, 31
Popular Democratic Party (PDP): commonwealth status and, 165, 169; on federal minimum wage increases, 45; financial crisis, requesting U.S. government intervention in, 4; Fomento and, 21–22, 41, 44, 46; GDB and, 102, 109–12; as "*jíbaro* party" (party of rural workers), 34, 40; on juridical defect, 35, 36; labor policy/employment/unions and, 90, 96, 120, 121, 122–23, 125, 128; mandate to govern, belief in, 86; *El Nuevo Día* and, 146; plebiscites and, 37–41, 133–34, 135; power-sharing with NPP, 111; retirement of Muñoz and election of Sánchez Vilella, 33–34; Pedro Rosselló on, 146; Section 936, repeal of, 60; Section 936 replacement initiatives and, 70, 212; statehood movement versus, 30–34, 49, 161; success of Operation Bootstrap and, 25; U.S. national politics in Puerto Rico and, 201, 202. *See also specific governors*
population levels in Puerto Rico, 7, 19–20, 52–53, 163, 192
PREPA (Puerto Rico Electric Power Authority), 88, 91, 92, 102, 105
PRIDCO (Puerto Rico Industrial Development Company). *See* Fomento

privatization of public corporations, 41, 93–94

PRMA (Puerto Rico Manufacturers' Association), 62, 64, 102, 111, 143, 144, 211–12

PROMESA (Puerto Rican Oversight, Management and Economic Stability Act, 2016) and PROMESA Fiscal Board: economic crisis and institution of, 4, 11, 70, 158, 204, 208; on existing condition of Puerto Rico, 52–53, 174; GDB, demise of, 116–17; labor reforms proposed by, 126–29; opposition in Puerto Rico to, 141–42, 159, 204–5; on pharmaceuticals industry in Puerto Rico, 211; Pierluisi and, 132, 142; political status of Puerto Rico and, 4–6, 9, 137, 172

Pryor, David, 61, 63, 65

PSP (Socialist Party), 32, 91, 162

public corporations, 83–96; administrative revolution, Puerto Rico's need for, 87; as borrowing agencies, 106; creation of, under Muñoz and Tugwell, 83–87, 89, 93; debt crisis, contribution to, 96, 130; defined and described, 84; electric power infrastructure and, 88–89, 91, 92, 96; GDB and, 84, 104–5; independence of, 88; labor unions of, 89–92, 93, 94–96, 124; privatization efforts, 41, 93–94; water supply and, 93–96. *See also specific corporations*

Puerto Rican Oversight, Management and Economic Stability Act. *See* PROMESA

Puerto Rico. *See* economic rise and fall of Puerto Rico

Puerto Rico: A Colonial Experiment (Carr), 173, 177

"Puerto Rico: Factors Contributing to the Debt Crisis and Potential Federal Actions to Address Them" (GAO, 2018), 92, 107, 115–16, 123, 126, 129

Puerto Rico Aqueduct and Sewerage Authority (AAA), 93–96, 105, 108, 125

Puerto Rico Development Funds Agency, 106

Puerto Rico Economic Relief Administration, 196

Puerto Rico Election Commission, 156

Puerto Rico Electric Power Authority (PREPA), 88, 91, 92, 102, 105

Puerto Rico Federal Relations Act, 55

Puerto Rico Highway and Transportation Authority, 79, 96

Puerto Rico Independence Party (PIP), 23, 25–26, 32, 38, 153, 159–60, 162, 164

Puerto Rico Industrial, Tourism, Educational, Medical, and Environmental Financing Authority (AFICA), 106

Puerto Rico Industrial Development Company (PRIDCO). *See* Fomento

Puerto Rico Investment Promotion Act, 70

Puerto Rico Manufacturers' Association (PRMA), 62, 64, 102, 111, 143, 144, 211–12

Puerto Rico Sales Tax Financing Corporation (COFINA), 113, 115

Puerto Rico Water Resources
     Authority, 17, 88, 89, 102
Puerto Rico–USA Foundation, 64, 69

Quebec, Puerto Rico compared to,
     149, 173

racial discrimination: independence
     movement and, 161, 163; under
     Spanish rule, 181; statehood
     debate and, 144–46
Ramos, Angel, 203
Rangel, Carlos, 10
Rangel, Charles, 62, 72
Reagan, Ronald, and Reagan
     doctrine, 58–59, 105, 201
Republican Coalition Party, 86, 101,
     196, 198
Republican Party, 17, 26, 31, 32–33,
     86, 136–39, 181, 184, 198,
     201–3. *See also* Statehood
     Republican Party
Richardson, Elliot, 153
Riggs, Francis E. (American police
     chief of San Juan), assassination
     of, 155, 161, 197
Rincón de Gautier, Felisa, 201
ringworm, 191
Rivera, Ignacio, 53–54
Rivera Casiano, Pedro, 50
Rivera Shatz, Thomas, 10, 127, 136,
     141, 147
Roberto Clemente Coliseum, 80
Rodriguez, Carlos, 143
Rodríguez, Guillermo, 98
Rodriguez, Ivan, 6
Roig, Antonio, 101
Romero Barceló, Carlos: on culture of
     Puerto Rico, 148; Fortuño

criticized by, 114, 115; on labor
     policy, 128; Moscoso, meeting
     with, 50; on plebiscite, 156;
     Section 936, repeal of, 60–63,
     65, 66, 72, 116; *Statehood Is
     for the Poor*, 28, 49–51, 63, 72,
     148; on statehood movement,
     Operation Bootstrap, and tax
     exemption, 27–28, 30, 36,
     48–51, 146; Tennessee Plan
     and, 136; U.S. national politics
     in Puerto Rico and, 202
Roosevelt, Eleanor, 18–19, 196, 197
Roosevelt, Franklin Delano, 16–17,
     18, 20, 83, 89, 102, 121, 161,
     195–99
Roosevelt, Theodore, 2, 178–79, 190,
     191, 198
Roosevelt, Theodore, Jr., 194–95
Roosevelt Roads naval base, 152, 154
Root, Elihu, 55, 188
Rosen, Jeffrey A., 156
Rosselló, Pedro: Calderón compared,
     109; Coliseum and other
     Olympics sites, construction of,
     80–81, 108; Fortuño defeating,
     112; government debt and
     GDB under, 81, 82, 108, 109;
     health care reforms of, 75–77,
     108; OAS/Inter-American
     Human Rights Commission
     petitioned for statehood by,
     138; plebiscites under, 133;
     public corporations, privatization
     of, 93; on public employee
     unionization, 123, 125; re-
     election as governor in 1996,
     73–75, 130; Ricardo Rosselló
     as son of, 116, 131, 132;

Rosselló, Pedro (*cont.*)
  Section 936, repeal of, 59–63,
  65–66, 69, 72, 116; Tennessee
  Plan for statehood and, 136;
  El triumvirato del terror (The
  Triumvirate of Terror) and anti-
  statehood conspiracy, 145–46;
  Urban Train under, 78–80; U.S.
  national politics in Puerto Rico
  and, 202; Vieques, U.S. Naval
  station on, 151, 153
Rosselló, Ricardo: GDB and, 116;
  Hurricane Maria, response to,
  136–37; labor policy under,
  118–19, 126–29; lack of
  political experience, 131; OAS/
  Inter-American Human Rights
  Commission petitioned for
  statehood by, 138; plebiscites
  under, 134–36, 139; political
  crisis and resignation as governor,
  6, 7–8, 208; as son of Pedro
  Rosselló, 116, 131, 132, 202;
  statehood movement and, 6, 9,
  131–32, 134–36, 138, 143, 144;
  U.S. national politics in Puerto
  Rico and, 202
Rough Riders, 178–79
Rousset, M. J., 173, 177
Roy, Avik, vii
Rubio, Marco, 209
rum excise tax, 22, 184
Ryan, Paul, 70, 71, 136

Salazar, Alfredo, 111
sales tax, 111, 112, 113
samurai bonds, 108
San Juan sports complex, 80
San Juan Star, 69, 200, 203

Sanabría, Edgardo, 141
Sánchez Vilella, Roberto, 34, 37–40,
  46, 47, 88
Sanes, David, 153
Santorum, Rick, 69
Schlesinger, Arthur, Jr., 149, 155
Schurz, Carl, 144–45
Seattle Times, 209
Section 931, approval and eventual
  elimination of, 55–56
Section 933A initiative, 70
Section 936, passage of, 3, 47–48,
  56–58
Section 936, repeal of, 52–72; abuses
  of Section 936, 57, 65, 70;
  Caribbean Basin Initiative
  forestalling, 58–59; Curet Cuevas
  on, 73–75; effects of, vii–viii,
  52–54, 66–69, 129; federal
  government opposition to
  Section 936, 56–58, 61, 64, 68,
  71; GAO 2018 report on, 116;
  GE on Puerto Rico and, 53–54;
  historical development of tax
  exemption in Puerto Rico
  and, 55–58; inevitability of,
  64–66; job creation versus
  unemployment rate, 52, 57, 62,
  64, 65; job loss due to, 67, 71;
  job creation grant proposed to
  replace, 57; Operation Bootstrap,
  end of, ix, 3, 11, 29, 72; Puerto
  Rican government requesting, ix,
  3, 11; reasons for, ix, 28, 56–58;
  replacement initiatives, 69–71,
  143, 211–15; reprieve of 1993,
  64; responsibility of Puerto
  Rican government for, 71–72;
  statehood, Section 936 viewed as

obstacle to, 28, 62–64, 69, 71–72, 140, 214; ten-year phase-out of, 28, 66, 81, 112; wage credit proposed to replace, 61, 62

Section 956 initiative, 69

Small Business Job Protection Act (1996), vii, 28

Socialist Party (PSP), 32, 91, 162

Spain and Spanish rule, 1, 9, 160–61, 178–81, 183

Spanish Autonomy Pact, 18

Spanish versus English language, 147–49, 186, 203, 204

Spanish-American War (1898), 158, 177–83, 187, 189, 191, 194

sports in Puerto Rico, 80–81, 149–50

SRP. *See* Statehood Republican Party

Standard & Poor's, 98, 105, 106

statehood for Washington, DC, 139

Statehood Is for the Poor (Romero Barceló), 28, 49–51, 63, 72, 148

statehood movement, ix, 30–51, 131–57; Alaskan/Hawaiian statehood compared, 143–44, 145, 156, 167; "blood tax" (military service by Puerto Ricans) and, 150–51, 154; Ciudadanos Pro Estado 51 (Citizens for State 51), 36, 39; commonwealth status viewed as backdoor for independence by, 33, 161; convergence of statehood and independence ideology, 146–47; culture of Puerto Rico and, 147–49; Democratic Party and, 200; economic viability of statehood, 139–44, 155–57, 195; *estadidad jíbara* (native statehood), 40,

148, 149; Estadistas Unidos (United Statehooders), 38–39; federal minimum wage increases and, 45; Ferré elected as governor, 30–31, 40; financial crisis and, 4, 130; Fomento, tax exemption, and Operation Bootstrap, 26–29, 34–35, 41–51; Fortuño tax exemptions viewed as betrayal of, 114; in historical context of U.S.–Puerto Rico relationship, 181, 188; history of statehood movement, 32–33; House bills and lobbying for, 6; Hurricane Maria and, 136–37; on ideological and political tightrope, 44–45; international sporting events and beauty contests, 149–50; juridical defect of restricted U.S. voting rights, 35–36; labor policy and, 122; likelihood of, 155–57; Miles proclamation at end of Spanish-American War and, 181; plebiscite of 1967 and birth of NPP, 36–41, 133, 168–69; plebiscites on, 6, 36–41, 133–36, 139, 156, 168; PROMESA/Fiscal Board and, 5, 137; racial aspects of debate over, 144–46; repeal of Section 936 viewed as removal of obstacle to, 28, 62–64, 69, 71–72, 140, 214; return of pharmaceuticals industry to Puerto Rico affected by, 213–15; Romero Barceló and, 30, 36, 48–51; Ricardo Rosselló's election as governor on statehood platform, 131–32;

statehood movement (*cont.*)
  self-determination, meaning of
    U.S. commitment to, 199, 200;
    Tennessee Plan, 136; Tydings
    bill (1936) and, 197–98; United
    States–Puerto Rico Commission
    on, 37–38, 48, 72, 132, 136,
    140–41, 144, 149, 155, 157,
    167–68; U.S. national politics
    in Puerto Rico and, 138–39,
    201–2; Vieques, Culebra, and
    U.S. national defense, 151–55;
    Yom Kippur oil crisis of 1973
    and, 46–48. *See also* New
    Progressive Party
Statehood Republican Party (SRP),
  38, 39, 40, 63, 87, 147, 168,
  201, 202
status politics. *See* political status of
  Puerto Rico
Stephansky, Ben, 168
Stephanson, Anders, 182
Stephen, Bret, 210
Stokowski, Leopold, 2
Stone, Edward Durell, 31
Stricken Land, The (Tugwell), 17, 20,
  85, 87
Suez/Ondeo Company, 93–94
Super Aqueduct project, 82, 95
supreme court, Puerto Rico, 8, 133
Supreme Court, U.S., 4, 164, 171,
  185, 187, 188, 227n25, 228n13,
  229n26
swine flu/H1N1 epidemic (2009), 210

Taft, William, 187, 191, 193
tax exemption in Puerto Rico: from
  economic to political battle over,
  44; extended to 1983, 45;

historical development of, 55–58,
  185; Laws 20 and 22 offering tax
  exemption to relocating
  enterprises, 114; Law 137,
  extension of, 111; Law 154
  imposing tax on tax exempt
  industries, 113–14; plan
  proposed by Moscoso, 20–24,
  27, 29, 103; under Puerto Rico
  Federal Relations Act, 55;
  Section 931, approval and
  eventual elimination of, 55–56;
  Section 936, passage of, 3, 47–48,
  56–58; Section 936 replacement
  initiatives, failure of, 69–71;
  statehood movement and,
  26–29, 34–35, 41–51.
  See also Section 936, repeal of
Tax Revenue and Anticipatory Notes
  Agency (TRANS), 106
Teamsters, 90
Tennessee Plan, 136
territorial clause, claim of congressional power over Puerto Rico
  due to, 4–6, 171–72, 183, 204
terrorist groups in Puerto Rico, 162
textile industry, 44, 121
Textron, 42
Thompson Bankwatch, 106
Time magazine, 104
Tobin, James, and Tobin Report,
  98–99, 105, 112, 123, 126, 174
tourism industry, 90, 103, 106, 113,
  124, 148, 154, 207
TRANS (Tax Revenue and
  Anticipatory Notes Agency), 106
Transportation Department, U.S., 79
Treasury Department, U.S., 7, 51,
  56–57, 61, 69, 114

Tren Urbano (Urban Train), 77–80, 82, 96

Trías Monge, José, 204

triumvirato del terror, El (The Triumvirate of Terror; Pedro Rosselló), 145

Trujillo, Carlos, 138

Trujillo, Rafael, 163

Truman, Harry, 162

Trump, Donald J., vii, 7, 8, 136–38, 147, 155, 163, 203, 209–11

tuberculosis, 194

Tugwell, Rexford: on Atlantic Charter and self-determination, 199; Descartes, appointment of, 23; fiscal policy on borrowing under, 76; GDB and, 100–103, 104, 105, 107; Moscoso and, 17, 21–22, 24; Muñoz and, 18, 85–87, 167; New Deal and, 18, 196; Operation Bootstrap, introduction of, 15, 16–20; public corporations under, 83–87, 89, 93; on statehood, 43, 139; *The Stricken Land*, 17, 20, 85, 87; on tax exemption proposal and Fomento, 20–22, 29, 43, 120; on U.S. national security and Puerto Rico, 151, 152–53

tutelage policy, 186

Twentieth Century Fund, 172

Tydings, Millard, and Tydings bill (1936), 161, 197–98, 199

UIA (Aqueduct Independent Union), 93, 94–96

unemployment rates in Puerto Rico, ix, 7, 25, 26, 46, 47, 64, 118, 119

"ungratefulness" of Puerto Rico, claims of, 191, 193

unincorporated territory, Supreme Court cases establishing Puerto Rico as, 185, 187

Union Party, 186, 187

unions. *See* labor policy and employment; *specific unions*

United States–Puerto Rico Commission on the Status of Puerto Rico, 37–38, 48, 72, 132, 136, 140–41, 144, 149, 155, 157, 167–68

United Workers Movement (Movimiento Obrero Unido; MOU), 91

Urban Train (Tren Urbano), 77–80, 82, 96

U.S. citizenship of Puerto Ricans, 18, 19, 28, 35, 135, 137, 144, 150, 155, 160, 163, 164, 186–88

U.S. Commerce Department, 141

U.S. Constitution, 5, 27, 37, 138, 143, 183

U.S. Financial Oversight and Management Board for Puerto Rico. *See* PROMESA

U.S. Food and Drug Administration, viii, 209

U.S. GAO. *See* General Accounting Office

U.S. imperialism, 10, 26, 178, 179. *See also* colonialism

U.S. Justice Department, 135–36, 146, 156–57, 171–72

U.S. national politics in Puerto Rico, 200–203

U.S. national security and Puerto Rico, 150–55, 179

U.S. naval stations in Puerto Rico, 151–55
U.S. Supreme Court, 4, 164, 171, 185, 187, 188, 227n25, 228n13, 229n26
U.S. Transportation Department, 79
U.S. Treasury Department, 7, 51, 56–57, 61, 69, 114
U.S. voting rights of Puerto Ricans, 4–5, 9, 35, 36, 137, 144, 150–51, 169–72
USS Oregon, 179
UTIER (Electrical Industry and Irrigation Workers Union), 91

"Vampirita, La" (income tax surcharge), 99
Vázquez Garced, Wanda, 8, 156, 202, 207, 214–15
Vieques, U.S. Naval station on, 151–55, 158
Vietnam War, 151
Virgin Islands, U.S., IOC separate recognition of, 150
Vivendi, 93, 94
Volkswagen, 119
voting rights, U.S., of Puerto Ricans, 4–5, 9, 35, 36, 137, 144, 150–51, 169–72

Wall Street Journal, 11, 16, 118, 159
Wanniski, Jude, 16, 166, 196

War on Poverty, 159
Warren, Earl, 170, 217n4 (introduction)
Washington, DC, statehood for, 139
water: Aqueduct and Sewerage Authority (AAA), 93–96, 105, 108, 125; Puerto Rico Water Resources Authority, 17, 88, 89, 102; Super Aqueduct project, 82, 95; UIA (Aqueduct Independent Union), 93, 94–96
Weekly Journal, 143, 213
West Side Story, 145
Westinghouse, 65
Wilson, Woodrow, 187, 191
Woodworth, Lawrence, 56
World Bank, 92, 129
World Herald, 102
World Journal, 100, 203
World War I, 161, 191
World War II, 17, 22, 84, 100, 150, 151, 152, 155, 194
Wyeth, 67–68

Yager, Arthur, 191–92
Yom Kippur oil crisis of 1973 and oil embargo of 1973–1975, 29, 46–48, 54, 98–99, 106, 126, 127, 129
Yulín Cruz, Carmen, 138

Zacalán, Fernando, 111

A. W. MALDONADO

is a retired journalist who spent more than fifty years covering Puerto Rico's
politics and economy as reporter and columnist for the *San Juan Star*
and editor of *El Mundo* and *El Reportero*. He is the author of several books,
including *Teodoro Moscoso* and *Puerto Rico's Operation Bootstrap* and
Luis Muñoz Marín: Puerto Rico's Democratic Revolution.

Lightning Source UK Ltd.
Milton Keynes UK
UKHW021050230721
387614UK00002B/120